WHAT IS IT THAT THEOLOGIANS DO, HOW THEY DO IT, AND WHY
Anglican Essays

Owen C. Thomas

The Edwin Mellen Press
Lewiston•Queenston•Lampeter

BT
78
.T375
2006

Library of Congress Cataloging-in-Publication Data

Thomas, Owen C.
  What is it that theologians do, how they do it, and why : Anglican essays /
by Owen C. Thomas
    p. cm.
  Includes bibliographical references and index.
  ISBN-13: 978-0-7734-5590-0
  ISBN-10: 0-7734-5590-6
  I. Title.

hors série.

A CIP catalog record for this book is available from the British Library.

The Edwin Mellen Press
Box 450
Lewiston, New York
USA 14092-0450

The Edwin Mellen Press
Box 67
Queenston, Ontario
CANADA L0S 1L0

The Edwin Mellen Press, Ltd.
Lampeter, Ceredigion, Wales
UNITED KINGDOM SA48 8LT

Printed in the United States of America

To Margaret

Sine Qua Non

WHAT IS IT THAT THEOLOGIANS DO, HOW THEY DO IT, AND WHY

TABLE OF CONTENTS

Part III — Applications

ACKNOWLEDGMENTS

I am happy to acknowledge and thank the many people to whom I am indebted over the years for inspiration, conversation, ideas, and criticism. They include my teachers, colleagues, and students at the Episcopal Divinity School, Columbia University, Union Theological Seminary, the Gregorian University and the North American College in Rome, the Boston Theological Society, the New Haven Theological Group, the American Theological Society, the American Academy of Religion, the North American Paul Tillich Society, the Pacific Coast Theological Society, the Graduate Theological Union, and the Center for Theology and the Natural Sciences in Berkeley. The number of individuals is too large to list here, but I must include my wife, Dr. Margaret R. Miles, with whom conversations over the past thirty years on matters historical, theological and existential have been fundamental in my thinking, writing and life, and to whom I dedicate this book. I am grateful to my friend Huston Smith for his comments on a draft of chapter 13. Needless to say, he is not responsible for any of my interpretations.

I am also indebted to Eileen Murphy for excellent help in the preparation of the manuscript, and to the following publishers, journals, and institutions for permission to publish the following essays:

T. & T. Clark: "Recent Thought on Divine Agency," chapter 2 in *Divine Action: Studies Inspired by the Philosophical Theology of Austin Farrer*, eds. Brian Hebblethwaite and Edward Henderson, 1990. (Copyright T. & T. Clark, 1990. Reprinted by permission of the Continuum International Publishing Group).

Wipf & Stock: an earlier version of "On Doing Theology During a Romantic Movement," in *The Subjective Eye: Essays in Culture, Religion and Gender in Honor of Margaret R. Miles*, ed. Richard Valantasis, 2006. Reprinted with permission.

The Journal of Religion: "Interiority and Christian Spirituality," 80:1 (2000), 41-60. (© 2000 by the University of Chicago. All rights reserved.)

INTRODUCTION

What is it that theologians do, and how do they do it and why? Colloquially and in public discourse "theology" and "theological" refer to something weird, irrational, and beyond discussion. Recently a columnist stated that the arguments about health care had become not just economic or political but rather "theological," that is, hopelessly arcane and ideological.

The purpose of this book is to deal with these questions about theology, and by means of some examples to give the reader a clearer idea of what theologians do, what is the point of theology, and why it is sometimes a necessity. I will be suggesting that theology is something that all Christians engage in off and on, something that can be very useful and occasionally necessary in the Christian life. For theology is simply thinking about your life and experience before God in the church and the world.

Such thinking, however, takes place on various levels of complexity. On the simplest level it is just recalling and understanding that we live in the presence of God, the God who made us, who loves us, and who leads us to our fulfillment. Our faith in God always involves an element of understanding, understanding who God is, and what is our relation to God. And theology on this simplest, yet infinitely mysterious, level is just recalling this understanding.

At another level of complexity we may wonder, puzzle, and reflect about some experience we have had or something that has happened, about its relation to God or how God was involved in it. Or we may reflect on the meaning of a prayer or a passage from the Bible that we hear in church. At a somewhat more complex level is the reflection of a teacher of a church school class, who must think about ways to interpret and explain the Christian faith and life in such a way that people will be able to grasp and affirm it.

More complexity is involved in the reflection involved in the work of a lay or ordained minister in preaching, pastoral care, and the conduct of worship. Then there is the level of thought involved in the work of the theologian who is asked to reflect on issues before the church, such as revision of the liturgy, the ordination of women and gay and lesbian people, and the blessing of same-sex couples. The theologian is also asked to interpret various aspects of the tradition of the church and to assess new developments in Christian thought, such as feminist theology, liberation theology, and process theology. At all these levels of complexity theology can be defined, following Anselm, as faith seeking understanding.

Now I have spoken of various levels of complexity in the work of theology, and I may have seemed to imply that the more complex levels are more important than the simpler. Not at all. In fact I believe that the opposite is the case. The simpler levels are the most important in the life of the church, and the work of theologians on the more complex level may well be the least important. In any case the main purpose of the work of theologians is to serve the Christian life in the church and in the larger society.

So my point is that theology is most important at the level where Christian people are reflecting on the questions and issues which arise in their lives in the church and the world. For this is how theology arose in the first place. This is clear from the Bible. The first major issue that the early Christians faced was how to understand the fact that the one they had come to know as the Messiah had been crucified. But there were many other issues: food offered to idols, ecstatic phenomena, the relation to governing authorities, sex and marriage, and one of the most important, what to do with gentile converts. All of these issues required careful theological reflection for their resolution, and we can see Paul, for example, doing just that in many places in his letters. My point is that this is how theology arose: from the necessity of dealing with issues that emerged in the lives of Christians and the church. I expand on this in the first essay.

Now it may have occurred to you that theology is really not this kind of thing, namely, Christians thinking about their lives before God, but rather that theology is large dusty tomes sitting in libraries or in the pastor's study, perhaps untouched since seminary. Well, something happened in the history of theology that transformed it.

As more gentile converts came into the church, they had to be instructed more carefully and thoroughly in the Christian understanding of God and the world and the Christian way of life, because as non-Jews they did not share the foundation of the Christian way in Judaism. This need for instruction led to the drawing up of what was called the rule of faith, a short summary of the main points of Christian faith. In the second century this developed into what we know as the Apostles' Creed, which was used as confession of faith at the baptism of gentiles.

Next interpretations and explanations of the rule of faith were drawn up for the guidance of those instructing new gentile converts. Then some of these converts were pagan philosophers, mainly Middle Platonists, for example, Justin Martyr, who became a Christian teacher in Rome in the middle of the second century. They were interested in spelling out the meaning of Christian faith in some detail to deal with their philosophical questions. Also some of the pagan philosophers attacked Christianity and wrote long treatises attempting to prove that it was a lot of nonsense. Christian teachers responded to these attacks in long and detailed defenses.

So these motivations led to the writing of extended and systematic treatments of Christian faith which became one of the main forms of theological writing in the Middle Ages and down to the present. Now although this form of theology served some useful purposes, it also had some unfortunate results. First, it turned the study of theology into the study of these great systems of theology. That is, it turned the study of theology into the study of the results of other people's thinking about Christian faith rather than one's own reflection on one's life before God. Second, it obscured the fact that theology had arisen in Christians puzzling about the questions that had emerged in their lives, and it was not much help in this. So in my teaching I attempted to turn this development around and focus on the issues and questions which arise in the lives of students.

4

(See my book *Theological Questions: Analysis and Argument* [Morehouse, 1983]).

It is important to recall that in the early church theologians were mainly clergy and monks.   In the medieval period more and more theologians became teachers at universities.   Today most theologians, especially in the United States, are professors in theological schools or departments of religious studies in colleges and universities.   This means that the enterprise of theology has tended to take on a life of its own that is relatively independent of the churches.   It has emerged as a profession, an academic discipline, a guild, with publishing companies and professional societies, such as the American Academy of Religion and the American Theological Society.

One of the results of this development is that theologians who, like myself, teach in seminaries and who are thus in closer touch with the concerns of the churches tend to work in two rather distinct areas, the concerns of the church and the concerns of the academy.   This is reflected in the essays in this volume.   Most of the essays in the first two parts treat issues which have arisen in the academy and the professional guilds, whereas most of those in the third part deal with issues which have emerged in the life of the church.   It is not as though these two areas are entirely unrelated, but that their relations are often fairly remote, claims to the contrary notwithstanding.   With that in mind it may be helpful if I offered a brief introduction to the subjects of these essays, the occasions of their writing, and their relations to each other and to the developments I have been discussing.

In the first part of this book I take up questions about the nature of theology and its methods, criteria, and social context.   In the first essay I offer some reflections on the theological scene as I have observed it over the past sixty years.   I have organized these reflections under the headings of the ways of doing theology and its social setting, or the methodology and sociology of theology.   I expand on some of the points I have just made about the origin of theology and its taking on a life of its own.

In the second essay I take up a question which is central in theological discussion today, namely, the place of experience in Christian faith and thought.

What is the relation of experience to theology? Should theological proposals be confirmed in experience? Should experience be the main criterion of theology? The pressing character of these questions is derived in large part from the current Romantic movement that began in the 1960s, that emphasizes the importance of experience, and which I address in the fifth and last essay in this part. I conclude that while experience is often decisive in an individual's theological judgments, it is very difficult to use as a criterion in theology.

In the third essay in this part I discuss a related question, namely, whether theology can and should be a public discipline in the sense of the natural sciences, that is, addressed to all people and using criteria acceptable to all. I focus on the work of David Tracy. I note that traditional definitions of "public" have tended to exclude the participation of women, minorities, and the poor. But with the breakdown of the public sphere, new groups of the formerly excluded are organizing what have been called "counter-public spheres" which point to the possibility of theology being public in a truer sense.

The criticism and reform of the Christian tradition raises the crucial question of continuity and change or development. Are we in the same church as the apostles, the medieval mystics, and the Reformers? Were they all in the same church? We believe that we have experienced something salvific in the Christian life in the church, something we associate with Jesus and the apostles, and we don't want to lose that. This requires some kind of continuity of what is essential in Christianity. What is the essence of Christianity and how can we know whether or not we have preserved it? These are the questions I discuss in the fourth essay in this part. I conclude that what is essential in Christianity may be more in practices such as worship, prayer, service, and action for justice and peace, than in doctrine.

In the fifth and last essay in this part I take up what I believe to be the most important influence on contemporary theology in the United States and England, namely, the current Romantic movement. I believe that a new Romantic movement began to emerge in the 1960s and has continued to gain strength and influence. I offer evidence for this new Romantic movement from historians, sociologists, philosophers, theologians, contemporary theology, the current spirituality movement, and from popular culture. Romantic movements are ambiguous, having both beneficial and destructive effects in society and culture. I believe that we need to become more aware of this movement and its influence so that we can affirm its positive side and avoid its negative results.

In the essays in the second part of this volume I move from preliminary questions about the norms and methods of theology to specific theological problems. The three essays deal with issues which are fundamental in Christian faith and life, namely, how we can use ordinary language to talk about the transcendent God, what is the most fundamental term we can apply to God, and how we can understand God acting in the world.

I noted above that theologians tend to function in two contexts, the church and the academy. The three essays in this part fall in the latter category and thus tend to be rather technical. The reasons for this are that theology, literally, talks about God, uses ordinary language in a very unusual way, stretching it way beyond it usual usage. This raises all kinds of complex questions about how theological language works and how it is to be assessed. The theological tradition often drawing on, as well as contributing to, the philosophical tradition has developed complex methods and concepts which are useful in the clarification and resolution of theological issues.

So in the first essay in this second part I explore the question of analogy, the use of ordinary terms in unusual ways to speak of God. How are these terms chosen and how do they refer to God? I conclude that the basic source must be the Bible, and that when these terms are brought together they can correct each other and point to God.

In the second essay I take up one of the key terms which has been used in the theological tradition to speak of God, namely, being or being-itself. It was used by the early Greek theologians, by Augustine, Aquinas, and by several followers of Aquinas in the last century, such as Karl Rahner and Bernard Lonergan, as well as by some Protestant theologians, such as Paul Tillich and Robert Neville. I discover that there is a great diversity and confusion in the application of these terms to God, and especially in their various equivalents in Greek, Latin, and English. I conclude, therefore, that it is not a useful concept for interpreting the reality of God.

To be sure this is a negative conclusion, but theologians and scientists generally recognize that negative conclusions are equally important with positive ones. As a former physicist I recall that the Michelson-Morley experiment helped to disprove the ether theory of the propagation of light. Also the Council of Nicea ruled out the creative and widely held Arian theory of Christ. Both of these judgments pointed out dead ends and guided reflection and research in more fruitful directions. I recently wrote a review essay of a major study of the significance of chaos theory for the interpretation of God's activity in the world, which study comes to an important and fruitful negative conclusion.

This leads directly to the third essay in this part which deals with the problem of how to understand God's activity in the world. Throughout the Bible and Christian history it has been asserted that God acts and does things in the world. But the question of how this should be understood was not much discussed until the medieval period, when the primary-secondary cause theory was developed which dominated Christian thought down into the last century when new theories began to be proposed.

Several years ago I was asked to prepare a book on this question which includes essays by twelve authors who present different views of divine action. In the conclusion of this book I suggest that these authors present five distinct views of divine activity in the world: God acts in a way analogous to the way a person acts in the world; God acts directly in miracles and indirectly through finite secondary causes; God acts persuasively and always in cooperation with finite causes; God acts uniformly and universally and the appearance of diversity derives from the diversity of human responses; God's actions and finite activities are simply two different ways of looking at the world.

In 1986 a conference was held at Louisiana State University which was based on my book and at which I presented a keynote address on theories of divine action which had appeared since the publication of the book. This address is the third essay in this part, and in it I focus on the question of double agency, namely, how we can understand an event in which both God and a finite agent are acting. I conclude that only two of the theories proposed constitute satisfactory analogies of double agency, namely, liturgical pardon, and the complex theory of quasi-formal cause.

In the third part I focus on issues in the application of theological ideas in the life of the church and the world. In the first essay I explore one of the central themes in the long history of Christian spirituality, namely, its focus on interiority or the inner life. My thesis is that this focus is a mistake, philosophically, theologically, and ethically. This emphasis on interiority is a cultural construct of the Western tradition and not a universal theme of human nature. It is derived largely from the Neoplatonist tradition or the perennial philosophy rather than from the Bible, and it tends to turn away from the body, society, and history, to which we are directed by the moral teaching of scripture.

In the second essay I take up an issue that has been raised and discussed often in the past few decades, namely, whether or not the moral life of a thinker is relevant to the assessment of the thinker's thought and writings. I discuss this issue in relation to two thinkers who have been very influential in theology, Heidegger and Tillich. Heidegger is one of the most creative and influential philosophers of the last century, especially in relation to theology. Yet he was a member of the Nazi party, supported the Nazi regime, and carried out its mandates as rector of the University of Freiburg. Tillich is one of the most creative and influential theologians of the last century. Yet his relations with many women were exploitative, obsessive, and destructive. Are these facts about these thinkers relevant to the assessment of their thought or not? Although a great debate has raged over Heidegger and a lesser one on Tillich on this issue, no one has approached is theoretically or systematically. I make an attempt to do this and come down tentatively on the negative side. I conclude that although the moral/political life of a thinker can alert us to potential problems in the thought, it cannot be decisive. This essay is the presidential address I gave at the Annual Meeting of the American Theological Society in 1993.

In the third essay in this part I take up an issue which is central in Christian theology today and which is the subject of more conferences, books, and essays than any other single topic. It is the issue of religious plurality and the relation of Christianity to the other world religions. I experienced this issue of pluralism first when I moved from the naturalistic humanism of my parents to Christianity while a graduate student in physics. Later I published one of the first books in the current discussion of religious plurality, namely, *Attitudes Toward Other Religions* (Harper & Row, 1969).

Why is this topic so central today? Christians have known of the plurality of religions from the beginning and have occasionally addressed themselves to this issue in past centuries. But it is only in the latter third of the last century that it has come into the center of attention of churches and theologians. The reasons for this are not only more widespread travel, rapid communication, and the greatly increased experience of other cultures, but also and primarily the vastly increased number of adherents of other religions in Western countries. There are Muslim mosques, Hindu temples, and Buddhist monasteries in or near every major Western city. There are now more Muslims in the United States than there are Episcopalians or Presbyterians. The new awareness of other great religions has raised many questions for Christians. What is the relation of Christianity to other religions, and what should be our attitude toward them? What is God's relation to them? Do all religions claim to be true? Is there one true religion? Are other religions ways of salvation?

In this third essay I expand on the meaning of inclusivism, the view that sees truth and salvation in other religious traditions but understands these as manifestations of the truth and salvation in one's own tradition. I contrast this with the main alternative view of other religions that is called pluralism. Pluralists affirm that all the great religious traditions are equal in regard to truth and salvation. I argue that there can be no coherent pluralist position, and that all pluralist views reduce to some form of inclusivism. I support this by examining theories of pluralism in contemporary philosophy.

The next two essays in this part are two parts of one extended essay. Their main theme is the relation between the two great types of religion. These have been called the emissary and exemplary types (Max Weber) or the confrontation and interiority types (Peter Berger). I refer to them as the biblical religion and perennial philosophy types. The former is more at home in the West in Judaism, Christianity, and Islam, and the latter in the East in Hinduism and Buddhism, although both types are now present in all the religions of the world.

My main thesis is that, although Christianity had its origin in the biblical religion type, it has almost always been an amalgam of the two types, sometimes with the emphasis on one type and sometimes on the other. The main question I raise is whether or not a real synthesis of the two types is possible. In order to explore this question in the second essay I examine the work of my former teacher Paul Tillich who has attempted such a synthesis, albeit from the point of view of the biblical religion type. I conclude that his attempt is only partially successful. This may indicate that it is not possible to achieve a full synthesis of these two great types of world religion.

The problem of the relation of romantic love and marriage has troubled Western societies and churches for at least two centuries. The modern Western imagination has been described as obsessed with romantic love as seen in novels and movies. On the one hand, romantic love has been seen as the fulfillment of the deepest human desire and the necessary basis of marriage (living happily ever after), and on the other hand it has been condemned as the deadliest enemy of marriage, because it glorifies adultery. The central theme of many great modern novels is adultery, witness *Madame Bovary* and *Anna Karenina.* So in the next essay I discuss a modern debate between Charles Williams and Denis de Rougemont on romantic love and its relation to marriage. They seem to hold contradictory views, de Rougemont that the myth of romantic love, as seen in the story of Tristan and Iseult, is a heretical subversion of marriage, and Williams, drawing on Dante, that romantic love is an experience of Christian salvation and the necessary basis of marriage. Further examination of their views, however, leads to the conclusion that they can be seen as complementary.

The last essay in this part treats the relation between Christian faith and science. This topic is of great interest to me, since science was my first, if brief, career. I majored in physics and mathematics in college and was working on a doctorate in physics when I was drafted into the Navy in World War II. I was sent to the Naval Research Laboratory in Washington, DC, where I carried on research and development in ultra-high frequency radiation, namely, radar and counter measures. The end of the war was the end of my career in physics, but my interest in science, especially in physics and cosmology, has remained strong. Recently I have worked regularly with the Center for Theology and the Natural Sciences in Berkeley.

This essay is an address I delivered at the dedication of the Dupont science building at St. George's School, Newport, RI. I suggest that the struggle between Christianity and the emerging natural sciences in the last four centuries was based on the mistaken notions that Christianity could answer scientific questions and more recently that science could answer religious questions. Moreover, historians of science have discovered in the last few decades that Christianity played a key role in the rise of modern science. It was the impact of the Christian idea of creation on the tradition of Greek science which opened the way to the combination of experiment and mathematics which is the essence of modern science. Thus science can be understood as a Christian vocation.

My hope is that in these essays the reader will gain a deeper and clearer understanding what theology is and how it can help to clarify and resolve issues which arise in the Christian life in the church and the world.

PART I

METHOD

CHAPTER 1

ON THE METHODOLOGY AND SOCIOLOGY OF THEOLOGY

I have been working in and observing the theological scene for about a half century now, and I have noticed some things which have struck me and which have aroused my curiosity. They are not things which have been much if ever discussed in the theological guilds. They fall under two general headings which I will call the methodology and the sociology of theology and they are complexly related. I will begin with the methodological things.

I understand the primary purpose of Christian theology to be the service of the Christian life in the church and society. I believe that there are also secondary purposes of theology but that they are dependent on this primary purpose. Thus I understand Christian theology to be reflection on our life and experience before God in the light of the gospel, especially reflection on the questions, issues, and problems which arise in our life and our work in the church and in society at large. This, I believe, is or should be the primary locus and the fundamental beginning point of theology.

It certainly has been the case historically, for this is how theology arose, namely, as the attempt to resolve unavoidable issues which emerged in the lives of Christians and the church. A major issue in the lives of the early followers of Jesus was the crucifixion of the one they were beginning to believe was the messiah of Israel. This was not supposed to happen. The messiah was supposed to lead Israel to victory against its enemies and usher in a new era of peace, justice, and prosperity. So what in God's name is going on? The first Christians resolved this issue in various ways. They interpreted Jesus' death as a sacrifice for sins on the analogy of Hebrew sacrifice, or as a victorious struggle with the powers of evil, or as an example of humble obedience to the divine will, and so forth.

Other issues with which the early Christians had to deal concerned food offered to idols, ecstatic phenomena, the relation to governing authorities, marriage and divorce. A classic paradigm of the emergence of theology was the issue of what to do with gentile converts. Should they be subjected to circumcision and the food laws or not, and why? This was a forced decision; the church had to go one way or the other. There was a debate and arguments on both sides. Paul takes up the issue in the letter to the Galatians and makes an extended argument against subjection to the law and in favor of justification through grace. This was a crucial turning point in the history of the church, in its self-understanding and in its relation to Judaism. And the path it took was the result, at least in part, of theological argument and decision. This I believe is a paradigm case of the emergence of Christian theology.

Later the task of instruction, the explication of the developing rule of faith, and the treatment of more speculative issues raised by contemporary Middle Platonism led naturally to a sea change in theology, namely, the writing of more extended and systematic treatments of the topics of Christian faith. This issued in works such as Irenaeus' *Demonstration of the Apostolic Preaching* and Origen's *On First Principles*, later in the medieval summae, and ultimately to the massive theological systems of the seventeenth to the twentieth centuries.

This type of theological writing which still seems to be in vogue, had two results. The first was to obscure the fact that theology arose as the attempt to clarify and resolve specific issues arising in the life and work of Christians and the church. The second was to turn the study of theology into the study of these great systems, that is, into the study of the results of theological reflection rather the actual carrying out of theological reflection itself on the issues actually arising in the lives of Christians and the church.

What I am suggesting is that theology has tended to take on a life of its own apart from its original locus and purpose and has become an academic discipline, a guild, a profession, a publishing enterprise, and occasionally a media event. That is, intrinsic interest in the subject matter of theology has led many of us to seek careers as theologians with all the necessary trappings of academic careers, namely, joining guilds, publication of books and articles in journals in order to gain positions, promotion, and tenure. This occasionally leads to attention in the media, such as the cover of *Time* magazine in 1964 inquiring, "Is God Dead?"

What I am suggesting is that if all Christian churches and Christians, except theologians, disappeared, Christian theology might well continue on its own indefinitely. Concretely what I mean is that if this were to happen, professional organizations of theologians might continue on as usual, although there would undoubtedly be a lot of papers on the meaning of this strange event! I am not bewailing theology gaining a life of its own; I am just trying to explain what I mean by such a development.

I have been aware of theology having a life of its own in my experience of doing theology on two levels or in two departments. On the one hand, for example, I am asked to write papers on the ordination of women, the ordination of gay and lesbian people, the blessing of same sex covenants, liturgical revision, and so forth. On the other hand, I find myself writing essays on God as being, the problem of analogy, experience as a criterion of theology, public theology, religious plurality, and so on. The former derive from pressing issues in the Episcopal Church, while the latter arise from current discussions in the theological guilds and journals. This latter is what I mean by theology taking on a life of its own.

Now when theology takes on a life of its own relatively independent of the church, it tends to become more deeply influenced by its context in the academy. This leads to some reflections on the sociology of theology. But I will postpone that and mention some other methodological developments which I have noticed.

First, I began to notice a long time ago that theology is usually done backwards. That is, although a piece of theological writing on some particular question may begin with the description of the method to be followed and then the step-by-step carrying out of this method to arrive at a conclusion, the actual process of theological reflection seems to begin with an intuition of an answer to a question or the solution to a problem followed by a casting around for arguments to support this intuition. I am not objecting to theology being done backwards. I am simply noting that it is not theological argument but rather theological intuition which seems to be decisive. Then argument becomes a way of supporting an intuition rather than proceeding toward a conclusion.

I believe that the main reason for this lies in confusion about the nature of theological method. Most of the writing on this topic in this century has dealt with the method of interpreting historical texts (Bultmann et al.) or with the method of developing a theological system (Tillich), or with method in the most general sense of rational criteria or sources of authority (Lonergan, Tracy). Little if any of it has dealt with how one actually goes about treating a theological issue. I mean this very concretely: What do you do the first half hour? Introspection and some conversation with colleagues has led me to realize that the way we theologians actually go about dealing with a specific theological question is quite haphazard, hit or miss, trial and error. It might be rather embarrassing to keep an honest log of the steps we actually take and how we spend the hours we do on some particular problem.

In any case theological writing on a particular issue usually does not take the form simply of assertion or confession of faith. It usually takes the form of argument, namely, the giving of reasons, evidence, grounds, or in the traditional term, proof, for its statements. From the beginning for guidance in the development of their arguments theologians turned to the discipline of rhetoric, the art of persuasive discourse. The apologists and theologians of the early centuries of the church studied classical rhetoric, often were themselves rhetors or teachers of rhetoric, for example, Gregory Nazianzen, Cyprian, and Augustine, and employed rhetorical methods, styles, and devices.

The study of rhetoric was always an essential ingredient of classical education. Along with logic and grammar, it formed the trivium of the medieval seven liberal arts, and it was an important element in liberal education down through the nineteenth century. From the time of the Renaissance, however, there was a steady decline in the intellectual status of rhetoric. It came increasingly to be identified with its stylistic and decorative aspects and with purposes of entertainment. One of the last great works written by a theologian in a consciously rhetorical style is Schleiermacher's *Speeches* (1799). Schleiermacher complained that most of the criticisms of the *Speeches* were mistaken because they were based on a failure to perceive its rhetorical character.

Today our ordinary usage of the term rhetoric is entirely pejorative, and very few theologians have evidenced any knowledge or use of the rhetorical tradition. The only exceptions known to me are Walter Ong and through him F. J. van Beeck, plus some recent work by David Cunningham. This is a serious loss to contemporary theology, because lacking clarity in our arguments and knowledge of the modes of argument available to us, we tend to lapse into forms of argument which are inappropriate in theology. More about that in a moment.

A major contribution in this area is Stephen Toulmin's *The Uses of Argument* which holds a unique position in the history of logic and rhetoric. Toulmin criticizes the logical tradition for its lack of concern for the forms of argument used in the everyday life of the world. He develops a pattern of informal argument based on a jurisprudential model which he believes is useful for the analysis of actual arguments on concrete matters. It is interesting to note that while Toulmin betrays no knowledge of the rhetorical tradition, contemporary rhetoricians have hailed his work as a major contribution to their discipline, and theologians such as Van Harvey and David Kelsey have seized upon Toulmin's work for an analysis of theological argument.

However, if we theologians are to use Toulmin's proposals or learn from other new developments in rhetoric such as the volume entitled *The New Rhetoric* by Chaim Perelman and Lucie Olbrechts-Tyteca (Notre Dame, 1969), we need an ethic of theological rhetoric. For our theological arguments are often inappropriate or unfair. Let me give same examples.

One of the most common is the straw person argument in which you describe only the most extreme version of your opponent's position, because it is much easier to argue against than his actual nuanced position. This is familiar to us from the outside critics of Christianity from Feuerbach to Flew who attack only the most traditional form of Christianity and deny that any liberal or nuanced form is worthy of the name. I have noticed it most recently in the debates between pluralists and inclusivists about religious plurality.

Another very common form of what I consider to be unethical rhetoric is what I will call the trend or consensus argument. In the trend version you assert that the opponent's position is passé and no longer tenable, although he or she doesn't seem to be aware of that. We are familiar with this version from assertions by the neoorthodox about the downfall of liberal theology and by claims by neoliberal theologians about the demise of neoorthodoxy. The latest version of this is perhaps the announcement by postmodern theologians that their opponents are (shudder!) modern if not premodern. The word "increasingly" is often the sign of the presence of such an argument.

The consensus version of this takes the form of the following. "It is now generally agreed by all knowledgeable and sophisticated persons that X." Or "X has come to be widely doubted and as a result that whole scheme has broken down and is now no longer a viable alternative." This of course is not an argument but simply a claim about an alleged theological development and thus an unethical rhetorical device. The hidden and false premise of all such non-arguments is that all developments in theology are in the right direction, and that later theology is better than earlier, certainly a dubious assumption. But this unethical move is often effective. Who wants to be considered out of date, passé, unknowledgeable, or unsophisticated? The opposite unethical rhetorical move is to put down a current movement in theology by referring to it as a fad or fashionable or trendy, thus implying that all sensible people either have already, or will soon, see through it.

Another form of what I take to be unethical theological rhetoric is more subtle and complex. It is the argument about the alleged historical results of a particular theological doctrine. For example, it is often alleged that a particular theological idea has led to destructive social and cultural results, and that the opposing theological idea has or will have a constructive and healthy impact on human life. You are familiar with this rhetorical move, for example, in the critique of various points in traditional theology by liberation theology and the critique of aspects of liberal theology by conservative theology. For example, my wife accuses me of always referring to the Nazis in theological arguments. A recent example of such a move is the claim that the traditional doctrine of the uniqueness of Christ has caused hatred and oppression of other religionists.

Yes, we would like to think that theology is of great import and has a major impact on society. But is this not an over grandiose estimate of the social and cultural significance and impact of theological ideas? Furthermore, the determination of the cause of a particular social or cultural phenomenon is an extraordinarily complex task involving the analysis of the innumerable factors that function in the social historical world. My impression of the current discussion of such questions among historians and social scientists is that ideas are pretty far down the list of important and determinative factors compared to other cultural, social, economic, political and psychological factors. Moreover when I have noted such arguments I have never seen the theologian even begin to look into the complexity of such claims. I am sure that you can think of other examples of unethical theological rhetoric. This is why we need an ethics of theological rhetoric.

Now I come to an item which bridges the methodology and the sociology of theology, something I call theology and life. I am referring to the question of the significance of a theologian's life for the assessment of his or her thought. I think this first came to my attention in 1973 when I was lecturing on Tillich's theology at the Gregorian University in Rome. One day a student showed me a copy of *Time* magazine with a story about Hannah Tillich's new book *From Time to Time*. It recounted Tillich's infidelities, his exploitive relations with women, and his fascination with sadism and pornography. The student asked me how this would affect my assessment of Tillich's theology. It was a good question, an important and very complex question, and I have been thinking about it off and on ever since.

Tillichians, that is, followers and defenders of Tillich, tend to argue that Tillich's relations with women are irrelevant to the assessment of his theology. Anti-Tillichians tend to argue that his exploitive relations with women cast serious doubt on all of his theology. An analogous debate has taken place about Heidegger and Paul de Man in regard to their anti-Semitism and support of Nazism, about the "*braun*" theologians, Althaus, Kittel, Hirsch, and Gogarten, and about philosophers and theologians who supported Stalinism.

So far as I an aware no one has treated this issue at any length in regard to theologians. How shall we approach it? There are obviously two extremes which we will probably want to avoid, namely, the idea that a theologian's life is entirely irrelevant to the assessment of the thought, and that the life is absolutely decisive in such assessment. On the one hand we have the New Critics and the postmoderns who argue that biography is irrelevant or that authors are non-existent and that all we have is texts. On the other hand we have the older critics and historicists and the Marxists and psychoanalysts who tend to hold that thought is an epiphenomenon or at least a manifestation of the economic, social, and cultural context.

I would suggest that on this question there is probably a spectrum running from mathematics on one end to art, philosophy, ethics, and theology on the other. A key question here is the unity and coherence of a life and the relation between a person's creativity in various areas and that person's relations to fellows and society. Another problem is what to do with the work of theologians about whose lives we know nothing, and who may have led either exemplary or reprehensible lives, such as Dionysius. A related question is, If we can argue from an evil life to an unsound theology, can we argue from a good life to a valid theology? Probably not (see chapter 10).

This leads me directly to the first of the items under the heading of the sociology of theology, and it too could be named the relation of theology and life. Let me explain. In 1968 the philosopher Jacob Needleman wrote an essay in the *Review of Metaphysics* entitled "Why Philosophy is Easy." He noted that in the ancient and early medieval worlds philosophy was thought to be anything but easy. One could aim to be a philosopher only after a lifelong discipline and training of mind, body, emotions, and will, an ascetical discipline. Today, however, all that is necessary to become a philosopher is a good mind and enough money to get through college and graduate school. Something similar has happened in theology. Edward Farley has touched on this in his book *Theologia* in which he refers to the early concept of theology as a sapiential habitus closely associated with monastic ascetical discipline and contrasted with the modern concept of theology as an academic discipline.

What are we to make of this alleged change? Has there really been that much of a change? If so, is it pure gain or pure loss or a mixed phenomenon? I believe that there has been a real change, especially in Protestantism in the modern period, perhaps somewhat less in Orthodoxy and Roman Catholicism. But it has not been a total change. Karl Barth attends somewhat to the discipline of the life of the theologian in his late book *Evangelical Theology* (1963). Also the Anglican tradition which I entered as an adult attends to the life discipline of its members including the theologian in its commendation of a rule of life based on the Book of Common Prayer including the Daily Office, the daily or weekly Eucharist, and the availability of penance and spiritual direction.

I suppose the basis of this concern is the Johannine axiom that in order to know the truth, one must do the truth, and the modern axiom that to understand a religious tradition, one must participate in it and practice it. My only point is that this issue is not much attended to among theologians today and that it probably should be.

In general the sociology of theology is based on the modern insight much sharpened in the last decade that theological reflection and writing always takes place in a particular social, economic, and cultural setting, and in a particular racial, sexual, and class context, which setting and context have an influence which is neither entirely irrelevant nor entirely determinative. This point has been made most recently and sharply by political and liberation theologians who have pointed out that Christian theology has usually been done by affluent, highly educated, white Euro-American males.

One aspect of this setting which has received a lot of attention recently is that theology is largely done in the academy in its various forms from the free-standing denominational seminary to the university divinity school or department of religious studies. The report on "Religious and Theological Studies in American Higher Education" by Ray Hart in the Winter 1991 edition of the *JAAR* is unintentionally an important study of the sociology of theology. According Robert Neville in his 1992 presidential address to the AAR this report reveals that the AAR is "at a crisis point in its self-definition" because many people in theological studies, particularly those who are committed to the practice of religion, feel that they are not welcome in the Academy of Religion. "They believe that the Academy defines the public objectivity of religious studies in terms of Enlightenment skepticism and holds in contempt the kind of thinking that requires long years of yogic or spiritual practice and that in the Christian tradition has been called 'faith seeking understanding.'" This is confirmed by a rumor that Harvard graduates with doctorates in theology are having an increasingly difficult time getting positions in departments of religious studies.

The point about the sociology of theology which comes through most, sharply in the Hart report is the embarrassment on the part of people in religious studies about being associated with theologians and the resentment of theologians at feeling unwelcome in the secular academy. I believe that this phenomenon derives from the long embarrassment about religion in the modern academy and from the hankering after academic respectability by religion scholars and theologians in a time when theology has taken on a life of its own which is largely in the academy rather than the church.

In a way this situation is surprising, because some of my recent experience seems to indicate the opposite situation, that is, more openness and less embarrassment about religion in the academy. My friend Sam Beer, the distinguished professor emeritus of government at Harvard, who has always been quite open about his religious commitment and practice, said to me in 1992 that in the fifties his colleagues were very embarrassed by this and wondered about his sanity, but that in recent years this had all disappeared. Also another friend,

Hilary Putnam, a senior Harvard philosopher, has recently come out as a believing and practicing Jew. This latter example, however, is rather different because the embarrassment I am referring to is mainly related to Christianity. The fact that a colleague is a practicing Buddhist would cause little if any embarrassment.

I am suggesting that this aspect of the sociology of theology is very influential in the way that theology is done today. I believe it is one of the main factors, for example, behind the current concern that theology should be a public discipline. (See chapter 3.) I think that this can be generalized to the statement that the influence of the secular academy is to move theology in a liberal direction. This is entirely appropriate if it is the result of theologians' taking account of philosophy, history, critical theory, literary criticism, and the natural and human sciences. But it is entirely inappropriate if it is simply matter of embarrassment about religious faith and thought and a hankering to be more acceptable in the academy.

An example of this aspect of the sociology of theology comes to mind. In the late fifties I had an outstanding student who wrote an excellent thesis with me on the various theological responses to the challenge of analytical philosophy, a chapter of which was published in *New Theology No. 1*, ed. Marty and Peerman. He was a Barthian Anglo-Catholic and went on to do a doctorate at St. Andrews on the theology of Bonhoeffer. Later for some reason he did everything except the dissertation for a second doctorate in theology at Yale. Then he got a job in the department of philosophy and religion at a large university in the Middle West. Since then his theology has moved steadily to the left until he now finds himself somewhere between agnosticism and left-wing Unitarianism and attends the Friends meeting. This movement has been recorded in several books and also in our correspondence. We agree that his movement has been largely (but not solely) the result of the setting in which he has been working.

Another example of the sociology of theology is the impact of the media. Several years ago the late lamented journal *Christianity and Crisis* published an issue devoted to the topic "Whatever happened to theology?" In the introduction to this symposium the editors explained the background. It seems that at an editorial meeting they were discussing what topics they should get articles about. They talked about both current national and world events and also the various fields of theological study: Bible, history, ethics, church and theology. Various suggestions were made for each topic, but when they came to theology, there was dead silence. They decided that nothing was happening in theology; thus the title "What ever happened to theology?"

The implicit assumption was that if nothing newsworthy was happening in theology, then it was dead. Now newsworthy means novelty, something new and different, exciting, radical, perhaps disturbing, shocking, even blasphemous. This attitude constitutes a pressure on theologians to produce something newsworthy. The radical or death of God movement is a good example of such a largely media event. In less dramatic form it may lead theologians to propose what they believe to be radical new proposals which will get published, get attention, and get promotion or tenure or at least get invitations to lectureships.

A final example of the sociology of theology is more in the cultural setting of theology. I am thinking of the current romantic movement which has been noted by a number of commentators but first I think by Theodore Roszak in his book *Where the Wasteland Ends* (Doubleday, 1972). His thesis is that the youth counter-culture movement of sixties was the beginning of a new romantic movement modeled on the first romantic movement of the last century.

W. T. Jones described romanticism as a "syndrome of biases" in the direction of the dynamic, the disordered, the continuous, the soft-focused, the inner, the this-worldly. Crane Brinton puts it this way:

> Sensitive, emotional, preferring color to form, the exotic to the familiar, eager for novelty, for adventure, above all for the vicarious adventure of fantasy, reveling in disorder and uncertainty, insistent on the uniqueness of the individual to the point of making a virtue of eccentricity, the typical Romantic will hold that he cannot be typical, for the very concept of 'typical' suggests the work of the pigeonholing intellect he scorns. (*Encyclopedia of Philosophy*, 7:206b)

This is epitomized for me in the comment made by a student in one of my classes who came to talk to me about my approach to theology and stated simply,

"I don't like distinctions." He explained that to distinguish is to separate, to dichotomize, to alienate, and thus to create a dualism. He could have quoted Wordsworth: "We murder to dissect."

Those of us committed to theological clarity will always find romantic theology mushy and vague. We are not drawn to Goethe's Faust who cries, "Gray, dear friend, is all theory." But I believe we have all been influenced by the current romantic movement, although those over sixty-five have probably been influenced less than those under that age. We know that romantic movements are always valuable reactions to and critiques of the over-rationalization, technologizing and bureaucratizing of society. But we also know that romantic movements are ambiguous. They can begin above Tintern Abbey, but they can end in Auschwitz. So we are ambivalent about them. College and graduate study in physics and math and later an extended study of analytical philosophy did not incline me to romanticism. On the other hand it was a reading of Wordsworth's *Prelude* my sophomore year in college that began a journey which led in the long run to my departing the naturalistic humanism of my parents and finding my way into the church. I am suggesting that many of the debates in contemporary theology derive from a generational difference in relation to the current romantic movement. (See chapter 5)

. In sum, the sociology of theology including its cultural setting always involves what I call a tilting of the table of argument in a particular direction thus making it always more difficult to argue in one direction rather than another. The tilt of the table varies from region to region and from institution to institution, but I think that there is some commonality to the tilt in a particular period. For example, during a romantic movement it is always more difficult to argue for theological clarity and rationality, the transcendence of God, the distinction of creator and creature, the value of social order, the value of science and technology, and so forth.

CHAPTER 2

THEOLOGY AND EXPERIENCE

The word "experience" is one of the most deceitful in philosophy.
— Alfred North Whitehead

However paradoxical it may seem, the concept of experience seems
to me one of the most obscure we have.
— Hans-Georg Gadamer

In the light of these warnings from two philosophers who are attended to very carefully by contemporary theologians it might be expected that theologians would use the term "experience" with considerable caution. Exactly the opposite, however, seems to be the case. Contemporary theologians are talking a great deal about experience and, as we shall see, without much clarity or precision. This is probably the result of the swing of the theological pendulum to the left in the latter half of this century. It is also probably determined by the "hunger for experience" (Gadamer, Biersdorf) which has emerged in Western culture since the sixties. This in turn I take to be an aspect of a contemporary romantic movement which, like its predecessor in the last century, is marked by a reaction against the effects of modern science and technology and their accompanying secularism and rationalization of society, and by a longing for a deeper experience of the self, the world, and the divine.[1]

---

1. See, e.g., Hans-Georg Gadamer, *Truth and Method* (trans. and ed. Garrett Barden and John Cumming; New York: Seabury, 1975): 57-8; Theodore Roszak, *Where the Wasteland Ends: Politics and Transcendence in Postindustrial Society* (Garden City, NY: Doubleday, 1972); John E. Biersdorf, *Hunger for Experience: Vital Communities in America* (New York: Seabury, 1975).

Whatever its source, several commentators have noted a remarkable increase in attention to experience among contemporary theologians.[2] A striking example is the extensive treatment of experience in the first part of Edward Schillebeeckx's book *Christ: The Experience of Jesus as Lord* which is introduced in the following way:

> At present it is clear that many believers and quite evidently a number of students of theology are reluctant to engage in theological activity which has its starting-point in scripture and tradition. . . . They are of the opinion that a modern, living theology must begin from men's present-day experience. They want to begin 'at the other end.'[3]

In this essay I want to explore this phenomenon of the increasing concern for experience in contemporary theology, and in particular to investigate the ways in which appeal is made to experience as a warrant in theological argument or as a criterion for assessing theological proposals. Since the phenomenon is so widespread, appearing in so-called secular theology, liberation theology, process theology, romantic countercultural theology, Roman Catholic fundamental theology, and forms of theology influenced by analytical philosophy, some limitation of scope is in order. I propose to focus on three theologians: Schubert Ogden, Langdon Gilkey, and David Tracy. I choose this group because as individuals they have devoted the most sustained systematic attention to this issue and as a group they have a good deal in common and refer positively to each other. My procedure will be to investigate the ways in which each of these theologians appeals to experience as a criterion of theological judgment or as a warrant in theological argument, to determine what they have in common, to assess this critically, and to make some constructive comments on the consequences.

---

2. For references see Dermot A. Lane, *The Experience of God: An Invitation to Do Theology* (New York: Paulist, 1981): chap. 1, esp. n. 30; Jean-Pierre Torrell, "New Trends in Fundamental Theology in the Postconcilear Period," in René Latourelle and Gerald O'Collins, eds., *Problems and Perspectives of Fundamental Theology* (trans. Matthew J. O'Connell; New York: Paulist, 1982): 20-2; Gerhard Ebeling, "Die Klage über das Erfahrungsdefizit in der Theologie als Frage nach ihrer Sache," *Wort und Glaube* 3 (Tübingen: Mohr-Siebeck, 1975): 3-28.
3. Edward Schillebeeckx, *Christ: The Experience of Jesus as Lord* (New York: Seabury, 1980): 29.

Ogden

In what ways does Schubert Ogden appeal to experience as a criterion of theology? His thought on this issue has developed considerably. In *Christ Without Myth* (1961) the only criteria referred to are scripture and internal consistency.[4] In *The Reality of God* (1964) a pattern emerges which has been followed since then, although with considerable development. The main criteria of the adequacy of theological statements are appropriateness to the witness of scripture and understandability in the sense of being meaningful and true.[5] The truth or validity of theological statements requires that they be logically consistent and also "warranted by our common experience as modern secular men," or by "the same general standards of experience and reason to which scientific thought is subject."[6] These references to experience are not elaborated here. They seem to point in somewhat different directions: the first in an existential direction and the second in the direction of sense experience.

In other parts of this book Ogden elaborates on his interpretation of experience which is derived largely from Whitehead and Toulmin, and which he defines as "the sum total of our observings, encounterings, and undergoings."[7] First, the "facts of our experience," that is, "its constant structure," include our experience of "our existence as selves, as those who . . . always experience themselves and the world as finite-free parts of the infinite whole."[8] Second, our experience at its deepest level involves an affirmation of the basic value and meaning of life, a faith or assurance that life is worth living, an original confidence in the final worth of our existence.[9] Therefore, third, "the reality of God is essential to, or constitutive of, . . . the common faith or experiences of all men simply as such. If God is the necessary existent, to experience anything at all, even as merely possible, is to experience it together with God as its ultimate

---

4. Schubert M. Ogden, *Christ Without Myth: A Study Based on the Theology of Rudolf Bultmann* (New York: Harper & Row, 1961): 17, 138.
5. Idem, *The Reality of God and Other Essays* (New York: Harper & Row, 1969): 6, 67, 109-10, 120-1.
6. Ibid., 20, 122.
7. Ibid., 105 n.
8. Ibid., 117; see 104-5, 114, 116.
9. Ibid., 33-4, 36-7, 114, 138, 140.

32

ground." "All our experience must be the experience of (God's) reality."[10] Thus when Ogden refers to "our common human experience," he is referring to a very specific philosophical interpretation of it, and one, moreover, which is deeply influenced by the Western Christian tradition. I will return to this point later.

In an essay entitled "Present Prospects for Empirical Theology" (1969),[11] Ogden defines Christian theology as the hermeneutical task of understanding the Christian witness at the level of reflective thought in a way that is fitting to the essential claims of that witness. The primary test of this fittingness is appropriateness to the testimony of scripture.[12] An empirical Christian theology, however, is one which also "would appeal somehow to our experience simply as men in providing the final justification for its claims," or which "would acknowledge no final basis for its claims except our common human experience."[13]

Ogden's argument for the necessity of such an empirical theology is based on the scriptural testimony to the universal immanence of God in self-disclosure in the creation and to the freedom of humanity and its responsibility for its existence. In everyone's experience of anything, God is experienced as its necessary ground. Therefore all people are able to verify or justify the claims of faith in their own experience.[14] Ogden again interprets experience, following Whitehead, primarily as the sense of being and value or worth which underlies all the rest of our experience and which comprises the experience of the self, the world, and the infinite whole which includes them.[15] He claims that this argument leads to the necessity of an empirical theology, although it seems to lead only to the necessity of the possibility of such a theology or perhaps its strategic necessity.

---

10. Ibid., 124-5; see 20.
11. In Bernard E. Loomer, ed., *The Future of Empirical Theology* (Chicago: University of Chicago Press, 1969): 65-88.
12. Ibid., 66.
13. Ibid., 66-7.
14. Ibid., 73-4.
15. Ibid., 81-6.

This terminology is modified somewhat in an essay of 1972 entitled "What is Theology?" [16] Here Ogden states that the two criteria for the adequacy of a theological statement are its appropriateness to the witness of scripture and its understandability which is determined by "the completely general criteria" which are "the relevant conditions of meaning and truth universally established with human existence." [17] It should be noted that there is no explicit reference to experience here, although it is presumably included under the reference to human existence.

It is therefore surprising to find that experience is made the focus of the discussion in an essay published in 1976 on the same general subject. In "Sources of Religious Authority in Liberal Protestantism" [18] Ogden expands on the significance of experience as a criterion in theology employing a general theory of authority.

He concludes that there are two ultimate sources of religious authority: "not only specifically Christian experience of God in Jesus the Christ but also our experience and understanding of existence simply as human beings both confirming and confirmed by the essential claims of the Christian witness," or the "universally human experience of the gift and demand of authentic existence." [19] In relation to Christian religious claims these are later described (in reverse order) in terms of "their implicit ultimate source, which can be determined only by critically interpreting the whole history of human culture and religion; and their explicit ultimate source, which can be determined only by critically interpreting not only the entire Christian tradition, including Scripture, but also, finally and decisively, the earliest witness of the church." [20]

The reason for the implicit ultimate source is that no authority can be a sufficient authorization for the meaning and truth of the claims derived from it. They can be authorized as meaningful and true only by some method other than

16. *JR* 52 (1972): 22-40.
17. Ibid., 39, 25. The same formulation is used in an essay entitled "The Authority of Scripture for Theology," *Int* 30 (1976): 244.
18. *JAAR* 44 (1976): 403-16.
19. Ibid., 412 and n. 12
20. Ibid., 415-16.

an appeal to authority, namely, by the appeal to "our universal experience simply as human beings."[21] It should be noted that the content of both these ultimate experiential sources of authority can presumably be determined only by historical-critical investigation and interpretation.

In an essay entitled "The Experience of God: Critical Reflections on Hartshorne's Theory of Analogy" (1984),[22] Ogden seems to retreat somewhat from his empirical emphasis. Now the criteria of theological statements are that they should be appropriate, that is, congruent with the apostolic testimony, and credible, defined as "worthy of being believed by the same standards of critical judgment as properly apply to any other assertions of the same logical type or types."[23] This is a shift from intelligibility to believability, which is something quite different. In our situation today these two criteria require the assertion of "the experience of God" in both the subjective and objective senses. "What we now take to be specifically required by the criterion of credibility" is that an appeal must be made "to the ultimate verdict of our common human experience. . . . This means, then, that God must be asserted to be in some way the object of human experience."[24]

Ogden goes on to state that theology is not "empirical at all in the strict sense in which science can be said to be so." Its assertions are "not subject to any strictly empirical mode of verification." The question of God "cannot possibly be adequately answered on the same basis in experience or in the same terms and concepts as any ordinary question." "The fact that 'God' must be understood to express a nonempirical concept means that no empirical evidence can possibly be relevant to the question of whether the concept applies and that, therefore, God must be experienced directly rather than indirectly through experiencing something else." Furthermore, "the experience of God is universal

---

21. Ibid., 413.
22. In John B. Cobb, Jr. and Franklin L. Gamwell, eds., *Existence and Actuality: Conversations with Charles Hartshorne* (Chicago: University of Chicago Press, 1984): 16-37. The essays in this book were presented at the Conference in Honor of Charles Hartshorne held at the Divinity School of the University of Chicago in November 1981.
23. Ibid., 17.
24. Ibid.

as well as direct — something unavoidably had . . . by every human being simply
as such . . . in each and every one of its experiences of anything at all."[25]

Ogden then notes that this is obviously a tendentious claim and turns to
Hartshorne's contribution. Hartshorne distinguishes

> two different levels of human experience, or of more or less
> conscious thinking about experience, on only the deeper of which
> is there an experience of God that is both direct and universal.
> Since such unavoidable experience of God need not be consciously
> thought about at the higher level, and, in fact, may even be absent
> or denied there, the assertion that God is directly experienced by
> every human being as such is in no way incompatible with the
> existence of non- or even a-theistic modes of thought.[26]

Ogden notes that this is close to the view of the transcendental Thomists Rahner
and Lonergan.

The most recent stage in Ogden's development of this theme appears in
The Point of Christology (1982). Here the two criteria of the adequacy of a
theological statement are its appropriateness to the apostolic witness and its
credibility which means "credible to human existence as judged by common
experience and reason."[27] Ogden explains that the credibility of a theological
assertion is the credibility of its metaphysical and moral or theoretical and
practical implications, whether they can be believed on the basis of our common
human experience and reason.[28]

He notes that the conditions of both aspects of credibility are variable and
dependent upon the historical situation,[29] whereas previously he has implied that
these criteria are invariable and independent of the situation by the use of such
terms as "generic," "universal," "general," and "human existence as such." While
the theoretical implications are assessed by demythologization and metaphysical
interpretation, the practical implications are assessed by deideologization and
political interpretation. The latter have previously been ignored because of the

---

25. Ibid., 18-9.
26. Ibid., 20
27. Schubert M. Ogden, *The Point of Christology* (San Francisco: Harper & Row, 1982): 4.
28. Ibid., 130, 148-9.
29. Ibid., 88.

class bias of theologians.[30] Thus the christology of liberation which Ogden is proposing is practically credible "only insofar as we ourselves, as individuals and as the community called church, also live up to the demand that it strictly implies — by involving ourselves in the ongoing struggles for basic justice."[31]

In summary it can be stated that Ogden's understanding of the criteria of Christian theology involves a two-fold appeal to experience.

1) A theological statement is appropriate if it is derived from or coherent with the specifically Christian experience of God in Christ as found in the earliest layer of the church's witness.

2) A theological statement is meaningful and true if it can be verified or justified or validated (a) by the common or universal experience and reason of modern secular people, or (b) by the standards of experience and reason to which scientific thought is subject, or (c) by the universally human experience of the gift and demand of authentic experience, or (d) by whether or not the church lives up to the demands implied by the theological statement.

It is clear that the first is determined solely by historical critical analysis of the New Testament. Thus it is not an appeal to experience except in the trivial sense that every appeal to anything is an appeal to experience, since otherwise it could not be known in order to be appealed to. In regard to the second, the problem is the diversity of the references. (d) seems to be the kind of appeal which could be tested by empirical research of the type carried out by the human sciences, and the problems it involves will be taken up later. (a) is the most common form and is found in several essays, whereas the others are found only in single essays. However (a) is ambiguous. It can refer to the actual experience of modern secular people as they themselves interpret it, or it can refer to a specific philosophical interpretation of experience or the conditions of experience, such as Whitehead's or Heidegger's.

So the fundamental question is whether or not Ogden believes that his claims could in principle be confirmed or disconfirmed by the actual experience

---

30. Ibid., 94, 96.
31. Ibid., 167.

of modern people. On the one hand, his phraseology as noted above often implies this, especially his references to "experiences in which we all inescapably share," "what each of us actually experiences," the "essential features of our experience which everyone must recognize," and to the fact that everyone can "verify the claims of faith in terms of his own experience."[32] On the other hand, many versions of his claims suggest a negative answer to this question. In these he implies that he is referring not to the actual experience of modern people as they themselves interpret it but to a quite specific philosophical interpretation of it.[33] So that to any people's testimony that their experience did not confirm his claims, he could reply that their interpretation of their experience was inadequate and not fully critical or reflective.

So I believe that we must conclude that with the single exception of (d) above, which will be explored later, Ogden's references to experience are misleading in the sense that they imply some kind of empirical claim which can be verified by anyone in his or her experience or through the testimony of people to their experience. We have found, however, that these claims are not empirical in that sense but only in the quite different sense of a very specific philosophical interpretation of experience with which honest, sensitive, and reflective people could disagree.

Gilkey

In what ways does Langdon Gilkey appeal to experience as a criterion of theological statements? In *Naming the Whirlwind* (1969), experience is referred to as a criterion of the meaningfulness and validity of theological assertions in three ways. First, a theological symbol is meaningful only if it thematizes or conceptualizes a dimension of common secular experience. Second, a theological statement is valid only if it thematizes a concrete particular experience in which

---

32. Ogden, *Reality of God*, 20; idem, *Empirical Theology*, 86-7, 74.
33. See, e.g., *Reality of God*, 20, 114, 125; and *Empirical Theology*, 77-86, where Ogden criticizes interpretations of experience that are derived from British empiricism, continental philosophy of life, and American radical empiricism, and commends Whitehead's interpretation of the nature of experience.

38

something new emerges which answers an existential question. Third, a theological statement is valid only if it is able to interpret and illuminate all other areas of experience.

In regard to the first, Gilkey carries out what he calls an ontic or phenomenological analysis of our felt or lived experience, our ordinary, day-to-day secular experience. Within the central elements of secular experience, namely, its sense of contingency, relativity, temporality, and autonomy, he finds a dimension of ultimacy which points to the source, ground, horizon, and limit of secular experience.[34] Thus he concludes that theological symbols are meaningful.

Gilkey characterizes the second way in which experience functions as a criterion as the reception of revelation. This occurs in concrete historical experiences of a particular religious community and tradition. Theology is the symbolic thematization of these existential experiences. Theological assertions are verified and validated only in the life of the religious community. Proof is not possible here but only confession and conviction based on the acknowledgment of a particular experience.[35] "The *validity* of positive religious discourse and the *reality* of its object are inescapably based on 'faith' as the apprehension of the sacred in and through the profane."[36]

The third way in which experience serves as a criterion of theology refers to the width of the relevance, and the adequacy of the explanatory power, of a theological statement or system. Gilkey describes this in terms of a Christian philosophy or ontology but does not explore it further.[37]

This scheme of the relation of theology and experience is expanded but not basically modified in *Reaping the Whirlwind* (1976). As he did in the first

---

34. Langdon Gilkey, *Naming the Whirlwind: The Renewal of God-Language* (Indianapolis: Bobbs-Merrill, 1969): 250, 296-7, 313, 362-4. It should be pointed out that Gilkey's language and arguments about experience are rather ambiguous. For example, it is unclear whether ultimacy does or does not appear directly in concrete human experience. See the careful critique of some of his arguments by Frederick Ferré, "A Renewal of God-Language?" *JR* 52 (1972): 286-304.

35. *Naming the Whirlwind*, 428, 451.

36. Ibid., 455. It is interesting to note that the point which Gilkey affirms here is exactly the point he criticizes in neo-orthodoxy on pp. 97-9. See also Langdon Gilkey, *Reaping the Whirlwind: A Christian Interpretation of History* (New York: Seabury, 1976): 147-8.

37. *Naming the Whirlwind*, 275, 451, 460, 463.

volume, Gilkey asserts that a religious symbol is meaningful for us only if it thematizes our actual experience and resolves an existential question for us.[38] Likewise there are two levels of truth in theological reflection. First, a symbolic account is true if it illuminates and brings to coherent understanding a wide variety of experience. Second, religious symbols become true for us when through them we experience the reality they symbolize communicating itself.[39] The first is a necessary but not sufficient condition for the establishment of the validity of a symbol system. The second is also necessary and is described as follows: "If theology is taken to be true, ultimately it is because its symbols are experienced to communicate a real encounter with God, because through them the divine presence, the divine activity, and the divine promises are communicated to our existence."[40]

To summarize, Gilkey appeals to experience as a criterion of theological statements in three ways:

1) A theological symbol or statement is meaningful only if it thematizes a dimension of common secular experience and constitutes an answer to or resolution of an existential question.

2) A theological statement is valid only if it is able to interpret all areas of experience in an ontology.

3) A theological statement is valid only if it mediates an experience of the divine presence and thus is verified in the experience and life of the religious community.

Gilkey does not explain how (3) could actually be used or applied to a particular proposal, but the difficulties involved in any such attempt will be explored below. Similar problems are involved in (2) as a criterion of a theological proposal. In fact, Gilkey presents it as a criterion for a total religious symbol system. Moreover, a method would have to be specified for analyzing all

---

38. *Reaping the Whirlwind*, 144.
39. Ibid., 146-7.
40. Ibid., 148.

experience and of assessing ontological categories. This constitutes a task for a lifetime and would be impossible to apply to a particular theological proposal.

Since Gilkey explores only (1) in some detail, let us inquire in what sense it is an investigation of actual ordinary human experience. His exploration is carried out largely through introspection and memory and through references to about twenty philosophers and theologians, most of whom are from past generations, and especially Heidegger, Whitehead, Tillich, and Reinhold Niebuhr. There are also references to four novelists and playwrights, two psychiatrists, one historian, and to one report of an actual interview (from a review of a collection of interviews from *Playboy* magazine). No doubt this is a sensitive interpretation of contemporary experience, but of a very narrow segment. By that I mean that it is clearly the experience of a particular elite: an academic, male, white, middle-aged, affluent elite. Sociologist Andrew Greeley comments in another connection: "The fallacy of equating what goes on in the intellectual community — and only a segment of that — with the whole society is one that has been so long enshrined among academics, that he who questions it is viewed as just a little odd. . . 'Western man,' 'modern man, 'technological man,' 'secular man' are to be found, for the most part only on university campuses, and increasingly only among senior faculty members."[41]

Gilkey's analysis of the experience of this elite may also be an accurate interpretation of the common experience of ordinary secular people. But the only way to find this out is to ask them. Gilkey's work does not indicate that he has done this. In fact, evidence suggests that his picture of the shape of ordinary secular experience is quite inaccurate.[42] So I must conclude that at the only point where Gilkey claims to carry out an investigation of ordinary secular experience, it turns out to be largely a matter of introspection, informal observation, and academic construction.

---

41. Andrew M. Greeley, *Unsecular Man: The Persistence of Religion* (New York: Schocken, 1972): 3.
42. See ibid., chap. 1; Ferré, "Renewal of God-Language?," 304; and Tom F. Driver, Review of *Naming the Whirlwind USQR* 25 (1970): 361-7.

Tracy

How does David Tracy appeal to experience as a criterion in theology? In *Blessed Rage for Order* (1975) he defines the task of fundamental theology as that of correlating the meanings found in common human experience and in the Christian fact. Common human experience is explored by a phenomenological method to determine the meaning and meaningfulness of that experience, and by a metaphysical or transcendental method to determine the truth status of the cognitive claims involved in that experience.[43] The phenomenological analysis is carried out by means of Jaspers' existentialist philosophy, Lonergan's transcendental Thomism, and Toulmin's analytical philosophy.[44]

This analysis of common human experience requires the explication of three sets of criteria: meaningfulness, meaning, and truth.

A particular experience or language is 'meaningful' when it discloses an authentic dimension of our experience as selves. It has 'meaning' when its cognitive claims can be expressed conceptually with internal coherence. It is 'true' when transcendental or metaphysical analysis shows its 'adequacy to experience' by explicating how a particular concept (e.g., time, space, self, or God) functions as a fundamental 'belief' or 'condition of possibility' of all our experience.[45]

Furthermore, the central metaphysical requirement of fidelity or adequacy to experience is fulfilled by an explication of the conditions of the possibility of the experiencing self in the metaphysical turn to the subject in process philosophy and transcendental Thomism.[46]

Tracy further refers to experience in connection with the assessment of symbol systems. They should be judged by their "relative experiential adequacy" and their adequacy for character transformation and praxis, also referred to as existential verification. In his later book *The Analogical Imagination* (1981)

---

43. David Tracy, *Blessed Rage for Order: The New Pluralism in Theology* (New York: Seabury, 1975): 52, 69.
44. Ibid., 94-115.
45. Ibid., 71. I will not pause to point out the confusion in this passage. But one wonders how an "experience" can be shown to be "adequate to experience" by the transcendental analysis of a concept, by explicating how it is a "condition of possibility of all our experience."
46. Ibid., chap. 8.

Tracy elaborates this emphasis on praxis and transformation in his treatment of practical theology. Here the criterion of truth is the authenticity of the praxis of the theologian. A more classical and theoretical form of this is found in Lonergan's theory of the necessity for intellectual, moral, and religious conversion on the part of the theologian.[47]

In summary, we find four different kinds of appeal to experience as a criterion of theological statements in Tracy's writings.

(1) A theological proposal is meaningful if a phenomenological analysis of experience, demonstrates that it discloses an authentic dimension of experience.

(2) A theological proposal is true if metaphysical or transcendental analysis shows that it is adequate to experience, by explicating how it functions as a condition of the possibility of all our experience.

(3) A theological proposal is true if it can be demonstrated to be experientially valid by producing character transformation and authentic praxis.

(4) A theological proposal is true if it is founded on authentic conversion and/or praxis.

(3) and (4) are related in a circular manner, and their difficulties as criteria of theology are the same as for Gilkey's third point. The criteria for authentic character transformation, authentic praxis, and authentic conversion must be determined before they can function as criteria. These criteria cannot be derived from the experience of these phenomena without vicious circularity.

(1) and (2) are not really appeals to the actual experience of people as they themselves interpret it, but to very specific philosophical analyses.[48] Although Tracy states that he is concerned to analyze our actual concrete experience, his access to this is through the particular analyses of philosophers and theologians. Although, he asserts, in connection with practical theology, the necessity of "strictly empirical analyses of our actual economic, political, cultural, and social

---

47. David Tracy, *The Analogical Imagination: Christian Theology and the Culture of Pluralism* (New York: Crossroad, 1981): 69 -71.
48. In this connection see the critique of the "fallacy of disguised idealization" by Robert C. Neville in *Reconstruction of Thinking* (Albany: SUNY Press, 1981): 87-8.

situation (i.e., the kind of analyses probably best represented by the empirical character of the best of American social analyses . . .),"[49] his own references to experience are quite nonempirical. Finally, though Tracy is concerned to treat our common, shared, or universal experience as human beings, it is clear that his construction of experience is quite narrow in the same sense as Gilkey's. He wants to adopt a point of view informed by the sociology of knowledge and in particular by the critical social theory of the Frankfurt school,[50] but he does not apply this to his own understanding of experience.

It might be objected at this point that my criticism of Gilkey and Tracy for being nonempirical is misplaced. They claim to be performing phenomenological analyses of common human experience, and proper phenomenological statements are generally agreed to be nonempirical in character. They are derived not from empirical investigation but from the intuition of essences. It would seem, however, that neither Gilkey nor Tracy is carrying out a phenomenological analysis in the pure or rigorous sense, but in the broad sense of a general philosophical interpretation of experience which, they imply, is empirical in the sense of appealing to people's experience.[51]

Summary

In large part Ogden, Gilkey, and Tracy appeal not to the actual experience of people as they themselves interpret it, but to an alleged common or universal experience, to an alleged transcendental analysis of experience or of the conditions of the possibility of all experience, or to various specific philosophical analyses and constructions of experience.

On this point a consensus is beginning to emerge which is highly critical of this understanding of experience, and in particular of the possibility of universal or transcendental judgments about the character of experience and of the

---

49. *Blessed Rage for Order,* 246-7.
50. Ibid., 246-8; *Analogical Imagination,* 72-7.
51. See Gilkey, *Naming the Whirlwind,* 243-6; Tracy, *Blessed Rage for Order,* 47-8, 64-9.

44

implied interpretation of the relation of language and experience.[52] This emerging consensus has its roots in the growing philosophical reaction to the transcendental turn to the subject and to the claims of transcendental or foundational philosophy, which is seen, for example, in the works of Stephan Körner and Richard Rorty. In theology the challenge to transcendentalism has come through political, liberation, and hermeneutical theology. Political theologians have argued that the transcendental approach overlooks the social conditioning of knowledge, the need for ideology criticism, and the relevance of practice in the formation of theory. Hermeneutical theologians have criticized transcendentalism for ignoring the interpretive dimension of experience.

Recent works by Francis Schüssler Fiorenza and George A. Lindbeck have elaborated these criticisms. Schüssler Fiorenza argues that experience is primarily an act of interpretation which takes place within the context of cultural history and is thus embedded in a cultural tradition. He summarizes his argument with specific reference to Ogden and Tracy.

> To take the conditioning of human experience by historical tradition as a hermeneutical principle is to challenge the notion of a transcendental experience or of a transcendental analysis of the religious dimension of experience. Within contemporary fundamental theology, an appeal is made to human experience of a common faith, a common trust in reality, and an underlying religious dimension. This appeal overlooks the extent to which any human experience takes place within a cultural tradition that provides concepts and paradigms according to which that experience is interpreted. There are no experiences of the religious dimension of reality that can escape the influence of the historical tradition in shaping religious experience.[53]

Lindbeck's point is similar. He argues for a cultural-linguistic interpretation of religion in which religions are seen primarily as languages or interpretive schemes with correlative forms of life. Thus religions produce or shape experience rather than being the expressions of experience. Language and symbol are necessary preconditions for feeling and experience. Therefore, with

---

52. See the summary of this development by Francis Schüssler Fiorenza, *Foundational Theology: Jesus and the Church* (New York: Crossroad, 1984): 259-64.
53. Ibid., 299.

specific reference to Tracy, Lindbeck criticizes any transcendental deduction of experience and argues that there cannot be "an inner experience of God common to all human beings and religions. There can be no experiential core because . . . the experiences that religions evoke and mold are as varied as the interpretive schemes they embody. Adherents of different religions do not diversely thematize the same experience; rather they have different experiences."[54]

Ogden, Tracy, and Gilkey do, however, make appeals to actual experience which can be summarized as follows: A theological proposal is meaningful and true if the church lives up to the demands implied by the proposal, or if it constitutes an answer to an existential question, or if it is verified in the experience of the religious community, or if it produces authentic character transformation or praxis. These are the kinds of appeal to actual experience which cannot be determined in advance by any philosophical interpretation or transcendental analysis but which can be determined only by empirical investigation. In that sense they are valid appeals to experience. However, as I have indicated above in connection with Gilkey's formulation, the problems involved in such appeals are formidable.[55]

For these appeals to function as theological criteria the following would have to be specified: how the church's moral life is to be assessed; the nature of the experience of an existential question and of its answer and whose experience is being investigated; what is involved in verification in a community and what are the limits of the religious community; what aspects of the experience of the members of the religious community are being considered; what are the characteristics of authentic character transformation and praxis; what research methodology is to be used, including the procedures for selecting a scientific sample, and for collecting, collating, and interpreting the data.

---

54. George A. Lindbeck, *The Nature of Doctrine: Religion and Theology in a Postliberal Age* (Philadelphia: Westminster, 1984): 40.
55. For a thorough analysis of the problems involved in an appeal to experience in theology, see Anders Jeffner, *Kriterien christlicher Glaubenslehre: Eine prinzipielle Untersuchung heutiger protestantischer Dogmatik im deutschen Sprachbereich* (Acta Universitatis Upsaliensis, Studia Doctrinae Christiane Upsaliensia 13; Stockholm: Almqvist & Wiksell, 1977): chap. 4.

Moreover, the grounds for these various judgments would have to be specified. Since some of these involve theological judgments, the criteria for them would have to be made clear in a way that is not viciously circular. I understand this to be the point of Tillich's well-known criticism of experience as a criterion of theology. The appeal to experience as a theological criterion must involve the use of a prior criterion to distinguish authentic experience from inauthentic. In the nature of the case this criterion cannot be derived from the experience in question but must be brought to it. Then this criterion functions as the theological criterion and the experience itself does not.[56]

Since none of the questions listed above is resolved by these theologians, we must conclude that although they propose appeals to actual experience in a limited sense, they have not indicated how these appeals could be carried out or assessed.

Conclusion

Is this not the result that we might have expected? To be sure, experience in the comprehensive sense confirms or disconfirms a theological proposal in an obscure and complex manner over the long term both in the individual and in the life of the community. This is what Tillich refers to as "experiential verification."[57] However, this refers more to a whole symbol system or religious worldview than to a particular doctrine, and it occurs over a period of years or even the course of a lifetime.[58] Thus it is not a process which an individual theologian can observe or investigate in a period of, say, a year while assessing a particular theological proposal. This process, however, is perhaps the cause of the fact that a theologian affirms or denies a particular theological proposal. That is, a theologian can be aware of such a tidal movement in his or her own convictions,

---

56. Paul Tillich, *Systematic Theology* 3 vols., Chicago: University of Chicago Press, 1951-63): 1.40-46.

57. Ibid., 1.44, 102-5.

58. See, e.g., B. L. Hebblethwaite, "The Appeal to Experience in Christology," in S. W. Sykes and J. P. Clayton, eds., *Christ, Faith and History: Cambridge Studies in Christology* (Cambridge: Cambridge University Press, 1972): 263-78, esp. 268; Richard Crossman, ed., *The God That Failed* (New York: Bantam, 1950).

and it can be the basis of testimony to the meaningfulness and validity of a proposal for the individual. Thus it may be that most theology is done backwards in the sense that it is the exploration of the possible grounds in scripture, tradition, and other authorities for a theological conviction which has been arrived at in some other way.[59] However, it is clear that the experience of one theologian, no matter how representative and universal it is believed to be, can hardly function as a warrant in a theological argument.

The fact that experience in the comprehensive sense confirms or disconfirms a theological proposal in an obscure and complex manner over the long term in the individual and the community is probably the basis of the further fact that appeals to experience in theology seem so weighty. Another reason for this is that in one sense a theological argument can appeal *only* to experience; that is, one cannot appeal to anything which cannot be experienced. However, when logically we can appeal only to experience, then the claim that we should appeal to experience becomes vacuous, since there is no alternative.

This is presumably the point of Tillich's dictum that experience is not the source of theology but rather the medium through which all the sources are received.[60] Tillich's dictum also indicates the way out of the dilemma, namely, to make distinctions in experience between the various sources available to us through experience, such as scripture, tradition, magisterium, and so forth.

Tillich's position has been confirmed and elaborated in a recent study on this question. Edward Farley argues that the criteria of theology are fields of evidence mediated by experience:

> Our thesis is that experience itself does not function in any interpretative enterprise, cognitive or otherwise, as a field of evidence. The field of evidence is available through experience and the entities of that field are apprehended as existing entities through experience. . . . Evidence for judgments is thus the activity, manifestation or behavior of the entity. Experience mediates but does not constitute that evidence.

---

59. See my essay "Where Are We in Theology?" in Martin E. Marty and Dean G. Peerman, eds., *New Theology* No. 9 (New York: Macmillan, 1972).
60. Tillich, *Systematic Theology*, 1. 42.

> Theologically this distinction is between the experiential world of
> faith and the criteria of theological judgments. It is not incorrect to
> say that theological judgments are grounded in experience. In a
> certain sense all judgments are. But as it stands, the statement is
> elusive, and it is utterly misleading if it is taken to mean that
> experience is that to which theology appeals to justify a judgment
> as true. The reason is the one just given. If theology is able to
> make true judgments at all, it must have some field of evidence to
> which it refers. That is, it must have some manifested activity,
> behavior, and structure disclosing itself through experience.[61]

Experience, however, is often distinguished from other sources of theology as an object of independent appeal. Ogden, as we have seen, appeals to scripture and reason as well as to experience. Therefore, experience here must refer to an area of experience different from that through which scripture or reason is mediated. This is probably a reference to what is usually called inner experience — the experience of oneself, one's body, one's emotions and feelings, the flow of one's awareness or consciousness — as distinct from one's experience of anything else. It should be noted, however, that the experience of rational reflection — the awareness of implication, contradiction, self-evidence, and so forth — is presumably an aspect of inner experience.

In any case, an appeal to experience in this sense means an appeal to a particular aspect of experience, and some grounds would have to be given for this choice. Or, as Tillich suggests, a criterion would have to be brought to experience as a whole to distinguish this more important or authentic aspect of it from the less important or authentic aspects. Thus neither this aspect of experience nor experience as a whole could be the ultimate object of the appeal.

Furthermore, there are other reasons why experience cannot function very well as an independent theological criterion.[62] One can hardly appeal to the Bible in support of religious experience as a criterion, given the prophetic attitude toward Israel's religious experience and Jesus' attitude toward his disciples' experience. The great variety and instability of Christian experience, including its

---

61. Edward Farley, *Ecclesial Reflection: An Anatomy of Theological Method* (Philadelphia: Fortress, 1982): 175-6.
62. For an elaboration of these points see my book *Theological Questions: Analysis and Argument* (Wilton, CT: Morehouse-Barlow, 1983): 28-31.

fascist, racist, sexist, and classist forms, hardly qualifies it to function as a theological criterion. As we have noted, a further difficulty is that without the proper symbols or concepts a subject matter cannot be experienced at all. So it can be argued that experience must appeal to concepts to be validated rather than the other way around. This latter point is particularly critical for Gilkey and Tracy, since both of them in their appeals to experience refer especially to what they call preconceptual, prethematic, or prelinguistic experience.[63] Finally, it can be argued that a valid theological proposal may contradict previous experience or transform present experience, or produce new and unforeseen experience. If this should be the case, then it would be difficult to argue that any existing state of experience should be the criterion of a theological proposal.

Must we conclude, therefore, that experience is entirely irrelevant to theological argument and judgment? Not necessarily. It is generally agreed that theology deals with God and God's relation to the world. Those who appeal to experience as a criterion of theology sometimes argue that the experience of God, however understood, is identical with the relation to God, and that therefore theology should attend to experience. Those who object to this approach often argue that the experience of God is not identical with the relation to God, and that therefore theology should not appeal to the former in order to interpret the latter.

One can argue, in distinction from both positions, that, while the experience of God is not identical with the relation to God, it is an aspect of it: the experience of God is informative in regard to the relation to God. This can be seen from the analogy of human relations — the most common analogy for the relation to God in the Bible and Christian history — especially as human relations are illumined by the insights of psychotherapy. It is clear that a person's experience of a relation with another person is not identical with the actual relation to the other person, yet it is an important aspect of that relation. Therefore, it follows from the analogy that theology must attend to experience as

---

63. See Gilkey, *Naming the Whirlwind*, 277-9; Tracy, *Blessed Rage for Order*, 47. For a critique of Gilkey and Tracy on this point see Thomas, *Theological Questions*, 30 n. 9; Schüssler Fiorenza, *Foundational Theology* 41, 296-300; and Lindbeck, *Nature of Doctrine*, chap. 2.

part of its task and can appeal to experience in some sense in support of its proposals. However, in order to clarify just what part experience might play in theological argument, we must gain a better understanding of the actual relation between experience and theological statements.

Since I have developed a theory of the relation between experience and theology in another place, I will only summarize it here.[64] The possible relations between a particular segment of religious experience and a particular theological proposal fall on a spectrum running from full complementarity through independence to contradiction. Complementarity involves a good fit or coherence between experience and a theological proposal. The proposal orders, makes sense of, illuminates, and thus successfully interprets the experience. The experience confirms, supports, and thus gives evidence for the proposal. Independence is a neutral relation between the two, and contradiction is the polar opposite of complementarity.[65] Thus experience can function as a criterion of a theological proposal by manifesting a certain degree of complementarity on such a spectrum.

This leads us to the most problematic aspect of the possible use of experience as a criterion in assessing theological proposals, or as an object of appeal in a theological argument, namely, the research aspect referred to above. This has received no attention whatever by theologians who talk about experience as a criterion in theology. By research I refer to all the problems involved in the investigation of the actual experience of people as they themselves interpret it, the issues of research methodology in the human sciences. This involves many questions in social science methodology which are beyond my competence. All that can be done here is to mention some of the problems which must be addressed in any such research project.

Let us assume that our project is to investigate the degree to which a particular theological proposal is confirmed or disconfirmed in the experience of

---

64. *Theological Questions*, 31-2.
65. For an excellent example of such a contradictory relationship see the study by Judith Plaskow of the relation between women's experiences and the doctrines of sin and grace in R. Niebuhr and Tillich: *Sex, Sin and Grace: Women's Experience and the Theologies of Reinhold Niebuhr and Paul Tillich* (Washington: University Press of America, 1980).

Christians. First, the meaning of the key terms in the proposal must be specified clearly. Second, the research method must be determined, probably what is known as the social research interview. For such interviews questions must be developed which will explore the various aspects of the experience of the person interviewed as they bear upon the theological proposal. Third, the survey sample must be determined.[66] Finally, the scope of the research must be decided, namely, whose experience is to be investigated? If it is to be limited to Christians, how will they be defined? Will they be only those who have been baptized with water in the triune name of God? Will they be limited to those who are active as defined by weekly or monthly attendance at public worship, private prayer, and contribution, financial or otherwise, to the work of the church? Will there be other limitations, such as to women, certain minorities, the poor, or the oppressed? If so, the limits of these groups would have to be specified and the grounds given for such limits. If major Protestant, Orthodox, and Roman Catholic bodies are to be included, is the research to be limited to one area in one nation, to a scientific sample of members of various churches in different areas in one nation or many nations? What is the minimum research project which could be considered significant in assessing a theological proposal? How is this to be decided?

Suppose that a large research project involving a dozen congregations in each of six nations in different areas of the world (and costing hundreds of thousands of dollars) concluded that the experience of the majority failed to confirm, in the sense discussed above, the particular proposal. What would the theologian make of this? Would the theologian assume that this settled the issue? I doubt it, especially if the theologian favored the proposal. Many reasons would occur to her or him as to why the research should not be taken seriously, reasons deriving, for example, from questions of the sociology of knowledge, and offering explanations as to why the people were mistaken or their experience

---

66. For the issues involved in the latter two points see the essays on "Interviewing: Social Research" by Robert L. Kahn and Charles F. Cannell, and "Sample Surveys" by W. Edwards Deming in *The International Encyclopedia of the Social Sciences* (ed. David L. Sills; 17 vols.; New York: Macmillan/Free Press, 1968): 8.149-61, 13.594-612, respectively.

misinterpreted. In other words, in such a situation all the limitations of experience as a theological criterion would surface in the mind of the theologian, and the results of the research would be outweighed by his or her own conviction.

Now it should be clear what is involved in apparently casual assertions that theological proposals must be tested by experience. Most of such assertions betray an ignorance of the magnitude of the implications involved.

If the scope of the necessary research makes such an enterprise unfeasible, then is there some other way in which the experience of Christian people can be brought to bear on theological proposals? This brings us to a consideration of the phenomenon of doctrinal development or tradition and its interpretation by the church, which has received most attention by Roman Catholic theologians. Ideally the picture presented is that the experience of members of the church filters slowly upwards through the hierarchy until after a period of generations or even centuries it comes to be proposed and acted upon in a council of the church or a papal declaration. The Dogmatic Constitution on Divine Revelation of Vatican II states:

> This tradition which comes from the apostles develops in the Church with the help of the Holy Spirit. For there is a growth in the understanding of the realities and the words which have been handed down. This happens through the contemplation and study made by believers, who treasure these things in their hearts (cf. Lk. 2:19, 51), through the innate understanding of spiritual things they experience, and through the preaching of those who have received through episcopal succession the sure gift of truth.[67]

A commentator adds, "Note that the first medium of this development is the consideration and contemplation of revealed truth by the faithful."[68] Although this is very far from a scientific process, it may be the only feasible way of determining the consensus of the experience of the members of the church, or at least the Roman Catholic Church.

---

67. Walter M. Abbot, ed., *The Documents of Vatican II* (New York: American Press, 1966): 116.

68. Ibid., 116 n. See also the commentary by Joseph Ratzinger in *Commentary on the Documents of Vatican II* (New York: Herder and Herder, 1969): 3.186; see also Yves M. J. Congar, *Tradition and Traditions: A Historical and Theological Essay* (London: Burns and Oates, 1966): 323-8.

At this point, of course, Protestants will object that exactly this process demonstrates the invalidity of the appeal to experience in theology, especially when it is not really tested by scripture and the tradition of the so-called undivided church. And they will point to the later Marian dogmas as examples of this.[69] Indeed it can be argued that this does confirm the criticism made above of Christian experience: that it is so various and unstable and determined by irrelevant factors as to be unusable as a theological criterion.

However, perhaps we must conclude that, if the resources for social scientific research are not available, the only way in which the actual experience of Christian people can be brought to bear as one factor in the assessment of theological proposals, in Tillich's sense of "experiential verification," is not in the short term, in which an individual theologian is assessing some proposal, but rather only in the long term process, as imprecise and rough as it is, of a truly ecumenical council in which attention is paid to the ascertaining of the experience of laity as well as clergy, and in which such consensus of experience is tested by the criterion of coherence with the testimony of scripture as understood in the light of tradition.

We have explored the ways in which three contemporary theologians appeal to experience as a criterion of theological judgment or as a warrant in theological argument. We have found that some of these ways were not appeals to the actual experience of people as they themselves would interpret it but rather to an alleged common or universal experience, to an alleged transcendental analysis of experience, or of the conditions of the possibility of all experience, or to various other specific philosophical analyses or constructions of experience. We have criticized these appeals as highly problematic.

We have noted that these theologians also appeal in various ways to the actual experience of people presumably as they themselves would interpret it. But we have found that they have apparently not been aware of the difficulties involved in the carrying out of such appeals. We have not investigated the ways

---

69. See idem, *Lay People in the Church: A Study for a Theology of the Laity* (trans. Donald Attwater; Westminster, MD: Newman, 1955): 287.

in which appeals to experience are made in feminist, liberation, process, and other theologies, but we suspect in the light of the above analysis that similar problems would emerge in these theologies as well.

Finally, we have concluded that, while the experience of the individual and the group is a decisive factor in their acceptance or rejection of a theological proposal, the investigation of this experience poses such complex problems as to make it practically impossible, except on a scale so small that the results would be of little significance. So we find ourselves in the paradoxical situation of realizing both the fundamentally determinative character of experience in regard to theology and also the practical unavailability of this experience for the purposes of assessment and argument in theology. Thus it turns out that the concept of experience is as "obscure" and "deceitful" in theology as Gadamer and Whitehead have found it to be in philosophy.

CHAPTER 3

PUBLIC THEOLOGY AND COUNTER-PUBLIC SPHERES

In the past decade a number of influential theologians have claimed, based on the analogy of modern science, that Christian theology is or should be public discourse, a public discipline which is addressed to all people and which uses criteria acceptable to all. This claim is usually contrasted with a view in which theology is understood as private, subjective, authoritarian, based on faith or a special revelation, and limited to a particular community. In this essay I shall explore in particular David Tracy's claim that theology should be public discourse, point out some difficulties with regard to this claim, and make an alternative proposal.

Although Tracy's thesis about theology as a public discipline was first broached in an essay in 1975,[1] his most complete statement is in *The Analogical Imagination.* He begins with a global assertion: "This book will argue that all theology is public discourse."[2] The addressee of any theological statement is "any fellow human being."[3] "Theology, by the very nature of the kind of fundamental existential questions it asks and because of the nature of the reality of God upon which theology reflects, must develop public, not private, criteria and discourse."[4] He describes publicness as involving "argument and evidence."[5]

---

1. See David Tracy, "Theology as Public Discourse," *The Christian Century 92* (1975): 280-4.
2. David Tracy, *The Analogical Imagination: Christian Theology and the Culture of Pluralism* (New York: Crossroad, 1981): 3.
3. Ibid., 4.
4. Ibid., xi.
5. Ibid., 6. See also David Tracy, "Afterword: Theology, Public Discourse, and the American Tradition," in Michael J. Lacey, ed., *Religion and Twentieth-Century American Intellectual Life* (Cambridge: Cambridge University Press, 1989): 193-203. For similar views of theology as public, see Robert C. Neville, *The Tao and the Daimon: Segments of a Religious*

Why is Tracy concerned that theology should be a public discipline? His commitment to a public theology derives from his concerns about the privatization of religion and about the situation of pluralism in religion. He believes that a public theology will avoid or overcome the privatization of religion and its relegation to a "marginal existence as one interesting but purely private option."[6] Furthermore, Tracy sees religious pluralism as a fundamental enrichment of the human condition, and "to affirm pluralism responsibly must include an affirmation of truth and public criteria for that affirmation."[7]

A major issue with regard to this thesis about the public character of theology is that Christian theology generally appeals to the normativity of Jesus and the particularity of the Christian tradition. On the surface, this does not seem to be coherent with the public character of theology. Tracy handles this issue by making a distinction between fundamental and systematic theology. The thesis about the public character of theology applies fully only to fundamental theology, not to systematic theology.

> In terms of modes of argument, *fundamental* theologies will be concerned principally to provide arguments that all reasonable persons, whether 'religiously involved' or not, can recognize as reasonable. It assumes, therefore, the most usual meaning of public discourse: that discourse available (*in principle*) to all persons and explicated by appeals to one's experience, intelligence, rationality and responsibility, and formulated in arguments where claims are stated with appropriate warrants, backings and rebuttal procedures. *Systematic* theologies will ordinarily show less concern with such obviously public modes of arguments.[8]

Inquiry (Albany: SUNY Press, 1982): 12, 16-17, 21; and idem, *Behind the Masks of God: An Essay Toward Comparative Theology* (Albany: SUNY Press, 1991): 35; also David Ray Griffin, *God and Religion in the Postmodern World: Essays in Postmodern Theology* (Albany: SUNY Press, 1989): xiv, 8. It should be noted, however, that there are other quite different interpretations of public theology with which we are not concerned here. See, for example, Ronald F. Thiemann, *Constructing a Public Theology: The Church in a Pluralistic Society* (Louisville, KY: Westminster/John Knox, 1991).

6. Tracy, *The Analogical Imagination*, xi.
7. Ibid. Tracy's many references to pluralism in this volume are, with one exception, to an intra-Christian pluralism. For different reasons for the concern that theology should be public see Neville, *The Tao and the Daimon*, 11-12; and Griffin, *God and Religion in Postmodern Theology*, xiii.
8. Tracy, *The Analogical Imagination*, 57.

This distinction is explained further in a note where it is asserted that systematic theology, "although not obviously 'public' in the first sense, is nevertheless public in a distinct but related sense. . . . Fundamental theology is concerned principally with the 'true' in the sense of metaphysics, systematic theology with the beautiful (and, as we shall see, the beautiful *as true)* in the sense of poetics and rhetorics."[9]

Tracy's argument for the qualified public character of systematic theology is that every claim to universality involves a particular perspective which derives from a particular tradition. The task of the systematic theologian is primarily hermeneutical, interpreting the classics of a particular tradition and correlating them with an interpretation of the human situation.[10]

Now let us look at Tracy's argument in more detail. On the face of it, the argument seems both obscure and misleading. In the first place, Tracy claims that the nature of the reality of God and of the kind of existential questions with which theology deals "logically" demand publicness, but he never presents or explains this logic.[11] This logic seems to be that both the doctrine of God and the existential questions are either universal in character or have universal significance. Tracy does not, however, explain why such universality "logically" requires publicness.

It may be that Tracy is working with two meanings of publicness which he does not clearly distinguish: (1) the nature of a claim, namely, to universality or universal significance,[12] and (2) the nature of the grounds offered for a claim, namely, evidence, warrants, and backing.[13] According to the first meaning, the nature of the reality of God and the nature of the existential questions "logically" demand publicness because their universality is identical with this meaning, but claims about them do not logically demand certain kinds of criteria, although

---

9. Ibid., 85.
10. Ibid., 64-9, and passim. See also David Tracy, "Defending the Public Character of Theology," in James M. Wall, ed., *Theologians in Transition* (New York: Crossroad, 1981). For another explanation of how theology can be both public and Christian, see Griffin, *God and Religion in Postmodern Theology,* 10; and idem, *A Process Christology* (Philadelphia: Westminster, 1973): 153-5.
11. Tracy, *The Analogical Imagination,* 3, 63, 86.
12. Ibid., 5-6, 51-2, 55, 62-3, 86.
13. Ibid., 6, 18, 21, 63-4.

certain kinds of criteria may be appropriate in certain circumstances. The connection between the two meanings of publicness is that the means of assessing universal claims are criteria that are or ought to be acceptable universally. The scope of a claim and the criteria for assessing it, however, are quite distinct. The problem is that Tracy goes back and forth between these two meanings of publicness without indicating the shift in meaning.

Furthermore, Tracy's global statement that all theology is public discourse depends on what he refers to as the ordinary or normal meaning of public, namely, that it appeals to all people on grounds that any reasonable person would accept. This normal meaning focuses on evidence and argument. Tracy draws on Bernard Lonergan to give his fullest definition. "The word 'public' here refers to the articulation of fundamental questions and answers which any attentive, intelligent, reasonable and responsible person can understand and judge in keeping with fully public criteria for argument."[14] Drawing on Toulmin, Tracy often summarizes these latter criteria as "evidence, warrants, and backing."[15] Moreover, in this normal interpretation of public, "personal faith or beliefs may not serve as warrants or backings or publicly defended claims to truth."[16]

When Tracy speaks of systematic theology, however, a problem appears. "Yet if the systematic theologian allows the public claims of Christian faith to be decided simply by public argument in the first and usual sense, a different dilemma occurs. What has happened to the event of giftedness which is the central claim and disclosure of the Christian classic?"[17] It becomes clear that the normal meaning of public does not apply at all, and a new meaning is proposed which is found in the phenomenon of the classic. "The classics are public in our second sense: grounded in some realized experience of a claim to attention, unfolding as cognitively disclosure of both meaning and truth and ethically transformative of personal, social and historical life."[18]

---

14. Ibid., 63.
15. Ibid., 18, 21.
16. Ibid., 64.
17. Ibid., 132.
18. Ibid.

In this new sense of publicness, the truth of a particular religious tradition is *assumed* rather than argued. *"Systematic* theologies will ordinarily assume (or assume earlier arguments for) the truth-bearing character of a particular religious tradition."[19] This assumption is obviously not public in the normal sense of the word, and it is explicitly denied by most of the other advocates of public theology, since it is precisely what they are arguing against in advocating the public character of theology. This new interpretation of publicness makes it possible to recognize "the essentially public character of any genuine work of art or any authentic religion."[20]

Finally, this leads Tracy to the strange conclusion that the systematic theologies that show the most promise of achieving classic and thus public status are the neoorthodox "giants": Karl Barth, Rudolf Bultmann, Paul Tillich, and H. Richard and Reinhold Niebuhr, as well as Bernard Lonergan and Karl Rahner. In fact, Barth's commentary on Romans, his retrieval of Calvin, and his *Church Dogmatics* are singled out as public in this new sense![21] Tracy even comes to see this new sense as the supreme sense of publicness.

> Christian theology, in fact, consists in explicating in public terms and in accordance with the demands of its own primary confessions, the full meaning and truth of the original 'illuminating event'. . . which occasioned and continues to inform its understanding of all reality. . . . Claims that a discipline, any discipline, can achieve more publicness than this for its truth are misguided. . . . Whatever publicness is humanly achievable to disciplined reflection, so the argument runs, is accomplished by all genuine Christian confessional systematic theology.[22]

Nothing is more public than confessional Christian systematic theology! Here we have a complete reversal of the original intention of most of the proponents of the public character of theology. Robert C. Neville and David Ray Griffin, for example, use the normal meaning of public precisely in order to argue against the type of theological method exemplified by Barth.

---

19. Ibid., 58.
20. Ibid., 67.
21. Ibid., 104, 132.
22. Ibid., 66.

Why is Tracy so concerned to argue for the public character of theology? We have seen that the reasons he gives are to avoid or to overcome the privatization of religion and to deal with the situation of pluralism in theology. For Tracy the opposite of public is private, rather than authoritarian or based on faith, special revelation, or a particular community. He defines private as "the realm of personal preference where *de gustibus non est disputandum.*"[23] This definition suggests that private means that which is not subject to argument. Other passages suggest that it also means the absence of a claim to universality or universal relevance or significance.[24]

Christian theology, however, has always involved argument and claims to universality. Why then is Tracy worried about theology being private in the sense of its being unarguable and lacking universal claims? The reason, apparently, is that he is referring to a danger for religion rather than theology, because religion in the modern world has often been understood to be only a matter of personal preference. In this understanding, argument about religion is irrelevant, and religion is understood not to make any universal claims.

Tracy's main concern, however, is for theology rather than religion. Thus we must look further for the source of his concern. Tracy seems to have a fixation on an honorific sense of publicness and a pejorative sense of privateness. Perhaps in a university divinity school he is uneasy about the fact that his discipline of systematic theology is not public in the usual or normal sense of the word, as in the sciences.

It may be the case, however, that the usual or normal sense of public applies to very few, if any, disciplines. It is generally accepted, as Tracy himself notes, that philosophy and the human sciences are fundamentally perspectival in nature and based on particular cultural traditions. Thomas Kuhn and his followers also argue that this perspectivism and involvement in a tradition applies also to the natural sciences, which have always been assumed to be the quintessentially public disciplines.

---

23. Ibid., 132.
24. Ibid.

Why then is Tracy concerned to argue that fundamental theology is an exception to this general situation and that it is perhaps even more public than the natural sciences? On the contrary, his argument should lead him to conclude that fundamental theology is at least as perspectival and based on a particular cultural (and religious) tradition as any other discipline, if not more so. Furthermore, Tracy should be satisfied to understand that systematic theology is simply in the same boat. Then he would be in a stronger position than the other proponents of public theology, such as Neville and Griffin, who argue that only the most general criteria should be used in theology.

In order to pursue this issue, it will be helpful to explore some of the history of the idea and reality of publicness or the public sphere, especially as it has been analyzed by Jürgen Habermas. Habermas defines the public sphere as "a realm of our social life in which something approaching public opinion can be formed. . . . A portion of the public sphere comes into being in every conversation in which private individuals assemble to form a public body."[25]

This notion developed in the medieval period into what Habermas calls the representative public sphere, in which feudal authorities (princes, nobility, and clergy) represented public power before the people rather than for the people. By the end of the eighteenth century, this representative public sphere had disintegrated, and the rise of the national state and mercantile individualism produced a new constellation, which Habermas calls the "bourgeois public sphere," mediating between the private sphere and the state.[26] The function of this sphere was to oversee the state by means of public discussion in newspapers, journals, and related organizations.

The Enlightenment ideology of this bourgeois public sphere was that it was open to all; as feminist and other critics have pointed out, however, it was in fact open only to propertied white males and educated nobility. That is, it was an

---

25. Jürgen Habermas, "The Public Sphere: An Encyclopedia Article (1964)," *New German Critique* 1 (1974): 49.

26. Jürgen Habermas, *The Structural Transformation of the Public Sphere: An Inquiry into a Category of Bourgeois Society* (trans. Thomas Burger and Frederick Lawrence; Cambridge: MIT Press, 1989).

allegedly public sphere strictly defined by gender, class, and race. More specifically, this bourgeois public sphere was defined as the realm of impartial and universal reason, whereas matters of the body, affectivity, and desire were supposedly relegated to the private sphere of marriage, family, and home. Since these matters were closely associated with women, people of color, and lower classes, these people were therefore excluded from the public sphere.[27]

Beginning late in the last century, the bourgeois public sphere began to disintegrate under the impact of advanced capitalism and industrialized mass society. The increasing power of state bureaucracies to regulate economic and social life led to a blurring of the distinction between the bourgeois public sphere and the state and thus to a depoliticization of public discourse and a loss of its critical function. The advent of mass media and the public relations industry has led to what Rita Felski calls a "debased pseudopublic sphere" defined by the "homogenizing and universalizing logic of the global megaculture of modern mass communication." This shift makes it increasingly difficult to find any arena for the discussion of public issues.[28]

According to Habermas, in this situation the public sphere becomes an arena of advertising and public relations and is "refeudalized."

> The public sphere assumes advertising functions. The more it can be deployed as a vehicle for political and economic propaganda, the more it becomes unpolitical as a whole and pseudo-privatized. . . . In the measure that it is shaped by public relations, the public sphere of civil society again takes on feudal features. The 'suppliers' display a showy pomp before customers ready to follow. Publicity imitates the kind of aura proper to the personal prestige and supernatural authority once bestowed by the kind of publicity involved in representation.[29]

---

27. See Iris Marion Young, "Impartiality and the Civic Public," in Seyla Benhabib and Drucilia Cornell, eds., *Feminism as Critique: On the Politics of Gender* (Minneapolis: University of Minnesota Press, 1987): 64-6. See also Carol Pateman, "Feminist Critiques of the Public/Private Dichotomy," in S. I. Benn and G. F. Gaus, eds., *Public and Private in Social Life* (London: Croom Helm, 1983): 281-303.

28. Rita Felski, *Beyond Feminist Aesthetics: Feminist Literature and Social Change* (Cambridge: Harvard University Press, 1989): 165-6.

29. Habermas, *The Structural Transformation of the Public Sphere*, 175, 195.

The final stage of this development has been the emergence of what some social theorists have called autonomous, oppositional, or counter-public spheres in response to the failure of the late capitalist welfare state to function for the well-being of various groups.[30]   John Keane notes that advanced bureaucracies seem to have self-destructive tendencies. They attempt to subject all social and political life to surveillance, regulation, and control and thus to suppress all attempts to criticize and change them.   "Within all spheres of contemporary life. . . bureaucratic structures generate oppositional public spheres that continually tend to contradict and thereby reshape these structures' mode of operation."[31]

Keane makes it clear that this development is neither a matter of Habermas's idea of the formation of "deception-free consensuses through rational speech," nor a matter of a mass movement of the dispossessed. "The autonomous movements institute a *plurality* of public spheres" which "signal the emergence of a new political theme under late capitalist, welfare state conditions."[32] Keane sees the approach of a generalized confrontation

> between, on the one hand, administrative-bureaucratic attempts (championed by the new liberalism and corporatism) to restructure the welfare state and social life for a new phase of capitalist accumulation and state power, and on the other hand, the autonomous movements' struggle to speak and to be heard, to repoliticize their everyday lives, to establish qualitatively new forms of social and political relations in which public spheres of mutuality, discussion, and concern with concrete needs predominate.[33]

It is important to note that Tracy has begun to take into account these critiques of the concept of the public sphere. In a recent volume he explores the impact of pluralism as well as postmodern literary and historical criticism, hermeneutics, and deconstruction on religion and theology, and discovers themes

---

30. Oskar Negt and Alexander Kluge apparently coined the term "counter-public sphere" (*Gegenöffentlichkeit*). See their book *Öffentlichkeit and Erfahrung* (Frankfurt: Suhrkamp, 1972): 7-8, 11.
31. John Keane, *Public Life and Late Capitalism: Toward a Socialist Theory of Democracy* (Cambridge: Cambridge University Press, 1984): 67, 26.
32. Ibid., 29.
33. Ibid.

64

that I believe are potentially fatal for his thesis about theology as public discourse. For example, he comments on Michel Foucault's analyses of different discourses in our history.

> What these analyses show is that every discourse bears within itself the anonymous and repressed actuality of highly particular arrangements of power and knowledge. Every discourse, by operating under certain assumptions, necessarily excludes other assumptions. Above all, our discourses exclude those others who might disrupt the established hierarchies or challenge the prevailing hegemony of power: . . . the poor, the oppressed, and the marginalized — all those considered 'non-persons' by the powerful but declared by the great prophets to be God's own privileged ones. All the victims of our discourses and our history have begun to discover their own discourses in ways that our discourse finds difficult to hear, much less listen to. Their voices can seem strident and uncivil — in a word, other. And they are. We have all just begun to sense that otherness. But only by beginning to listen to those other voices may we also begin to hear the otherness within ourselves. What we might then begin to hear, above our chatter, are possibilities we have never dared to dream.[34]

It should be noted that the "we" in this passage apparently refers to established academic white males. Tracy goes on to note that modern consciousness pinned all its hopes on "rational consciousness." The growing awareness of "systematic distortion," however, calls for the strategy of the "hermeneutic of suspicion" in regard to reason. The postmodern consciousness now "deeply suspects the optimism concealed in Western notions of reason."[35] "Feminist thinkers have demonstrated that language was never innocent — especially the phallocentric language of the 'man of reason.'"[36] "Reason can be so driven by a debilitating optimism that it will not dwell for long upon either the radical interruptions of history or the unconscious distortions of self and culture. It is not merely that reason will not sometimes stay for an answer, but that it will not even wait for a question."[37]

---

34. David Tracy, *Plurality and Ambiguity: Hermeneutics, Religion, Hope* (San Francisco: Harper & Row, 1987): 79.
35. Ibid., 73-4.
36. Ibid., 77.
37. Ibid., 78.

It would seem that Tracy's new insights have spelled the doom of his thesis about theology as public discourse, because these "others" and their discourses stand outside his definition of public discourse. This is probably why he does not refer to the thesis in *Plurality and Ambiguity*. He has returned to this issue, however, in an important essay entitled "Theology, Critical Social Theory and the Public Realm."[38] In the first paragraph of this essay, it is surprising to read a strong emphasis on the necessity of reason as the basis of a public sphere.

> A public realm, by definition, is dependent on a shared concept of reason. . . . A public realm is that shared rational space where all participants, whatever their particular differences, can meet to discuss any claim that is rationally redeemable. Any strictly relativist reading of the nature of reason cannot inform a public realm as public.[39]

He notes and rejects Richard Rorty's relativism, Jean-François Lyotard's postmodern critique of reason, and the advice of some theologians to withdraw from the public realm because of the emptiness of the modern concept of rationality that is based on a foundationalism.

Tracy takes special note of liberation, black, and feminist theologies which have appealed to the "counter-experiences and counter-ideologies of oppressed peoples whose discourse has been marginalized by the dominant groups."[40] In particular he refers to feminist criticism of Habermas's failure to account for the gender-specific nature of many modern social realities.[41]

He states that the challenge of liberation theologies to public theologies lies in their ability to develop "new theological resources (centered on the symbol of liberation) from groups and movements too often marginalized by both critical theorists and public theologians."[42] Their weakness is that they are still "relatively unconcerned with the debates on rationality. . . . But without such explicit and

---

38. David Tracy, "Theology, Critical Social Theory and the Public Realm," in Don S. Browning and Francis Schüssler Fiorenza, eds., *Habermas, Modernity, and Public Theology* (New York: Crossroad/Continuum, 1992): 19-42.
39. Ibid., 19.
40. Ibid., 24.
41. Ibid., 34.
42. Ibid., 25.

systematic analysis, it is difficult to see how the crucial contributions and challenges of liberation theologies can be fully redeemed in a pluralistic reality."[43] Unless liberation theologies enter more explicitly into the debates on rationality and modernity, they "could be driven, despite their clear intentions, to those enforced 'reservations of the spirit' where a reigning technical rationality wishes to place all our countermovements."[44]

What are we to make of this apparently sudden reversal on the status of reason and its relation to the public sphere and public theology? Why is the public realm now dependent by definition on a shared concept of reason? What definition of the public realm does this imply? Whose concept of reason is being employed? Who decides what it means to be "rationally redeemable"? Richard Bernstein comments on such proposals:

> It is the very appeal to something like the idea of a rational consensus that has always been used to block, stifle, or rule out 'revolutionary' turns in the conversation. To speak of the argumentative redemption of validity claims through the appropriate level of discourse is either potentially stifling or sheer bluff.[45]

It seems that Tracy has a deep ambivalence about reason and its relation to the public sphere and public theology. On the one hand, he is sensitive to and impressed by all the postmodern critiques of reason. On the other hand, he is also deeply influenced by the long Roman Catholic tradition of natural and fundamental theology, especially through his earlier studies of the transcendental Thomism of Bernard Lonergan. The occasion of a conference on Habermas has apparently offered Tracy the opportunity to retrieve this latter tradition by means of Habermas's interpretation of rationality.

Tracy's main proposal is to use Habermas's critical social theory as the basis of new concepts of rationality and modernity for a public theology. In

---

43. Ibid.
44. Ibid., 26.
45. Richard Bernstein, *Philosophical Profiles: Essays in a Pragmatic Mode* (Cambridge: Polity Press, 1986): 80. I am indebted to Professor Barry A. Harvey of Baylor University for drawing my attention to this passage.

particular he attempts to show how Habermas's theory of communicative action can serve as the basis of a theory of rationality that can survive the above-mentioned critiques and supply the foundation for a public theology.

In brief, Tracy's argument is that on the basis of the linguistic turn of modern philosophy it can be shown that "in every communicative action, whatever the other particularities of its context, there is an exercise of self-transcending dialogical reason with language as the necessary medium of that self-transcendence."[46]

> If language is not a mere instrument of consciousness but the basic medium of all human understanding, then every act of understanding is intrinsically intersubjective, never purely subjective; every communicative action is dialogical, not monological. If understanding is dialogical, it is also, as hermeneutics and critical theory alike attest, both historical and contextual. But insofar as reason is genuinely dialogical or communicative in any historical context, it is not, in principle, limited to that context.[47]

Tracy's point here is that there is something about human reason that transcends not only the individual consciousness but also any particular social, cultural, and historical context. Reason is thus in some measure universal and can form the basis of public discourse and public theology in particular.

The contrast between this essay and the volume *Plurality and Ambiguity* is quite sharp. The preface of the latter begins with the statement, "The theme of this small book is conversation" and how it functions as "a model for all interpretation."[48] There are no limitations on the possibility of this conversation in terms of a "shared concept of reason" on which a public realm "by definition" is dependent. Thus it is not clear why liberation theologians, for example, must adopt a concept of reason that is recognizable and acceptable to traditional theologians before conversation can begin. In fact, this conversation has been going on for some time without such an explicit agreement.

---

46. David Tracy, "Theology, Critical Social Theory and the Public Realm," 23.
47. Ibid.
48. Tracy, *Plurality and Ambiguity*, ix.

In any case Tracy is clearly ambivalent about this proposal, since, as we have seen, he is aware of the fact that such proposals have always excluded and repressed those who would "disrupt the established hierarchies or challenge the prevailing hegemony of power."[49] Moreover, he has called "us" to begin listening to "those other voices" apparently without requiring the acceptance of any "shared concept of reason" on which a public realm "by definition" is dependent.

I believe that the way forward in the face of a radical pluralism in theological positions is suggested by the social theorists' concept of counter-public spheres mentioned above. These "critical oppositional forces," mentioned by Felski,[50] represent the areas of human experience that have been ignored and marginalized by the political and theological traditions.

Counter-public spheres of theological reflection have emerged among women, African-Americans, and the poor of Latin America. Similar counter-public spheres are beginning to emerge among other racial, ethnic, and sexual groups. The critical role of these counter-public spheres should not obscure their constructive roles, but these constructive roles must be based on their own public representation.

Margaret Miles has argued that such representation in the case of women requires at least three conditions.[51] It must be self-representation rather than representation by the various stereotypes of the male public sphere. This representation must have a public space in the institutions that shape society. Furthermore, it requires the construction of a collective voice rather than individual statements which can be easily ignored.

The various counter-public spheres in theology are at different stages in the development of these conditions in the United States. Women and African-Americans are probably ahead of other groups in these matters. In churches, ecumenical groups, and divinity schools, women, lay and ordained, teachers and students, have been meeting, discussing, organizing such institutions as the

---

49. Ibid., 79.
50. Felski, *Beyond Feminist Aesthetics*, 165.
51. Margaret R. Miles, *Carnal Knowing: Female Nakedness and Religious Meaning in the Christian West* (Boston: Beacon, 1989): 170-2.

Women's Theological Center in Boston, publishing such journals as the *Journal of Feminist Studies in Religion*, and in other ways developing self-representation, public space, and a collective voice. Within these developments the voices of women of color, lesbians, and poor women are beginning to be heard as well. Similar points could be made about African-Americans. Other groups have not yet progressed as far in developing these conditions for representation in theological discourse.

As these other counter-public spheres emerge there can be a vision of a new kind of public sphere of conversation in theology. Conversation is the key word here. Richard Rorty sees the maintaining of such a conversation between different discourses as the proper function of philosophy today: similarly, this could be applied to the developing situation in theology. This function, which he calls hermeneutics,

> sees the relations between various discourses as those of strands in a possible conversation, a conversation which unites the speakers, but where the hope of agreement is never lost so long as the conversation lasts. This hope is not a hope for the discovery of antecedently existing common ground, but *simply* hope for agreement, or, at least, exciting and fruitful disagreement.[52]

As we have noted, Tracy also sees conversation as fundamental in his idea of public theology. He understands conversation essentially as questioning. Conversation is "questioning itself. It is a willingness to follow the question wherever it goes."[53] "Conversation in its primary form is an exploration of possibilities in the search for truth. In following the track of any question, we must allow for difference and otherness. At the same time, as the question takes over, we notice that to attend to the other as other, the different as different, is also to understand the different as possible."[54] This kind of conversation assumes equality among the conversation partners, equality of power and access to self-representation, public space, and collective voice. This is something that does not

---

52. Richard Rorty, *Philosophy and the Mirror of Nature* (Princeton: Princeton University Press, 1979): 318.
53. Tracy, *Plurality and* Ambiguity, 18.
54. Ibid., 20.

yet exist, but it is a goal worth striving for. Responsibility for making this equality possible rests not only with the groups seeking public space and collective voice, but especially with those — for the most part white males — who now largely control institutional space and voice.

If such a goal can be envisioned, public theology or theology as public discourse will take on a quite different meaning from that proposed by the public theologians. It will not mean an agreement on a concept of reason or on specific criteria of argument and evidence. It will mean both a commitment to accept one another as equal partners in conversation and a commitment to continuing the conversation. Such a conversation will be so unusual in Christian history that the resulting agreements and disagreements are quite unpredictable. Finally, however, there will be a theology that is a truly public discourse.

CHAPTER 4

ON STEPPING TWICE INTO THE SAME CHURCH: ESSENCE, DEVELOPMENT, AND PLURALISM

All things flow; nothing abides. . . . You cannot step twice into the same river.
— Heraclitus

Can you step twice into the same church? Are we in the same church as the apostles, the authors of the New Testament, the early Christian councils, the medieval scholastics, the Reformers, the liberal theologians of the last century? "The question at stake is whether and how we can prove that we are still the selfsame Church" (Van Ruler). This is one way to approach the question of the development of doctrine. Has Christianity perhaps undergone *a metabasis eis allo genos?* Some have argued that historical change always means just that, a change into a different kind of thing. Others from Vincent of Lérins to Karl Barth have claimed that the church is always and everywhere essentially the same.

One can understand the concern of average Christians as to whether they are in the same church as the apostles or whether the church has undergone a change into another kind of thing. They have experienced something salvific in the Christian life in the church, something they associate with the origins of Christianity in Jesus and the apostles, and something they don't want to lose. In one sense, of course, given the ineradicable diversity manifest in the New Testament from the very beginning, not even the apostles (or at least the New Testament authors) were in the same church. And, since the church is constantly changing in all its aspects, it is impossible to step into the same church from one day to the next. In another sense it is also clear that most Christians are in the same church as the apostles in that they are in one of the communities or institutions which are historically continuous with those of the first century. The question before us, however, is somewhere in between these extremes. Namely, given the continuity or even the lack of it in some cases, has there also been a continuity of whatever it is that is most fundamental or essential in Christianity? And how is this to be determined?

Furthermore, is this a historical or a theological question? It has been addressed by both disciplines. Historians have tended to answer the question of continuity in the negative and theologians in the positive. The historian and theologian Ernst Troeltsch struggled with it and concluded that it is a theological question deeply informed by historical study.[1] Troeltsch notes that the essence of Christianity has been differently understood in every age. Which of these is the true essence is clearly a theological question. But the historian presses the point that the understanding of this true essence has changed constantly.

How then do we know that we participate in what is essential in Christianity? Is it by affirming the apostolic faith, participating in word and sacrament in corporate worship, practicing the Christian moral life, participating in the life of the church and its ministry in the world? And how do we know that we do these things in a form and with an interpretation which are appropriate developments for today of what we believe has been fundamental or essential from the beginning? Furthermore, are all these elements essential or only some, and, if the latter, which ones and why?

Many commentators have noted the close connection between the issues of the development of doctrine and the essence of Christianity. Although the essence question has a nineteenth-century ring about it, it has come back into prominence again as the theological pendulum has swung to the left since mid-century. Two recent discussions of the essence question deserve attention. Stephen Sykes argues that Christianity is essentially diverse and conflicted in character.[2] He reviews the essence discussion from Schleiermacher to Barth and suggests a distinction between an externality tradition and an inwardness tradition

---

1. See his essay, "What does 'Essence of Christianity' Mean?" in *Ernst Troeltsch: Writings in Theology and Religion*, ed. Robert Morgan and Michael Pye (London: Duckworth, 1977): 124-79.
2. Stephen Sykes, *The Identity of Christianity* (Philadelphia: Fortress, 1984).

which are held together by a dialectical tradition. This is exemplified in three models: foundation and superstructure, spirit and body, and center and circumference.

Given the diversity of Christianity, Sykes inquires about its possible unity. He sees the basis for the unity and continuity of Christianity in the undeviatingness of God, and concludes with a formal definition of the Christian as "one who gives attention to Jesus whose achievement is contextualized by God" in the two horizons of creation and eschatology (255f). Furthermore, the continuity of Christianity is preserved through corporate worship. Sykes notes that this is a formal definition of the essence of Christianity and that from the beginning there has never been agreement on a material specification of this. Any definition of the unity of Christianity will be in the form of "a containment of diversity within bounds" (246).

The other discussion of the essence of Christianity is by Edward Farley.[3] His project is to describe theological judgment after the collapse of the house of authority, the traditional theological criteriology of scripture and tradition. His proposal stands in the tradition of Schleiermacher and the attempt to determine the essence of Christianity. He describes the first dimension of theological reflection as theological portraiture, which is the "process of building up by inquiry of various sorts a portrait of ecclesiality as a type of historical existence" (197). Ecclesial existence emerges in the period of its origins in the first century and develops various aspects in different periods. But it essentially involves redemption or the transition from a sin-distorted historical existence into a new type of historical existence. The historical study of the development of ecclesial existence plus the study of its symbolic universe and its "depth sociality" or intersubjective meanings constitute theological portraiture.

Furthermore, this ecclesial existence has a continuity through change, because "a certain ideality and teleology presides over comprehensive types of existence" (212). How is this continuity of ecclesial existence maintained?

---

3. Edward Farley, *Ecclesial Reflection* (Philadelphia: Fortress, 1982).

Farley states, "Somehow in the period of its origins [ecclesial existence] obtained a form that enabled it to endure as a social type of existence" (217). What is this form? It involves the remembrance and celebration of the originating events through linguistic sedimentations in the writings of Israel and the early Christian kerygma and their interpretation, and vehicles of social persistence in certain institutions, namely, activities and social structures.

However, according to Farley, on the one hand this process may lead to a new and different paradigm and on the other a failure of correspondence or integration of the elements of social duration will threaten the continuance of a particular society (372f). Thus he implies that continuity of ecclesial existence is not assured and is a question which must be explored.

Both Sykes and Farley seem to assume that the continuity of Christianity has been maintained, that the Christian form of life has not undergone a radical change into something quite other. They explain the structures by which this has been achieved, but they do not argue that continuity has in fact been maintained. Among historians today, however, a fundamental change has been taking place in regard to their attitude toward continuity and development in history. Nicholas Lash, for example, has noted that evolutionary conceptions of history are being replaced by more episodic views.[4] He suggests that the cultural context imposes limits on the questions that occur to historians. Thus in the recent past ideas of evolutionary and linear development have led to the result that discontinuities and radical change are not expected and are overlooked. For example, almost all theories of doctrinal development have tended to assume a unified process of continual expansion illuminated by organic metaphors. Now, however, a shift in historiographical perspective common to all areas of contemporary inquiry is taking place from the evolutionary model to a new model which sees discontinuities and interruptions rather than continuities and developments.

Lash refers here to Michel Foucault's *The Archaeology of Knowledge*,[5] which is the foremost example of this shift. Foucault claims that in the history of

---

4. Nicholas Lash, *Change in Focus* (London: Sheed & Ward, 1973).
5. Michel Foucault, *The Archaeology of Knowledge* (New York: Pantheon, 1972).

ideas (philosophy, science, literature) attention has turned away from vast unities and continuities to the phenomena of rupture and discontinuity of various kinds. "[This mutation] has broken up the long series formed by the progress of consciousness, or the teleology of reason, or the evolution of human thought" (8). Whereas in traditional history discontinuity has been the problem to overcome, now it has become one of the basic elements of analysis.

> One of the most essential features of the new history is probably this displacement of the discontinuous: its transference from the obstacle to the work itself; its integration into the discourse of the historian, where it plays no longer the role of an external condition that must be reduced, but that of a working concept; and therefore the inversion of signs by which it is no longer the negative of the historical reading (its underside, its failure, the limit of its power), but the positive element that determines its objects and validates its analysis (9).

Foucault refers to this new history as archaeology and traces its origin to Marx, Nietzsche, and Freud and their decentering effects upon the subject and reason. He notes the great resistance of the history of thought in particular to the ideas of discontinuity, difference, separation, and dispersion. He points to the reason for this resistance in the concern for the sovereignty and founding function of consciousness or the subject. Foucault is here attacking the ideological use of history by classical humanism, which seeks a safe shelter for human consciousness and reason in a sacralized idea of history in which they undergo continuous teleological development. Thus "archaeological description is precisely . . . an abandonment of the history of ideas, a systematic rejection of its postulates and procedures, an attempt to practice a quite different history of what [people] have said" (138).

So Foucault proposes a new method for the analysis of history, one which is freed from the assumptions of the continuity of discourse with its ideas of influence, evolution, and teleology. This archaeological analysis involves the description of the elements of discourse, namely, the objects, modes, concepts, and strategies which make up a discourse.

Foucault sees four main points of divergence between archaeological analysis and the traditional history of ideas: the attribution of innovation, the analysis of contradictions, comparative descriptions, and the mapping of transformations. Archaeology does not distinguish between original and traditional formulations, because precession and resemblance are not autonomous but entirely relative to particular discursive formulations.

Archaeology does not, as does the history of ideas, assume coherence in its object and thus try to resolve all apparent contradictions. Nor does it assume that a basic contradiction is the source of all discourse. Rather it sees contradictions as objects to be described, which occur in different types, at different levels of discourse, and with different functions in a discourse. Archaeology compares discourses not in order to reduce their diversities but rather to explore them. It does not pursue influences, causes, and expressions but rather seeks analogies and differences at the level of the rules of formation of a discourse.

Although archaeology seems to ignore the temporality of discourses, Foucault argues that it treats change more carefully than does the traditional history of ideas. Archaeology deals with change through an analysis of the various kinds of transformation which occur in change: transformation of the elements of discourse, of the relations of these elements, of the rules of formation of a discourse, and of the relations between discourses. Although archaeology discovers discontinuity, interruptions, differences, separations, and dispersions, it also recognizes the phenomena of permanence, continuity, repetition, and sequence of the elements of discourse. Foucault jeers at "the agoraphobics of time and history" who "confuse rupture and irrationality" and who, in trying to preserve continuity from discontinuity, misunderstand both (174). Foucault with his new analysis of discourse is attempting to discover how both are formed according to the same rules of discursive practice.

What are the implications of Foucault's archaeology and his critique of the history of ideas for the question of the development of Christianity? In the first place it seems clear that Foucault is undermining many of the ideas held dear by those who want to affirm ideas of continuity and development. He is mainly critical of what he calls an ideological view of history which presupposes a deep origin, continuity, and goal of the development of reason and consciousness. As against this view he proposes a neutral phenomenological quasi-structuralist analysis of the various discourses and their elements and transformations which underlie and inform the history of ideas.

Would Foucault deny the possibility of the continuity of Christianity? No. Archaeology recognizes the phenomena of permanence, continuity, and sequence when they are found in the elements of various discourses. It simply does not presuppose them. Furthermore, archaeology is exploring a different level of discourse than the history of ideas or of institutions. It is examining the system of neutral elements which make up and determine a way of talking about a subject matter, a system of which the talkers are entirely unaware. As two commentators on Foucault have put it, "[Archaeology] shows that what seems like the continuous development of a meaning is crossed by discontinuous discursive formations." "[The task of archaeology] is to substitute for [the disciplines'] apparent internal intelligibility a different intelligibility, namely their place within the discursive formation."[6]

Dreyfus and Rabinow offer an example of Foucault's concept of rules of discourse.

> The functioning of the university is dependent upon a great many primary relations — these include economic, political, familial, institutional, architectural, and pedagogical practices — but these diverse elements can coalesce into the modern university only because of something which has been called 'the idea of the university.' But this concept, which administrators, professors, and students share to some extent, is itself a 'secondary relation' conditioned by something else. This final unifying factor cannot be described in objective nor in mentalistic terms. It is rather a certain currently acceptable way of talking (describing, discussing, demanding, announcing) which is taken seriously in a domain called higher education. This specific type of discourse is no doubt related to what administrators, professors, and students think about

---

6. Herbert L. Dreyfus and Paul Rabinow, *Michel Foucault: Beyond Structuralism and Hermeneutics* 2d ed. (Chicago: Univ. of Chicago Press, 1983): 106, 117.

university education, but these ways of *thinking* no more organize all the factors that make up the university system than do the various social and economic forces. What organizes the institutional relations and the thinking is finally the system of rules which govern what sort of *talk* about education (and which talkers) can, in a given period, be taken seriously. It is these rules 'governing' what can be seriously said that, counterintuitive as it may first seem, ultimately 'effect' or 'establish' university life as we know it (66).

However, Dreyfus and Rabinow have concluded that Foucault's archaeological project has failed and that he has given up the attempt to work out a theory of rule-governed systems of discourse.[7] They argue that his theory of the causal power attributed to the rules governing a discourse is unintelligible and that he could have stuck to his phenomenological project of a pure description of the facts of discourse. They note that since writing *The Archaeology of Knowledge* Foucault has added to his archaeological project the enterprise of genealogy, which is a new method for the analysis of the relations of power, knowledge, and the body in society. Genealogy is the analysis of that which conditions, limits, and institutionalizes discourses. It involves a critique of continuities and development similar to that of archaeology. What is added is a critique of the relation of power and knowledge.

In fact, genealogy in its exploration of origins and development may be more negative than archaeology. "Genealogy does not look to origins to capture the essence of things, or to search for some 'immobile form' that has developed throughout history; the secret disclosed by genealogy is that there is no essence or original unity to be discovered. When genealogy looks to beginnings, it looks for accidents, chance, passion, petty malice, surprises, feverish agitation, unsteady victories, and power."[8]

So the bearing of Foucault's project on the question of the development of doctrine and the continuity of Christianity must await the archaeological and

---

7. Ibid., xxivf, ch. 4.
8. Arnold I. Davidson, "Archeology, Genealogy, Ethics," in *Foucault: A Critical Reader*, ed. David Couzens Hoy (Oxford: Basil Blackwell, 1986): 224. I am indebted to F. S. Fiorenza for this reference.

genealogical study of the history of Christianity, the uncovering of the various discourses at work and their transformations. This will certainly clarify the course of Christian history and illuminate the questions of development and continuity. But this work has barely begun.[9]

Foucault, however, exemplifies one other development which invites further inquiry. In *The Archaeology of Knowledge* and previous works Foucault places theory over practice. In his studies of the human sciences, the practices and the practitioner's theories are subordinated to a theoretical structure which governs them. The task of the archaeologist is to describe in theoretical terms the rules governing discursive practice. But after *The Archaeology of Knowledge* this order is inverted, and in Foucault's later works practice is always considered more fundamental than theory. The intelligibility of the human sciences is not found in their theories but in the sets of practices of which they are a part. His new method of genealogy is a way of diagnosing and grasping the significance of social practices. Archaeology is still employed but it is now subordinated to genealogy.[10]

This priority of practice over theory is part of a general movement or tendency today in a number of disciplines including history, linguistics, literary criticism, sociology, and anthropology. This is the thesis of an essay by Sherry B. Ortner on anthropological theory. She claims that the practice theorists in anthropology seek to explain the relation between human action and the social-cultural system, which she defines as "a set of organizational and evaluative schemes embodied in institutional, symbolic, and material forms."[11] The practice theorists explore how the system shapes practice and how human action reproduces the system through socialization practices. The system is changed when different groups come to power and when traditional strategies are deployed

---

9. George A. Lindbeck, in his book *The Nature of Doctrine* (Philadelphia: Westminster, 1984), has begun something like an archaeology of Christian thought, although he does not refer to Foucault. His theory of doctrine as rule corresponds roughly to Foucault's theory of the rules of discourse.

10. See Dreyfus and Rabinow, *Foucault*, 102f.

11. Sherry B. Ortner, "Theory in Anthropology since the Sixties," *Comparative Studies in Society and History* 26:1 (January 1984): 148.

in relation to novel situations. She states, "Change comes when traditional strategies, which assume traditional patterns of relations . . . are deployed in relation to novel phenomena. . . . Change . . . is failed reproduction" (155f). Thus practice theorists see major social changes not as the result of intended action but rather as a by-product, an unintended consequence of action. Ortner quotes Foucault: "People know what they do; they frequently know why they do what they do; but what they don't know is what they do does" (157; quoting from Dreyfus and Rabinow, *Foucault*, 187). It may be that changes in Christianity, both in doctrine and practice, occur unintentionally, as "failed reproduction," when traditional strategies are applied to new situations.

This priority of practice over theory is also reflected in contemporary theology. In an unpublished paper entitled "The Role of Doctrine in Judaism," Professor David Novak of Jewish Theological Seminary states, "Judaism regulates action more strictly than it does the formulation and expression of ideas. Action is the immediate subject of communal norms, whereas ideas . . . are more in the domain of individual thought." George Lindbeck, in an unpublished paper entitled "Doctrine in Christianity: A Comparison with Judaism" responding to Novak's paper, suggests that "Christianity has been and could again be much like Judaism in this respect." He asks, "Why have ideas tended to replace narrative and worship, not to mention behavioral rules, as the primary authoritative structure through which Christianity has been identified?" He suggests that the accidents of history have caused the doctrinal emphasis to be primary in the West, namely, the development of scholastic theology and the religious struggles of the sixteenth century. Eastern Orthodoxy (and to a lesser extent Anglicanism), however, has had a more doxological understanding of doctrine and creeds and has adhered more closely to the principle *lex orandi lex credendi*, thus subordinating doctrine to practice. Lindbeck continues, "The primacy of doctrine is not part of the internal logic of a religion which inherently centers more on narrative (including that of Israel), law (including the decalogue and the prophet's calls for justice and mercy), and liturgy (including major elements of Jewish worship)."

Lindbeck's affirmation of the priority of practice is confirmed and elaborated in his book *The Nature of Doctrine*. He suggests that a religion is like "a set of acquired skills," like a language. Religious doctrines do not make first-order truth claims but rather are second-order rules for such claims. In Christianity, he says, "the cognitive aspect, while important, is not primary. . . . To become religious . . . is to interiorize a set of skills by practice and training . . . The primary knowledge is not . . . *that* the religion teaches such and such, but rather *how* to be religious in such and such ways" (35). "The ontological truth of religious utterances . . . is only a function of their role in constituting a form of life, a way of being in the world" (65). "The only way to assert [Christ's lordship] is to do something about it, i.e., to commit oneself to a way of life" (66; see also 67-9, 99f).

Political theology and liberation theology also affirm the priority of practice to doctrine. By this they mean at least three things. First, doctrine should be reflection on practice, the clarification of what is learned in practice about the situation of oppression and God's relation to it. Second, therefore, the theologian must be involved in practice as the struggle of the oppressed for liberation. And, third, doctrine is to be tested and evaluated in practice by whether or not it illumines and guides practice.

The priority of practice in the Christian life has a long history in the Christian tradition. The Johannine Christ teaches that it is they who do the truth who will know the truth, that understanding derives from obedience. The Matthean Christ teaches that we will be judged on the basis of how we have responded to those in need. It has usually been a principle of catholic ascetical theology that it is the practice of the Christian life that leads to the understanding of the Christian faith rather than the other way around. Newman argued that right practice is a necessary condition of true development.[12]

A more recent example is found in a report commissioned by the House of Bishops of the Episcopal Church in connection with the censure of the Rt. Rev. James A. Pike in 1966. It states:

---

12. See Nicholas Lash, *Newman on Development* (London: Sheed & Ward, 1975): 141-5.

When Episcopalians are questioned about the supposed orthodoxy or heterodoxy of one of their number, their most likely response is to ask whether or not [this person] wishes — sincerely and responsibly — to join them in the celebration of God's being and goodness in the prayers and worship of the Prayer Book. Assuming [this person's] integrity, they would not be likely to press the question beyond that point.[13]

So as an experiment in thought I would like to explore briefly how the problem of development looks when practice is seen as prior to doctrine in Christianity. But when we speak of the priority of practice over theory or doctrine, what do we mean? Religion is generally understood as a way or form of life with many aspects. Ninian Smart notes six aspects or dimensions: the ritual, mythological, doctrinal, ethical, social, and experiential dimensions.[14] Now assuming that practice includes the ritual, ethical, and social dimensions of a religion, what does it mean to say that practice precedes or is prior to doctrine? (So far as I can discover, no one who makes this point has ever explored this question.)

Precedence or priority can refer to logic, temporality, urgency, identity, or decisiveness. Logical priority would mean that doctrine is founded on or derived from practice. Temporal priority would mean that practice must be engaged in before doctrine can be reflected on or developed. Priority of urgency would mean that practice is a pressing requirement at all times while doctrinal reflection is necessary only occasionally. Identity priority would mean that Christianity is to be identified more by its practice than by its doctrine. Priority of decisiveness would mean that, for example, in God's eyes or in the final judgment practice is weighed more heavily than doctrinal affirmation. Some of these meanings are related to or derived from others. For example, it may be that identity or urgency priority is derived from priority of decisiveness, and so forth.

Now in suggesting the priority of practice over doctrine in regard to the development of Christianity, which meaning of priority is referred to? It is

---

13. *Theological Freedom and Social Responsibility*, ed. Stephen F. Bayne (New York: Seabury, 1987): 21.
14. Ninian Smart, *The Religious Experience of Mankind* (New York: Scribner, 1969): 6-12.

probably the priority of identity which is paramount here. That is, the priority of practice over doctrine means that Christianity can best be identified by the forms of its practice (the ritual, ethical, and social dimensions) rather than by its doctrine. (It should be noted in passing that, of course, theological reflection and doctrinal affirmation are activities and thus aspects of practice. So the distinction of practice and doctrine cannot be a sharp one.)

Now what bearing does this proposal of the priority of practice to doctrine have on the questions of development, the continuity of Christianity, and whether or not we are in the same church? It is clear that Christian practice has developed and changed as much as, if not more than, Christian doctrine, and also that today there is probably more agreement on doctrine than on practice. So the emphasis on practice does not simplify, let alone solve, our problem. In any case, the question of development would become one concerning the proper or valid development of practice, orthopraxy rather than orthodoxy, in the face of new situations and demands. The question of the continuity of Christianity would become that of the continuity of Christian practice or of the essentials of Christian practice. And the question of whether or not we are in the same church would be reduced to the prior question of the continuity of essential practices.

This raises the decisive question of the diversity of practice and the norms of practice. We have defined Christian practice to include the ritual, ethical, and social dimensions of the Christian life; in brief, what the Christian and the church are called to be and do in the world. Christian practice in this sense has been reflected upon in a number of diverse and relatively unrelated disciplines: ascetical, liturgical, homiletical, and moral theology, as well as the study of church discipline, order, and polity. Should we not look to the discipline of practical theology for the discussion of the essential elements of practice and the norms of practice? Although Schleiermacher described practical theology as "the crown of theological study," a unified discipline of practical theology simply does not exist today, although some proposals have been made in this direction.[15]

---

15. See David Tracy, *The Analogical Imagination* (New York: Crossroad, 1981): 69-79, 390-8; Edward Farley, *Theologia* (Philadelphia: Fortress, 1983), 190f et passim; Don

Since Christian practice today must look to a variety of diverse and unrelated disciplines for guidance, there is an urgent need for these to be brought together in a unified practical theology.

At this point, however, a critical question arises. If practice is held to be prior to doctrine in Christianity, this cannot mean any practice that happens to prevail at the time. It must mean valid or authentic practice, and this implies a norm or norms of validity or authenticity. What is the source of such norms? If they are the norms of valid worship, moral action, and church order, then they must derive from theological reflection on these areas of practice, that is, from doctrine. Then it would seem that practice becomes again subordinate to doctrine, and we return to the priority of doctrine in Christianity.

Stephen Sykes discusses this point in the following way. He argues that it is inconceivable that there ever was complete agreement about the identity of Christianity, that there have always been conflicts about this. Furthermore, these conflicts concern each and every aspect of Christianity, but they can be debated and possibly resolved only by means of doctrinal discussion. That is, the conflicts can be made explicit and manageable only by means of theological reflection. This, however, does not reduce worship or moral action to doctrine any more than literary criticism reduces a poem to the philosophical, political, or aesthetic views of its author. This does not mean, therefore, that doctrine is the most fundamental aspect of Christianity. Rather it means that what is most fundamental or essential can be determined only by doctrinal discussion or theological reflection.[16]

Where does this leave us on the question of development, the continuity of Christianity, and of whether we are in the same church? Our tentative proposal at this point is that, because practice is more important in regard to the identity of Christianity than is doctrine, our concern is with the development and continuity of Christian practice in its various forms. Although practice is prior in regard to

---

Browning (ed.), *Practical Theology* (San Francisco: Harper & Row, 1983); Owen C. Thomas, "Some Problems in Theological Education," *Theological Education* 5 (1969): 346-56.
    16. *Identity*, 28-32.

the identity of Christianity, its priority, content, and norms can be clarified and warranted only by means of the practice of theological reflection.

How then do we go about making decisions in regard to practice in such a way as to maintain the continuity of Christianity? The problem here resides in the diversity of practice, historically and at the present, and in the lack of clarity and unity in regard to the norms of practice. Again the question of essential practices arises as it always does in regard to doctrine.

At this point a development in modern analytical philosophy may be of some help, namely, the critique of essentialism in language and the reference, following Wittgenstein, to the phenomenon of family resemblances.[17] Essentialism is the view that all instances of a general term must have some common property which allows them to be counted as such instances. Wittgenstein argues against this view and suggests that such instances must have family resemblances rather than some common property. Phenomena most susceptible to family resemblance analysis are those which are complex and also marked by lack of any single common property. Wittgenstein uses the metaphor of a rope which hangs together not because of any single fiber which runs through its whole length but because of a large number of overlapping and interlacing fibers. Later interpreters have added the necessity of a "quorum factor." No one particular property is necessary for every instance of a general term, but a certain number of relevant properties is necessary, although that number cannot be fixed in advance but must be determined for each case.

Wittgenstein saw such family resemblance analysis as purely descriptive and not normative, but he allowed for the possibility in such analysis of a normative drawing of boundaries and setting of limits for particular purposes. Such purposes might include, for example, an ecumenical venture in which two or more churches from different traditions are exploring the possibility of some joint action or limited intercommunion.

---

17. For many of the following points I am indebted to John Powell Clayton, *The Concept of Correlation* (Berlin: De Gruyter, 1980): 236-48.

The practices in any list of family resemblances among churches would include public worship, the reading and interpretation of scripture, baptism, eucharist, the use of ancient creeds, private prayer, service of those in need, community life and organization, and ordered ministry. Not all Christian bodies have all of these practices. A quorum factor for some particular purpose might be that any body that does not have at least four of these practices would not be included in the purpose in question.[18]

Although we have been considering ecumenism between contemporary churches, the problem of development is concerned with ecumenism in time rather than space, the proper continuity in history of the identity of Christianity. And our proposal is that we should focus on a quorum of practices as the mark of continuity rather than on adherence to essential doctrine.

It is clear that this view of development may involve quite radical change. Old practices may disappear and new practices may emerge. Recent commentators have seen development and continuity as involving compression and simplification (Rahner), pruning and purgation (Bévmot), demolition (Schillebeeckx), and even revolution (Wiles). Maurice Wiles suggests that the most important changes in a tradition occur when someone sees the subject matter from a new perspective. "It is a new frame of reference rather than new particular facts (though the former is often set off by the latter) which is most productive of advance."[19]

The new perspective or frame of reference of liberation theology is relevant here. We have noted its emphasis on the priority of practice in the Christian life. Its critique of the traditional view of development goes beyond this, however, and is four-fold. First, the Christian tradition of doctrine and practice has always been produced by an elite, a white, male, western, literate,

---

18. The Chicago-Lambeth Quadrilateral of 1888, which lists "as essential to the restoration of unity among the divided branches of Christendom" the scriptures, the Apostles' and Nicene creeds, baptism and eucharist, and the historic episcopate, is not an example of a quorum of practices, since it specifies four particular practices as essential. Furthermore, it describes scriptures and creeds as standards of faith rather than practices, although their use could be stated as practices.

19. Maurice Wiles, *The Remaking of Christian Doctrine* (London: SCM, 1974): 7.

often celibate, relatively affluent elite. Second, Christian tradition represents directly or indirectly the interest of this elite in maintaining the status quo especially in regard to its power and authority in church and society. Third, this elite tends to universalize its point of view and experience by asserting that it is the normative human perspective, thus ignoring the point of view and experience of the majority of Christians. Fourth, therefore, its concern about development, the continuity of Christianity, and being in the same church is often an expression of its interest, just mentioned, in maintaining its power and authority in church and society.

In one sense, of course, the groups excluded from this elite, namely, women, the poor, and minorities, are not at all interested in the continuity of the Christianity defined by the elite or in remaining in the same church. They would like to step into a different church tomorrow. In another sense, if they stay in the church, they want to be in a reformed church in which they will participate in the development of practice and doctrine to illuminate their experience of oppression and to point the way to overcoming it. This, they believe, is the original purpose of the church in its prophetic calling.

Thus the message of liberation theology to the rest of the church is that there must be attention to the voices and experience of the excluded in the church, and a rediscovery of the prophetic and liberation traditions of Israel and Jesus that concern about the continuity of Christianity must focus on the continuity of liberating practice, and that concern for the proper development of Christianity must attend to the experience of those who have been marginalized, and to that which interprets and supports liberating practice.

CHAPTER 5

ON DOING THEOLOGY DURING A ROMANTIC MOVEMENT

I believe that we, in the United States and England at least, have been in a Romantic movement since the late 1960s, similar to the first one in the late eighteenth to the mid-nineteenth centuries. This movement influences in varying degrees all aspects of our lives and our culture. Since this is not widely recognized, this influence is all the more effective. Romantic movements are ambiguous, having both beneficial and destructive effects in society and culture. They have been usually correct in their criticism of the cultural situation and dubious in their extremes and some of their assumptions. Many of the negative effects result from the fact that Romantic movements are based in part on what has been called the perennial philosophy, the traditional esoteric metaphysics which has been at the foundation of Gnosticism, later Neoplatonism, theosophy, and related movements. The current Romantic movement has influenced Christian theology as carried on by scholars and also by others reflecting on their faith. This has tipped the table of argument in a particular direction making it easier to argue in one direction and more difficult in another, or making some theological proposals seem more plausible and others less so. We need to become more aware of the current Romantic movement and its influence on us so that we can affirm its positive side and avoid its negative results.

This is clearly a tall order for a short essay, especially since Romantic movements are highly amorphous and debatable in their definition, themes, and extent. Arthur Lovejoy has complained about the sloppy use of the term and warned against its careless application.[1] Nevertheless I will hazard some generally accepted descriptions of Romanticism. W. T. Jones has described Romanticism as a complex syndrome of "biases" in the direction of what he calls the dynamic, the disordered, the continuous, the soft-focused, the inner, and the other-worldly. He exemplifies this through an analysis of the poetry of Coleridge, Goethe, Keats, Wordsworth, Shelley and Byron, the metaphysics of Schopenhauer, and the political theory of Edmund Burke.[2] Crane Brinton portrays the Romantic temperament as "sensitive, emotional, preferring color to form, the exotic to the familiar, eager for novelty, for adventure, above all for the vicarious adventure of fantasy, reveling in disorder and uncertainty, insistent on the uniqueness of the individual to the point of making a virtue of eccentricity." The phases of Romantic thought include "exaltation of intuition, spirit, sensibility, imagination, faith, the immeasurable, the infinite, the wordless."[3]

A number of cultural analysts have argued that we are involved in a new Romantic movement. The main one is the historian Theodore Roszak in his books *The Making of a Counter Culture* (1969) and *Where the Wasteland Ends* (1972). In the first book Roszak explores the youth movement of the 1960s, but the interpretation of it as a new Romantic movement is only a sub-theme. In the second volume, however, this interpretation of the youth movement is the major thesis. To support his thesis Roszak offers an analysis of the themes of the first Romantic movement in the work of Blake, Wordsworth, and Goethe. Then he shows how these themes have been adopted by the youth movement, seen especially in its critique of the dominance of science and technology in industrial society and the resulting rationalization, secularization, bureaucratization, and dehumanization of life. Furthermore, Roszak finds the basis of both the old and new Romantic movements in what he calls the "Old Gnosis." This includes the hermetic tradition, Islamic and Hindu mysticism, Kabala, Zen, I Ching, Tarot,

---

1. See Arthur O. Lovejoy, "On the Discrimination of Romanticisms," in *Essays in the History of Ideas* (Baltimore: Johns Hopkins Press, 1948): chap. xii.
2. W. T. Jones, *The Romantic Syndrome: Toward a New Method in Cultural Anthropology and History of Ideas* (The Hague: Martinus Nijhoff, 1961): chaps. v-vii.
3. Crane Brinton, "Romanticism," *The Encyclopedia of Philosophy* 8 vols. (New York: Macmillan, 1967): 7:206b, 209b.

Taoism, magical, alchemical, and occult traditions, astrology, shakra yoga, Buddhist Tantra, as well as ancient Gnosticism.[4] Rozak often appeals to Jung, especially in the latter's studies of hermeticism and alchemy. Philip Rieff offers an interpretation of the Romantic themes in Jung's writings, namely, feeling versus intellect, spontaneity versus restriction, the unconscious as savior, introversion, the creative disorder of the interior life, and especially fantasy, which Rieff describes as "the Jungian successor to Christian faith."[5]

In a 1977 volume on the holocaust there is a section entitled "The New Romanticism and Biblical Faith." In this section theologian Michael D. Ryan finds evidence for the new Romanticism in Robert Jay Lifton's concept of "protean man" who embraces many loyalties and commitments in a single life. He also finds it in Charles Reich's book *The Greening of America* in which Consciousness I represents the old Romanticism, Consciousness II the technocratic managerial revolution, and the emerging Consciousness III which rejects Consciousness II and reaffirms Consciousness I. Ryan finds further evidence of the new Romanticism in William Irwin Thompson's book *At the Edge of History* (1971). Thompson's book is a wide-ranging critique of scientific, technological, industrial society which he believes has blinded itself to the possibilities of a deeper understanding of human life and history which is available in the myths of Atlantis and native Americans, in the prophecies of the famous psychic Edgar Cayce, the poetry of William Blake, and the science fiction of J. R. R. Tolkien, C. S. Lewis, and Arthur Clarke, author of "2001: A Space Odyssey."[6]

In the same section of this volume in an essay entitled "Romantic Consciousness and Biblical Faith" philosopher Edith Wyschogrod contrasts these two by describing Romanticism as a metaphysics of consciousness and biblical faith as a metaphysics of event. She argues that the metaphysics of consciousness expands the role given to individual consciousness with the goal of unlimited

---

4. Theodore Roszak, *Where the Wasteland Ends: Politics and Transcendence in Postindustrial Society* (Garden City, NY: Doubleday, 1872).
5. Philip Rieff, *The Triumph of the Therapeutic: The Uses of Faith After Freud* (New York: Harper & Row, 1966): 118.
6. Eva Fleischner, ed., *Auschwitz: Beginning of A New Era? Reflections on the Holocaust*, (New York: KTAV Publishing House, 1977): part vii.

freedom and the tendency to identify the self with God as in Hegel. This leads Romanticism to an apotheosis of the undetermined, of chaos, and finally to a valorization of death, which, she argues, was the contribution of Romanticism to Nazism. Wyschogrod states, "In the cult literature of the New Romanticism Hitler's orgies of destruction are interpreted as a regrettable but necessary antidote to Western rationalism, as demonic possession [is] the price man must pay to inaugurate the new age of giants."[7] She continues: "Another strategy [of the New Romanticism] is to return to a Neoplatonic or Vedantic devaluation of the body by acquiring spiritual powers which bypass the body and depend upon transcendent principles. . . . The true self and the body are radically dichotomized, the demise of the body is no way experienced as jeopardizing the life of the spirit."[8]

It is interesting to note that in his first book Roszak also worries about this darker side of the new Romanticism. He is concerned that "liberating the non-intellectual powers of the personality," which he favors, may lead to a "rampant, antinomian mania, which in the name of permissiveness threatens to plunge us into a dark and savage age." Here he refers to Peter Viereck's book *Metapolitics: The Roots of the Nazi Mind* which he describes as a "thorough attempt to spell out the connections between Nazism and Romanticism."[9] Roszak's worries, however, disappear in *Where the Wasteland Ends.*

Also, in an unpublished essay written in 1971 and entitled "Romanticism as a Religious Movement" the historian Sydney Ahlstrom states,

> Many observers have pointed to a pronounced romantic element in the new interests that mark the 1960s. A short unelaborated enumeration will suffice as a reminder: 1) the revival of Novalis' plea that youth must bring in the new day; 2) the surge of interest in Far Eastern religion that Herder and Friedrich Schlegel pioneered; 3) the commitment to history that Hegel personified and which Herbert Marcuse and the Marxist revival betoken; 4) the renewed interest in astrology, hermetic philosophy and the occult

---

7.   Ibid., 335.
8.   Ibid. Here she cites the influence of the work of Sri Aurobindo.
9.   Theodore Roszak, *The Making of a Counterculture: Reflections on the Technocratic Society and Its Youthful Opposition* (Garden City, NY: Doubleday, 1969): 73.

which Saint-Martin and Oettinger championed; 5) the interest in subjectivity, the subconscious, and openness to others associated with Rousseau's *Confessions* and dozens of romantic autobiographical expositions; 6) the search for the meaning and realization of an organic sense of community and a general enlivening of organic metaphors as an antidote to materialism, individualism, and mechanism; 7) a widespread attack on conventional morality which also reverberated in [Rousseau's] *La Nouvelle Héloise* and [Schlegel's] *Lucinde*; 8) a return of interest in Hermann Hesse who himself recapitulated many of these themes — not least a deep regard for Hölderlin — in his poetry and fiction; and 9) a new reverence for Nature.

Although these two historians refer solely to the German and English versions of Romanticism, a similar case could be made from the American version exemplified in the work of Ralph Waldo Emerson and the Transcendentalists. They were influenced by the European versions as well as by the perennial philosophy tradition and combined them in novel ways.

Finally, three British sociologists confirm the judgment of these historians. Bernice Martin states, "At the heart of the radical movement which will be the focus of my attention is the so-called 'counter-culture' of the late 1960s. My argument is that it served as a dramatic embodiment of certain crucial Romantic values which in the subsequent decades became intimately woven into the fabric of our culture." Frank Musgrove and Colin Campbell make similar arguments.[10]

It should be noted that postmodernism in literary and cultural critical theory which emerged in the 1960s can be considered to be an aspect of the current Romantic movement. Postmodern authors often refer to figures in the first Romantic movement, such as Goethe, Blake and Burke, as forerunners of postmodernism. This is not surprising since both movements involve a strong critique of the Enlightenment tradition.

---

10. Bernice Martin, *A Sociology of Contemporary Cultural Change* (New York: St. Martin's Press, 1981): 2. See also Frank Musgrove, *Ecstasy and Holiness: Counter Culture and the Open Society* (Bloomington, IN: Indiana University Press, 1974): 65; and Colin Campbell, *The Romantic Ethic and the Spirit of Modern Consumerism* (Oxford: Basil Blackwell, 1987): 3. I will return below to Campbell's thesis about the relation of the New Romanticism and consumerism.

I turn now to more specific evidence of the current Romantic movement in American cultures.[11] Over the past three years I have collected many examples of this from the media. I will mention a few of them. A reviewer of "The Lord of the Rings" in *The New York Times* attributes its success to the fact that "fantasy has become the order of the day in contemporary popular culture." Picking up on a phrase of Crane Brinton's mentioned above, namely, the Romantic preference "above all for the vicarious adventure of fantasy" I refer to the vast popularity of novels, movies, television shows since the 1960s focused on fantasy, involving mythic places, plots, young characters with magical powers in epic struggles with evil powers, the supernatural and paranormal, aliens, ghosts, angels, and so forth. In an article entitled "A Hunger for Fantasy, an Empire to Feed It" A. O. Scott notes that four recent movies, "Spider-Man," "Star Wars: Episode II — Attack of the Clones," "Harry Potter and the Sorcerer's Stone," and "Lord of the Rings: The Fellowship of the Ring," had by mid-2002 already earned more than one billion dollars in domestic sales alone, not counting overseas box office, DVD and video sales, and the vast merchandizing of all the paraphernalia of these box office hits. Moreover, three of these are parts of series and the fourth will probably follow suit. Scott concludes: "Perhaps more than ever before, Hollywood is an empire of fantasy."[12] A reviewer in *The New Yorker* describes the devotees of Harry Potter as "obsessed, incurable diehard romantics."[13] Another reviewer summarizes the significance of the "Lord of the Rings" trilogy in this way: "They revive the art of Romantic wonder."[14] Furthermore, sales of video games based on these movies and similar science fiction fantasies approached thirty-five billion in 2002. These examples of a current Romanticism in popular culture are, of course, rather sketchy, and I will leave it to the readers to assess whether or not their experience of contemporary culture confirms my thesis.

---

11. When I searched "new Romantic movement" on the web, I received 217,000 items in .07 seconds treating the new Romanticism in art, music, literature, criticism, and so forth.

12. A. O. Scott, "A Hunger for Fantasy, an Empire to Feed It," *The New York Times*, 6/16/02, Arts and Leisure, 1.

13. Bruce McCall, "Not Scared of Harry Potter," *The New Yorker*, (12/10/01): 54.

14. Alex Ross, "The Ring and the Rings," *The New Yorker*, (12/22 & 29/ 03): 162b.

Closely associated with these manifestations of the new Romantic movement is a new intensity of consumerism. In 1970 psychoanalyst Erich Fromm stated, "Man is in the process of becoming a *homo consumens, a* total consumer. . . . This vision of the total consumer is indeed a new image of man that is conquering the world."[15] Noting that American consumer debt now exceeds $2 trillion, one commentator states, "U.S. shopping centers now outnumber high schools and attract twenty million shoppers a month. In as many as a dozen states, the biggest tourist attraction is not a historical site or a cultural attraction: It's a mall. . . . The Nation's largest temple to malldom [is] the 4.2 million-square-foot Mall of America in Minnesota."[16]

British sociologist Colin Campbell sees this consumerism as a manifestation of the current Romantic movement, even as the first Romantic movement facilitated the emergence of the consumerism which fuelled the Industrial Revolution in the late eighteenth and early nineteenth centuries. He states that although consumption would seem to be at the opposite pole of life from Romanticism, "There is one significant modern phenomenon which does indeed directly connect the two. This, of course, is advertising, for even the most cursory examination of the pages of glossy magazines and the contents of television commercials will serve to reveal how many advertisements are concerned with the topic of 'romance,' or with images and copy which deal with scenes which are 'remote from everyday experience,' 'imaginative' or suggestive of 'grandeur' or 'passion.' [The phrases in quotation marks are from the definition of 'romantic' in *The Oxford English Dictionary*.][17]

I believe that the influence of the current Romantic movement can also be seen in the contemporary neoconservative movement which informs the

---

15 Erich Fromm, "Problems of Surplus," in *The Essential Fromm*, ed. Rainer Funk (New York: Continuum, 1995).

16 Vicki Haddock, "Lessons in Human Buy-ology," *San Francisco Chronicle*, (12/19/04): D1. See also these important studies of the new consumerism: Juliet Schor, *Do Americans Shop Too Much?* (Boston: Beacon Press, 2000); idem, *Born to Buy: The Commercialized Child and the New Consumer Culture* (New York: Scribner, 2004; and Juliet B. Schor and Douglas B. Holt, *The Consumer Society Reader* (New York: The New Press, 2000).

17. Colin Campbell, *The Romantic Ethic and the Spirit of Modern Consumerism*, 1.

administration of George W. Bush. The mentor of the neoconservative theorists and their disciples in the Bush administration is the political philosopher Leo Strauss (1899-1973). Strauss's impact has been described as the largest academic movement in the twentieth century, and he has been called the godfather of the Republican party's 1994 Contract with America. Strauss's political thought shows the influence of the Romantic political philosophers Edmund Burke and Jean Jacques Rousseau, and he praised Romanticism as the strongest German protest against liberal modernity. He is also influenced by the Romantic reactionaries such as Oswald Spengler, Carl Schmitt, Ernst Jünger and Martin Heidegger. His thought is marked by certain Romantic themes and tendencies: the esoteric character of his teaching, (which has been described as having a profound similarity to that of the Kabbalists — see below for a discussion of the current fascination with Kabbalah), anti-modernity, rule by an elite who are considered god-like, the state as sacred, an hierarchical ordering of society, antipathy to liberal democracy, abhorrence of egalitarianism, the importance of religion as the basis of a society, and an emphasis on rootedness in the soil, and on militarism and war.[18] I am suggesting that Strauss's political thought was influenced by first Romantic movement and that its widespread influence today is strengthened by the current Romantic movement. It represents the darker side of Romanticism mentioned above.

How has the current Romantic movement influenced Christian theology? I believe that the emphases of Romanticism mentioned by Jones and Brinton are apparent in some areas of contemporary theology. I have observed a suspicion of clarity, precision, analysis, and rationality, and a favoring of vagueness, complexity, the irrational, the anarchic, the chaotic, the wild, the Dionysian, the exotic, the esoteric, the heretical, the ancient, the primitive, the apophatic, the holistic, the mystical, and the divine darkness. Some years ago a graduate student in theology stated to me that she did not like distinctions. When I tried to explain

---

18. See Shadia Drury, *Leo Strauss and the American Right* (New York: St. Martin's Press, 1997): 2, 3, 41; idem, *Alexandre Kojève: The Roots of Postmodern Politics* (New York: St. Martin's Press, 1994): 155; idem, *The Political Ideas of Leo Strauss* (London: Macmillan, 1988). Professor Drury has stated that she agrees with my interpretation of Strauss.

that the making of distinctions was an essential of rational thought, she responded that rational thought always dichotomizes and creates separations and alienations, whereas she preferred holism. I have encountered several examples of these romantic attitudes among younger theologians. It should be noted, however, that the influence of the current Romantic movement on contemporary theology is limited largely to middle class mainline theology, rather than to liberation or conservative theology.

In 1980 the Dean of a seminary published an essay on theology and religious renewal which exemplifies the current Romantic movement. He stated that renewal requires us "to move, at times, to the edge of chaos," to have "a confrontation with the abyss." "Felt and intuitive meaning borders on chaos, whereas thinking is several steps removed from chaos." Theology and religion need "the willingness to get dirty together." Also he calls us to embrace "the threat" and "the antistructural." "We must intentionally move into the darkness, the surd, the unknown behind our systems." He offers three illustrations of the darkness into which we must intentionally move: "our grim fear of our own sexuality," the need for the archaic, the bizarre, and the vulgar in the liturgy, and "formation in the wilderness." He says that academic theologians will accuse him of "Romanticism, Transcendentalism, alchemy, the neo-Gothic revival" and so forth.[19] (This latter was in response to a critique I posed to an earlier version of his essay.) He was correct in this prediction since his essay illustrates many Romantic themes.

More recently a professor of spirituality and editor of a major journal of spirituality has published an article exploring "what it means to see the wild and the sacred as part of a single, indissoluble mystery," and "learning again to see and imagine the wild world as alive and sacred and whole."[20] There are many positive references to mystery, immersion in the larger whole, sacred yearning, ground of being, and negative references to the arrogance of knowledge and

---

19. Urban T. Holmes, "Theology and Religious Renewal," *The Anglican Theological Review* 62:1 (1980): 3-19; see esp. 16-19.
20. Douglas Burton-Christie, "The Wild and the Sacred," *Anglican Theological Review* 85:3 (2003): 494, 501, 509.

objectifying perception. He focuses on the environmental movement and especially on trees "those wild, ancient luminous beings which are for me the most necessary traces of the sacred in the world." He continues "The *trees* hold me. And I hold them. . . . I find myself increasingly asking myself this: what does it mean to hold and be held by a tree? . . . To ask this question is really to ask: what is a tree? . . . Perhaps it is time to begin thinking of and responding to trees, as, well, trees."[21] (I will suggest below that the current spirituality movement is major manifestation of the current Romantic movement.)

Both Jones and Brinton mention a bias toward the disordered or reveling in disorder as an aspect of Romanticism. One example of this theme appears in contemporary theology in the current interest in creation out of chaos and criticism of the traditional view of creation out of nothing. This is based on an interpretation of Gen 1:2: "The Earth was formless and void (*tohuwabohu*) and darkness covered the face of the deep (*tehom*)." Historians generally see this passage as a reflection of the Babylonian creation myth, the *Enuma elish*, in which the young male god Marduk defeats the primeval mother goddess Tiamat (= *tehom*) in a story of rape, murder, and dismemberment, and out of this primeval chaos creates the world order. Paul Ricoeur interprets this myth as one of the four great myths of evil, in which evil is identified with the chaos out of which the world is made. Thus evil is built into the order of things, is not a matter of human responsibility, and is irredeemable.[22]

Sjoerd Bonting criticizes the doctrine of creation out of nothing and affirms creation out of chaos on the basis of the Genesis texts, Justin Martyr, Clement of Alexandria, and modern chaos theory in physics. He applies this to all the main topics in theology and concludes that, although chaos itself is morally neutral, it is also the cause of moral and physical evil.[23]

---

21. Ibid., 506-7.
22. See Paul Ricoeur, *The Symbolism of Evil* (Boston: Beacon Press, 1967): part ii, chap. 1.
23. See Sjoerd L. Bonting, *Chaos Theology: A Revised Creation Theology* (Ottawa: Novalis, 2002). For a similar view from the perspective of process philosophy, see David A. Griffin, "Creation out of Chaos and the Problem of Evil," in Stephen T. Davis, ed. *Encountering Evil: Live Options in Theology* (Atlanta: John Knox Press, 1981).

A more fully developed theology based on a theory of chaos is presented in James Huchingson's book *Pandemonium Tremendum: Chaos and Mystery in the Life of God* which was discussed by a panel at the 2002 Annual Meeting of the American Academy of Religion.[24] In it the romantic themes of imagination, disorder, anarchy, complexity, mystery, and critique of the Enlightenment receive special emphasis. He makes creative use of information, communication, and systems theory to offer a perspective and vocabulary for the development of a novel theology of chaos as the basis of God and creation. Like Bonting Huchingson begins with an interpretation of Gen 1:2 which speaks of the formless, the void, and the deep.

Huchingson's main thesis is that chaos or the *Pandemonium Tremendum* is the foundation of both God and the creation. He states that chaos is "an infinite field of variety, of complete indeterminateness filled with potency, the source of all created things and one aspect of divine abundance"(105). Furthermore, "The *Pandemonium Tremendum* is the state antecedent to the creation, the comprehensive, unconditioned, and indeterminate source or ground of diversity among determinate things. It is the formless and the void of the *tohuwabohu* and the agitated deep of the *tehom*" (109).

What then is the relation of the chaos or *Pandemonium Tremendum* to God? It is the source of "grounding" for the "chaos-God-creation system" (131). "The chaos is the *Ungrund* [Boehme], the fundament and basin [basis?] of the divine life, the ground and groundlessness of God, eternal and uncaused, at once the answer to the cosmological question and the most profound mystery"(132). God must, however, shield the creation from chaos. For the *Pandemonium Tremendum* is "nothing but trouble. . . . It cannot behave itself" (127). God therefore must "contain the chaos" (127). "The order of the cosmos is divinely protected from being swept away" by the chaos (128). Furthermore, God can release the chaos or the *Pandemonium Tremendum* as the instrument of divine judgment, wrath, and retribution (127f).

---

24. James E. Huchingson, *Pandemonium Tremendum: Chaos and Mystery in the Life of God* (Cleveland: Pilgrim Press, 2001).

Huchingson is aware that "chaos is traditionally identified as evil" (210). But he argues that "the primordial chaos, the *Pandemonium Tremendum*, suffers the undeserved reputation of being evil. Evil is to be located in the character of systems that generate destructive chaos, the chaos that does not liberate but obliterates" (210). It is not clear how this is different from the *Pandemonium Tremendum*.

Catherine Keller follows a similar line but with suite different sources and style in her book *Face of the Deep: A Theology of Becoming*.[25] She offers a different argument against creation out of nothing and for creation out of chaos which is more clearly an expression of contemporary Romanticism than either Bonting or Huchingson. Many Romantic themes receive constant reiteration: depth, darkness, chaos, disorder, fluidity, multiplicity, mystery, mysticism, gnosticism, apophasis, and silence. Also various authors often cited by Romantics are regularly quoted: Dionysius, Eckhart, Nicholas of Cusa, the author of *The Cloud of Unknowing*, Blake, and Schelling.

Keller's goal is to develop what she calls a tehomic (deep) theology which constitutes a fundamental critique of the tradition of creation out of nothing which has promoted the "dominology" of the transcendent male person structure of Christian orthodoxy and its destructive effects on all of creation. Although her style is meditative, allusive, poetical, vague, and often elusive, her central theological proposal, which she calls "apophatic panentheism," is fairly clear. She affirms Whitehead's concept of "creativity from which both creator and creature emerge as mutual differentiations." "Creator and creature create, effect *each other*. . . . This radical interdependence would take place within the 'infinite creativity" (218). "The tehomic deity remains enmeshed in the vulnerabilities and potentialities of an indeterminate creativity. As Tehom it is that process; as deity it is *born from and suckles* that process" (226).

Finally, Philip Hefner, drawing on Plato, the Enuma Elish, Boehme, Berdyaev, and Tillich, also affirms creation out of chaos. He analyzes the types

---

25. Catherine Keller, *Face of the Deep: A Theology of Becoming*, (London & New York, 2003).

of experience which are associated with the second law of thermodynamics on entropy. These are the experiences of running down, degeneracy, chaos, the irreversibility of time, and the emergence of new possibilities. In the tradition of Plato they have usually been interpreted negatively and dualistically. Hefner, however, sides with the tradition of Boehme, Berdyaev, and Tillich that interprets them positively. Hefner concludes that our experience of the basic polarity of being and non-being, order and chaos, good and evil, possibility and actuality, point to the very foundation of reality in God.[26]

The main problem in these four interpretations of chaos, besides their lack of clarity, is whether or not they can overcome the dualistic implications of creation out of chaos, which have been analyzed in detail by Paul Ricoeur. In any case, however, they illustrate the fascination with chaos which is characteristic of the current Romantic movement.

Another bias of romanticism has been in favor of complexity, richness, and mystery as against rational simplicity and unity. I believe that this bias can be seen in the revival in contemporary theology of the ancient Eastern doctrine of the trinity which now seems to have become the majority view. This is the social analogy of the trinity emphasizing the distinctions of the persons in the godhead as contrasted with the Western psychological analogy emphasizing the unity of the godhead. This can be seen especially in the work of Jürgen Moltmann, Catherine La Cugna, and Elizabeth Johnson. Here the ancient concepts of *perichoresis* and *circumincessio* are sometimes interpreted as the dance of the divine persons in the eternal godhead that constitutes the mystery of the trinity. Moltmann, for example, sees monotheistic Christianity as heretical, as in the cases of Arius and Sabellius. He describes the inner life of the trinity in the following way: "John Damascene's doctrine of the eternal *perichoresis* or *circumincessio* of

---

26. Philip Hefner, "God and Chaos: The Demiurge Versus the *Ungrund*," *Zygon* 19:4 (1984): 469-85; see also Stuart Chandler, "When the World Falls Apart: Methodology for Employing Chaos and Emptiness as Theological Constructs," *Harvard Theological Review* 85:4 (1992): 467-91; and James I. McCord, "Editorial: The Blurred Vision," *Theology Today* 28:3 (1971): 271-77, in which he refers to our "moving out of one age into another," and to one reaction to this as the "romantic left" which in its fears of the "promised land of technology" represents a "flourishing romanticism."

the trinitarian persons . . . grasps the circulatory character of the eternal divine life. An eternal life process takes place in the triune God through the exchange of energies. . . . It is a process of the most perfect and intense empathy."[27] This kind of fascination with the mystery of the divine complexity is redolent of romanticism. (See O'Regan on Moltmann in the next paragraph.)

I expect indirect confirmation of the influence of Romanticism in contemporary theology in the work of Cyril O'Regan. He has begun a vast seven-volume project described by the title of the first volume, *Gnostic Return in Modernity*.[28] His thesis is that the Valentinian Gnosticism of the second and third centuries has returned in the philosophy of the seventeenth century German mystic Jacob Boehme, in the philosophy of Hegel and Schelling, in German and English Romanticism, and in the twentieth century theology of Berdyaev, Tillich, Altizer, and Moltmann. O'Regan states that "the essentially Valentinian [Gnostic] narrative is trinitarianly framed and landscaped" in Moltmann.[29] I say indirect confirmation, because, if as O'Regan argues, Romanticism is a manifestation of Gnosticism and Gnosticism is present in contemporary theology, then the latter will constitute *prima facie* evidence of the influence of Romanticism in contemporary theology.

I believe, however, that the clearest and most massive evidence of the current Romantic movement in contemporary theology is the current spirituality movement. It emerged about three decades ago, and it has grown very rapidly into a vast multimillion dollar industry involving thousands of full-time professional specialists, many new training, retreat and conference centers, a large number of new professorial chairs of spirituality in seminaries and other graduate schools, a vast new publishing enterprise producing hundreds of new books on spirituality every year, and the creation of new sections on spirituality in almost all bookstores. There is, of course, some overlap between the new spirituality

---

27. See Jürgen Moltmann, *The Trinity and the Kingdom* (San Francisco: Harper & Row, 1981): 174-5.

28. Cyril O'Regan, *Gnostic Return in Modernity* (Albany: State University of New York Press, 2001).

29. Ibid., 233.

movement and the continuing tradition of the churches' practice of teaching about and formation in the Christian life. They shade into each other. This is a result of the fact that Christianity has almost always been an unstable synthesis of what can be called the biblical religion tradition and the perennial philosophy tradition, on which one side of romanticism has been based.[30]

The marks of the current spirituality movement include many of those of the first Romantic movement mentioned by Jones and Brinton. I will focus on a few of them: an emphasis on the interior life as distinct from the outer life of the body, the community and history; a focus on the individual and private life rather than public life; an emphasis on feeling rather than rationality; and a sharp distinction between religion, which is disparaged, and spirituality, which is honored. Robert C. Fuller notes that a 1997 survey indicates that those people who are self identified as "spiritual but not religious" were "associated with higher levels of interest in mysticism, experimentation with unorthodox beliefs and practices, and negative feelings toward both clergy and churches."[31] Along with these more fundamental marks of Romanticism go more tangential elements: a fascination with the ancient, the primitive, the exotic, the esoteric, the mystical, the apophatic, and the heretical. All of these characterize both the current spirituality movement and the new Romantic movement of which it is in large part a product.

First, both the current spirituality and Romantic movements strongly emphasize the importance and centrality of interiority or the interior life.[32] Jones has noted its centrality in the first Romantic movement.[33] One of the most important publications of the spirituality movement is the twenty-five volume series entitled *World Spirituality*. In the "Preface to the Series" in each of the volumes the general editor, Ewert Cousins, states, "This series focuses on that inner dimension of the person called by certain traditions 'the spirit.' This

---

30. See chapter 12.
31. Robert C. Fuller, *Spiritual But Not Religious: Understanding Unattached America* (Oxford: Oxford University Press, 2001): 6.
32. See chapter 9.
33. See Jones, *The Romantic Syndrome*, 125-6.

spiritual core is the deepest center of the person."[34] In a recent study Michael Downey comments on contemporary currents in Christian spirituality as follows: "The common perception is still that spirituality is primarily concerned with the life of the soul, the inner life, one's prayer life, one's spiritual life, as a separate compartment of the Christian life. The tendency to equate the spiritual life with the interior life is particularly prevalent in our own day."[35]

Brinton has noted the emphasis in Romanticism on the individual and the fundamental importance of individuality. Jack Forstman states that the early German romantics were "overwhelmed and exhilarated by the awareness of individuality."[36] This appears in the current spirituality movement in its similar emphasis on the individual spiritual life as distinct from communal and historical life, an emphasis on private life rather than public life. Any consideration of the implications of spirituality for politics, for example, is extremely rare.[37]

One of the key affirmations of the current spirituality movement is the sharp distinction it makes between spirituality and religion, a distinction in which religion is disparaged and spirituality honored. While spirituality is understood to deal with the inner life, religion is seen to treat the outer life of institutions, creeds, traditions, and moral codes. Recent surveys of religious attitudes have often come across statements such as the following: "I'm probably not very religious, but I consider myself a deeply spiritual person."[38] Roszak is quite clear that the Christian religion is one of the main problems rather than the solution, which he finds in the "old Gnosis."[39] This is taken to an extreme in the thought of Diarmuid Ó Murchú, a Roman Catholic monk who is a leader of the spirituality

---

34. Ewert Cousins, *World Spirituality: An Encyclopedic History of the Religious Quest* (New York: Crossroad, 1985-).

35. Michael Downey, *Understanding Christian Spirituality* (New York: Paulist Press, 1992): 105.

36. Jack Forstman, *A Romantic Triangle: Schleiermacher and Early German Romanticism* (Missoula, MT: Scholars Press, 1970): xii.

37. See my essay "Political Spirituality: Oxymoron or Redundancy ?" *Journal of Religion and Society*, 3 (2001) (an electronic journal).

38. See Meredith B. McGuire, "Mapping Contemporary American Spirituality: A Sociological Perspective," *Christian Spirituality Bulletin* 5:1 (1997): 1c; see also Wade Clark Roof, *The Spiritual Marketplace: Baby Boomers and the Remaking of American Religion* (Princeton: Princeton University Press, 1999): 81, 173-9.

39. See Roszak, *Where the Wasteland Ends*, xxxi, 391, 405.

movement. (He was the keynote speaker at the annual conference in 2002 of Spiritual Directors International, the largest professional group at the heart of the spirituality movement with over four thousand members.) According to Ó Murchú spirituality emerged forty thousand years ago in the paleolithic period as "a cosmological synthesis imbued with a highly developed holistic, intuitive and spiritual consciousness" devoted to the worship of the Great Mother Goddess.[40] Religion, however, appeared only five thousand years ago and has been the source of all our alienation and inhumanity. "Religion in its essential essence is about alienation from the Earth and the cosmos." "Religion thrives on perpetuating that state of exile and alienation." The end of religion is "a likely possibility and a highly desirable one." Ó Murchú hails "the probable decline of formal religion and the revival of spirituality."[41]

In general in the current Romantic movement traditional Christianity is often seen as a massive conspiracy against anything new, fascinating, liberating, and heterodox. This is exemplified in the wide popularity of Elaine Pagels' books *The Gnostic Gospels* (1979) and *Beyond Belief: The Secret Gospel of Thomas* (2003) and the 2003 fiction best seller *The Da Vinci Code* by Dan Brown whose theme is the marriage of Jesus to Mary Magdalene, the birth of their child, and the desperate suppression of all this by the church. This is a repetition of the attitude toward religion which often appeared in the first Romantic movement. For example, the intended audience of Schleiermacher's *Speeches on Religion* appears in the subtitle, *To the Cultured Among its Despisers*, especially his friends, Schlegel and Novalis, the founders of the German Romantic movement, who had turned away from organized religion toward Gnosticism and theosophy.[42]

A new study brings together three themes of the current Romantic movement which have been mentioned above, namely, spirituality, consumerism, and neoconservatism. The authors argue that the spirituality movement has been taken over and further individualized, privatized, and commodified by what they

---

40. Diarmuid Ó Murchú, *Religion in Exile: A Spiritual Vision for the Homeward Bound* (Dublin: Gateway, 2000): 29.
41. Ibid., vii, 14, 65-6.
42. See Forstman, *A Romantic Triangle*, chaps. 2 & 3.

call neo-liberal, multinational, corporate capitalism in order to sell its worldview and its products. This has removed any concern in spirituality for community, social justice, or politics. This privatization and commodification has been accomplished through contemporary humanistic psychology and the colonization of Asian religious traditions in New Age forms. In order to further the goals of neo-liberal corporate capitalism this individualized and privatized spirituality is now widely used in educational and professional institutions, including health care, counseling, business training, management theory, and marketing.[43]

Another theme of the first Romantic movement was the emphasis on feeling, passion, and sentiment. The hero of Goethe's *Faust*, the "Bible of the [first] Romantic movement," (Barzun) cries, "Feeling is all." Sentiment, emotion, and the heart are constantly praised over against reason and the mind in Rousseau's Romantic novel *La Nouvelle Héloise*. This theme has been strongly echoed in the current spirituality movement and the Romantic movement of which it is a product. This is also exemplified in the human potential movement of the 1960s and 1970s and its focus on feeling, emotion, and sensitivity training pioneered by the National Training Laboratories and the Esalen Institute.

I mentioned above the fascination in the spirituality movement with the ancient, the exotic, the mystical, and the esoteric. This reflects the similar attitude in the first Romantic movement exemplified in Novalis' idealization of the Medieval, Schwenhauer's devotion to Hinduism, and the interest of Saint-Martin and Oettinger in astrology, hermetic philosophy, and the occult, mentioned by Ahlstrom. In the spirituality movement this fascination can be seen in the new found interest among Protestants in such figures and movements as the Desert Fathers, Celtic spirituality, the Kabbalah, Eckhart, and the medieval mystics. It is also exemplified in the great popularity of the new multivolume series *Classics of Western Spirituality*, which includes volumes on *The Cloud of Unknowing*, Pseudo-Dionysius, Boehme, and Swedenborg, who were deeply influenced by the perennial philosophy tradition. This can also be seen in the program of the 2001

---

43. See Jeremy Carrette and Richard King, *Selling Spirituality: The Silent Takeover of Religion* (London: Routledge, 2005).

Annual Meeting of Spiritual Directors International which featured institutes and workshops on such topics as the Kabbalah, the sacred labyrinth, and two on the Enneagram, as well as "Praying through the great elements of Earth/Air/ Fire/Water."

Especially typical of the new Romantic movement is the recent surge of interest in Kabbalah, the collection of texts of medieval Jewish mysticism with alleged sources in the second century. It arose in Provence in the thirteenth century and was influenced by the Neoplatonist and Gnostic traditions. A recent newspaper article described Kabbalah as "arcane, obscure, and inaccessible. . . . Its inaccessibility is what makes it attractive."[44] Kabbalah has been taken up by various celebrities, such as Madonna, Barbra Streisand, Courtney Love, Roseanne Barr, and Britney Spears. It is promoted by the Kabbalah Centre International which has twenty-three offices worldwide and claims 18,000 students in its classes, 90,000 active members in the United States and 90,000 visits to its website every month.[45] Kabbalah as ancient, esoteric, mystical, heretical, and exotic is a perfect example of and vehicle for the current spirituality and Romantic movements.

Although perhaps not central to the spirituality movement but constituting its left wing and clearly a manifestation of the current Romantic movement are phenomena such as the Fourth International Conference on Science and Consciousness held in 2002 and sponsored by thirty-five organizations including the Parapsychology Foundation, The Anthroposophic Press, The Mind Science Foundation, the Holographic Repatterning Association, the American Society for Psychical Research, the Academy of Intuitive Studies and Intuition Medicine, and the International Society for the Study of Subtle Energies and Energy Medicine. The conference featured workshops on many aspects of the relation of spirituality and science including "Electromagnetism and Sacred Indwelling," "The Science of Alchemy and the Art of Tantra," "The Genome Approach to Spiritual

---

44. Patricia Yollin, "New interest in Jewish Mysticism," *San Francisco Chronicle*, (12/26/03): A21, 25.
45. See Debra Nussbaum Cohen, "A Surge in Popularity in Jewish Mysticism," *The New York Times*, (12/13/03): A15.

Transformation," "Trance Surgery," "The Chakras of Telecommunication," "The Frequencies of Higher Consciousness," and "Accessing Noumenal Consciousness." This conference and many similar ones are examples of the spirituality movement, its basis in the current Romantic movement, its foundation in the perennial philosophy, and the fascination of all of these with the exotic and the paranormal.

This conference and other points mentioned above indicate an important difference between the two Romantic movements in their diverse attitudes toward science. The first Romantic movement in its emphasis on disorder, uncertainty, the soft-focused, the exotic, fantasy, the inner, and the otherworldly, attacked the Newtonian science which was celebrated by the Enlightenment. This was more the case in England than in Germany where Goethe and Schopenhauer had some interest in and knowledge of science. In England, however, Blake and Wordsworth in particular were unremitting in their attack on Newtonian empirical science.

In the current Romantic movement, however, the attitude toward science has occasionally been more affirmative. The main reason for this has been the emergence early in the last century of what has been called post-modern science, in particular relativity and quantum theory and later chaos theory. Relativity theory holds that there is no absolute and fixed space-time system as in Newtonian physics. Quantum mechanics is usually interpreted to mean that our knowledge of the most fundamental level of matter is strictly limited by the uncertainty principle, that events with no physical cause are pervasive in matter, and that non-locality or unmediated action at a distance is also pervasive.

These developments in modern physics were quickly adopted by the current Romantic movement, since they seemed to support the main emphases of this movement. One of the first was Fritjof Capra's book *The Tao of Physics* (1976) which argued that modern physics demonstrated the truth of Eastern mystical religious thought. This was followed shortly by Gary Zukav's book *The Dancing Wu Li Masters* (1979) with a similar argument. More recently we have Danah Zohar's books *The Quantum Self: Human Nature and Consciousness*

Defined by the New Physics (1990) and (with Ian Merchall) *The Quantum Society: Mind, Physics, and a New Social Vision* (1994). Most recently we have Diarmuid Ó Murchú's book *Quantum Theology: The Spiritual Implications of the New Physics* (1997) which explores these ideas further. All these works are examples of the current Romantic movement and its spin-off in the spirituality movement. The appendix in Ó Murchú's book on "Principles of a Quantum Theology" is a fine summary of both.

I suggested above that Romantic movements have tended to be correct in their criticisms of the contemporary culture and dubious in their extremities and some of their assumptions. The first Romantic movement was valid in its criticism of the one-sidedness of the Enlightenment and neo-classical traditions. W. T. Jones describes the Enlightenment as a syndrome of biases toward the static, order, discreteness, a sharp focus, the outer, and the this-worldly.[46] We have noted above that according to Jones the biases of the first Romantic movement were the exact opposite of these and constituted a critique of their exaggerations.[47] Friedrich Schlegel, the leader of the German version of the first Romantic movement, was "convinced that the day of enlightened rationality and detachment, of neo-classical ideals and decorum was over." He and his colleagues "challenged the cool rationality and spectator attitude of the Enlightenment."[48]

As mentioned above the English Romantics were appalled at the scientific-technological attitude toward the natural world. Blake chastised the "single vision" of Bacon, Newton, and the new natural science. Wordsworth cried that natural scientists "murder to dissect" nature. All of this was a valid criticism of the ideals of the Enlightenment and of the worldview of modern science and technology. The Romantics attempted at least to restore a measure of balance by emphasizing the place of feeling, emotion, intuition, fantasy and imagination in

---

46. See Jones, *The Romantic Syndrome*, 117.
47. See ibid., chaps. vi, vii.
48. Forstman, *A Romantic Triangle*, x.

human life and culture. But of course, they went to extremes, since extremity was their middle name.

The same can be said of the current Romantic movement. It is a valid critique of the dominance of scientism, technology, and industrialization and the resulting over-rationalization, bureaucratization, and dehumanization of human society and culture. As to the dubiousness of their extremities and their assumptions, we have noted Wyschogrod's and Roszak's warnings about the dark side of Romanticism, its tendency toward a valorization of chaos and death, and its antinomian mania which tends toward savagery. To this we should add its tendency to melancholy, disenchantment, and to political messianism, extreme nationalism, racism, militarism, imperialism, and racism which became evident in the hate groups of the past century.

I believe, however, that the most significant problem in Romanticism and the main source of its negative implications is its grounding in the perennial philosophy, in what Roszak calls "the old Gnosis." By the perennial philosophy I refer to a Weberian ideal type, a heuristic construct which serves to organize certain historical data. This particular ideal type was described by Weber as the exemplary type found mainly in Eastern religion in distinction from the emissary type which is found in biblical religion in the West.[49] Peter Berger refers to these as the interiority and confrontation types.[50] The perennial philosophy is the religio-philosophical worldview exemplified by later Neoplatonism and Vedanta and by the philosophical foundations of Gnosticism, Rosicrucianism, Theosophy, and similar movements, and propounded in the modern period by such philosophers as René Guénon, Frithjof Schuon, S. H. Nasr, Huston Smith, and many others. The implications of the perennial philosophy are that individuality or personhood tends to be understood as ambiguous, evil, or unreal, that bodily life and the natural world are viewed with suspicion, that human communal life and history lack any meaning, and that human fulfillment is found only in escape

---

49. See Max Weber, *The Sociology of Religion*, (Boston: Beacon Press, 1963): 456-50.
50. Peter Berger, ed., *The Other Side of God: A Polarity in World Religions* (Garden City, NY: Anchor, 1981): vii-viii, 3-6.

from the body and the world and reunion of the human spirit (which is divine) with the divine.[51]

It is clear that one side of the first Romantic movement was grounded in the perennial philosophy. Goethe, the father of the German Romantic movement, states in his autobiography that he was influenced by Arnold's *History of the Church and of Heretics*, and that "what particularly delighted me in his work was, that I received a more favourable notion of many heretics." He states that every man has his own religion and that he was moved to form his too. He describes it as follows: "The Neo-Platonism lay at the foundation; the hermetical, the mystical, the cabalistic, also contributed their share." He goes on to describe "a Godhead which has gone on producing itself from all eternity." First is produced a Second which is the Son; then a Third which completes the circle of the Godhead. But the work of divine production continues with the appearance of a fourth which is Lucifer, who embodies a contradiction as unlimited but contained in the Godhead, and who creates the angels who are contained in him. Then Lucifer forgets his higher origin and attempts to find himself in himself, and this causes the Fall of the Angels and the production of matter which is heavy, solid and dark. But since matter is descended by filiation from the Divine Being it is unlimited and eternal. Next the Elohim give to the Eternal Being the power of expansion to produce the creation and also man who acts the part of Lucifer and produces the second fall. Finally, in order to restore the creation the Divinity takes the form of man. Thus "the whole creation was nothing but a falling from and returning to the original."[52] This seems to be a version of the Valentinian Gnosticism analyzed by O'Regan.[53]

Novalis (Friedrich von Hardenburg), the leader of the first German Romantic movement, was a follower of Jacob Boehme, Plotinus, and what he called "the mysteries of the East." As a Neoplatonist he envisioned all of reality

---

51. For a fuller elaboration of these points see chapters 12 and 13.

52. See John Oxenford, trans., *The Autobiography of Johann Wolfgang von Goethe*, (New York: Horizon Press, 1969): 379-82.

53. See his summary of "Valentinian narrative grammar" in *Gnostic Return in Modernity*, 137.

as a process of separation from the primordial unity and an ultimate return to a higher and richer unity. He saw this world as a prison, a realm of polarity, opposition, separation, and boundedness, from which we are released only by death. It is only the poet who through the power of imagination can lift the veil which the world casts over the true reality of the spiritual world. This, however, requires deification, since "God is known only by a god." According to the mystery tradition this is accomplished by an initiation which involves the recognition and enhancement of that part of man which is divine. Then the poet, the divinized high priest of this cosmic religion, lifts the veil of illusion by means of dream, fantasy, imagination and magic and leads us back to our eternal home. Novalis is a perfect example of the perennial philosophy.[54]

Arthur Schopenhauer, the "arch Romantic" (Brinton), was attracted by Buddhism and mystical elitist esotericism, but he was primarily a Vedantist. He referred to the Vedas as "the most profitable and sublime reading that is possible in the world." The Upanishads were his main devotional literature. He held a dualistic view of the body and the world, which he said was created by a devil. He held that the world is a hell surpassing that of Dante. He said No to the Romantics who delighted in nature. The eternal soul had been banished into the body, but the better and eternal self could be saved by turning away from life in the body and the world through renunciation and resignation aided by art, especially music.[55]

As was suggested above, Roszak also argues that the current Romantic movement is founded on "the old Gnosis" or the perennial philosophy, more specifically on the hermetic tradition, Islamic and Hindu mysticism (Sufism and Vedanta), and ancient Gnosticism. Ahlstrom sees hermetic philosophy and Eastern religion at the basis of the current Romantic movement. Wyschogrod finds a foundation of the new Romanticism in Neoplatonism and Vedanta. Finally, since O'Regan argues that the first Romantic movement was at least in

---

54. See Forstman, *A Romantic Triangle*, chaps. 3, 4; and Jones, *The Romantic Syndrome*, chap. 6.

55. See Rudiger Safranski, *Schopenhauer and the Wild Years of Philosophy*, (Cambridge: Harvard University Press, 1990): 58-9, 63, 93, 201-2, 228, 235, 321.

part a manifestation of Gnostic return, then he would presumably agree that a current Romantic movement would be subject to the same interpretation.[56]

It should be stated, however, that there is a side of both the old and the new Romanticism that is not based on the perennial philosophy in any of its versions. It is quite clear, for example, that Schleiermacher, although clearly a Romantic and the first Romantic theologian, opposed and distanced himself from the views of Novalis.[57] And O'Regan considers Coleridge, the most philosophical of the English Romantics, among the anti-Gnostic authors. Moreover, some of the themes of the perennial philosophy seem to be less evident in at least one side of the current Romantic movement, for example, a dualistic attitude toward human nature and the natural world, and human fulfillment as escape from the body, the community, and the world.

If the above argument has any validity, what are the implications for Christian theology, both lay and professional? In sum we need to become aware of the current Romantic movement in its various aspects and influences, to assess how much we have been influenced by it, to affirm what we believe to be the positive aspects without their extremities, and to avoid what we judge to be the negative aspects. Among the positive aspects I have mentioned, first, the critique of the dominance of scientism, technology, and industrialization and the resulting over-rationalization, bureaucratization, and dehumanization of life and culture; second, the affirmation of the centrality in human life and culture of feeling, emotion, sentiment, intuition, and imagination; third, the affirmation of the fundamental importance of individuality and subjectivity; and fourth, the affirmation on one side of Romanticism of the goodness and beauty of the natural world and the human body. However, the extremes of these aspects must be avoided: a Romantic retreat from modern life and responsibility, an overemphasis on feeling to the exclusion of a proper rationality, the extreme individualism of

---

56. See O'Regan, *Deranging Narrative: Romanticism and its Gnostic Limit* (Albany: State University of New York Press, forthcoming).
57. See Forstman, *A Romantic Triangle*, chap. 6.

contemporary life noted by many commentators, and the Romantic divinization of nature often found in Neo-pagan movements.

The negative aspects of the current Romantic movement, including the overemphases which have been mentioned, which should be avoided, are, first, the darker side mentioned by Roszak and Wyschogrod exemplified in the prevalence of many hate groups based on racism, nationalism, and militarism; and, second, the negative influences of the foundation of one side of the current Romantic movement in the perennial philosophy which have been mentioned above. It is clear, however, that one side of the current Romantic movement has avoided some of these results.

So our responsibility as theologians is, as always, to assess new theological proposals with generosity, that is, in the best possible light, and then subject them to critical analysis in the light of our norms. Now this may be difficult, since the influence of the current Romantic movement on theology has been to tend to disparage clarity, precision, analysis, and coherence, and to tend to commend vagueness, the irrational, the chaotic, the apophatic, the heretical, and mystery. The task of theology, however, has always been difficult, and in fact recent Romantically influenced theology has in fact sometimes given us examples of important critical and constructive theological work.

PART II

TOPICS

CHAPTER 6

ANALOGY AT IMPASSE

[The question of analogy] has been and still is perhaps the most complex and difficult question the theologian faces. Its difficulty is felt with particular force today because it is widely believed by contemporary philosophers and theologians that the classical theory of analogy cannot be maintained, since it fails to solve the problem it purports to solve. . . . I, too, hold that the classical theory of analogy is untenable.[1]

Most recent writers in philosophical theology have made some reference to the theory of analogy current in medieval times, and almost universally these writers have judged it hopeless.[2]

I find myself using ordinary language about God in prayer, worship, preaching, teaching, and in reflection on these. However, this language is odd in the sense that its usual meaning is being stretched or transcended. This language is being used metaphorically, symbolically, or, in traditional theological terms, analogically. How does one decide which analogies are the most appropriate, the most fundamental? How do these analogies refer to God? Is some non-analogous assertion about God necessary for the meaningfulness of these analogies? Is it possible? A doctrine or theory of analogy is an attempt to resolve these questions and to clarify, explain, and control analogical usage.

In contemporary theology and philosophy the doctrine of analogy is at something of an impasse. It is variously held to be necessary, in need of radical reformulation, invalid, and unnecessary in theology. In this chapter I shall

---

1. Schubert M. Ogden, *The Reality of God and Other Essays* (New York: Harper and Row, 1963): 174.
2. James F. Ross, "Analogy as a Rule of Meaning for Religious Language," *International Philosophical Quarterly* I (1961): 468.

explore some of the criticisms which are being made of the doctrine of analogy by contemporary theologians and philosophers, investigate various reinterpretations of the doctrine, and assess whether they successfully meet the criticisms. I shall suggest that attention to the doctrine of revelation will help us to resolve one of the crucial difficulties with the doctrine

Criticisms of Analogy

Some theologians and philosophers hold that the doctrine of analogy in its traditional form is valid and necessary to theology. Others assert that the traditional doctrine is invalid because it is contradictory or vague and that it must be radically reinterpreted. A third view adds that the doctrine should play only a subsidiary role in theology. Others assert that the doctrine cannot and need not be formulated clearly.

Schubert M. Ogden and Leslie Dewart hold that the classical theory of analogy is untenable. Both assert that there is an implicit or explicit contradiction between the positive affirmations about God and the denial of literal meaning in them. Both see the origin of this difficulty in the classical metaphysical doctrine of God. Dewart argues that the classical doctrine of analogy is based on an outmoded theory of knowledge. Furthermore, no theory of analogy is necessary in theology, because God can be adequately conceived by us in the univocal concepts of empirical intuition.[3] Ogden, on the other hand, notes that the classical metaphysical outlook is oriented to the objective world and sense perception and not to the primal phenomenon of our existence as experiencing selves. He believes that Heidegger and Hartshorne point the way to a consistent theory of analogy.[4]

In his most recent discussion of analogy Ogden still finds the classical doctrine untenable but for quite different reasons. Unless God is already known immediately, there is no way to establish whether a term can be applied to God as

---

3. *The Future of Belief: Theism in a World Come of Age* (New York: Herder and Hercer, 1966): 178-80.

4. Ogden, *The Reality of God*, pp. 156-7, 174-7.

a proper analogy as distinct from being merely a symbol. Since there can be no immediate knowledge of God, the application of analogies to God is impossible. This difficulty applies also to Hartshorne's doctrine of analogy, which Ogden therefore finds to be as inadequate as the classical doctrine. Ogden now defends the possibility of a strictly transcendental metaphysical theism which dispenses altogether with analogy.[5]

Humphrey Palmer and Frederick Ferré argue that the traditional analogy of proportionality is uninformative about God. The "equation" of this form of analogy (e.g., the divine goodness is to the divine nature as human goodness is to human nature) contains two variables or unknowns (the divine goodness and the divine nature) and thus is insoluble and gives no new knowledge of God. They also argue that the analogy of attribution, which is based on an alleged resemblance between creator and creatures, is excessively permissive and allows us to predicate almost any quality of God and yet to remain in ignorance of the way in which any analogue applies to God. However, the doctrine of analogy is appropriate as a way of explaining how religious language functions and as a way of controlling its usage.[6] William T. Blackstone makes a similar criticism of the analogy of proportionality and adds that it would be informative about God only if we had some literal or non-analogical knowledge of God, e.g., God's nature or goodness.[7]

Robert Neville elaborates on this latter point. This positive non-analogical affirmation has a dual role in relation to an analogy.

> On the one hand, as Scotus pointed out, the affirmation is the standard that establishes what is to be denied of the analogy, that determines what parts are not similar. On the other hand, it must be the ground for asserting the analogy itself, for if the analogate

5. *The Point of Christology* (San Francisco: Harper & Row, 1982): chap. 7.

6. Humphrey Palmer, *Analogy: A Study of Qualification and Argument in Theology* (London: Macmillan, 1973): chap. 5, 82-4; Frederick Ferré, *Language, Logic and God* (New York: Harper and Brothers, 1961): pp. 72-4; idem., "Analogy in Theology," *Encyclopedia of Philosophy*, 8 vols., ed. Paul Edwards (New York: Macmillan Co., 1967): 7:94-7. See Dorothy Emmet, *The Nature of Metaphysical Thinking* (London: Macmillan & Co., 1953): 179, 187.

7. *The Problem of Religious Knowledge: The Impact of Philosophical Analysis on the Question of Religious Knowledge* (Englewood Cliffs, NJ: Prentice-Hall, 1963): 65-7.

could be known *only* through the analogue, how could it be known that *any* analogy applied?[8]

Neville argues further that being must be predicated univocally of God and creatures. If this were not the case, then nothing at all could be predicated of God and creatures univocally and as a result nothing at all could be predicated analogically. From this Neville concludes that our knowledge of God, which cannot be of God in himself but only of God in relation to the world, is univocal.[9]

Neville allows, however, that there are legitimate functions of analogy consistent with the univocity of being itself.[10] One is the articulation of a new domain to which we do not have direct access and which we can compare with some familiar domain. Another is the offering of an inference claim on a univocal foundation which is supplied by dialectic. A third is that an analogy allows us *"to detach the conclusion in thought from the argument that sets the conditions it must fulfill.* For instance, the analogy of the creator to a father allows us to treat the creator without in the same breath considering the product."[11] This makes it possible to focus on the conclusion of an argument apart from the premises from which the conclusion was derived. Thus, "the conclusion of a dialectical argument can be worshipped, prayed to, and so forth."[12] This also allows us to move the conclusion into contexts different from that of the original premises and argument. The analogy here is an "organon of discovery" and can be employed to suggest new connections that might cast light on the conclusion. These, however, must finally be interpreted in a univocal way.

Hartshorne

Ogden in his earlier work stated that "Hartshorne has amply demonstrated that a consistent logic of analogy can be developed and that the ancient dilemma of anthropomorphism and agnosticism can be resolved without in any way

---

8. *God the Creator: On the Transcendence and Presence of God* (Chicago: University of Chicago Press, 1968): 19; 139-42.
9. Ibid., pp. 20, 77.
10. Ibid., pp. 139-42.
11. Ibid, p. 142.
12. Ibid.

prejudicing the claims of Christian faith."[13] Let us see whether Hartshorne has in fact developed a consistent logic of analogy which is able to deal with the difficulties mentioned above.

In *Man's Vision of God* (1941) Hartshorne states that "the relation of God to the world must necessarily be conceived, if at all, by analogy with relations given in human experience."[14] He proceeds to analyze this relation in terms of the analogies of the human to human and the mind-body relations. In *The Divine Relativity* (1948), however, we find strong assertions of both the analogical and the literal character of language about God. God has a metaphysically unique status and character, namely, one whose distinctions can be defined through purely universal categories. "Thus God is the *one individual conceivable a priori*. It is in this sense that concepts applied to him are analogical rather than simply univocal, in comparison to their other applications."[15] "So both 'relative' and 'non-relative' are analogical, not univocal in relation to deity."[16] But then he goes on to state that the categories of relativity, absoluteness, necessity, and accidentality can be applied strictly or literally only to God, whereas they can be applied to creatures only in a "middling" manner. Hartshorne is attempting to indicate the way in which concepts are applied differently to God and to creatures, but he is not clear as to which is the prime and which the secondary analogate. Then in a section entitled "Literalness of Theism" he states that theology is "the most literal of all sciences of existence."[17] God loves and knows literally. God is literally wise, unborn, everlasting, socially aware, and person. Finally, this is apparently contradicted in a section on "The Principles of Eminence" in which he affirms that "whatever is good in the creation is, in superior or eminent fashion, 'analogically not univocally,' the property of God."[18]

13. Ogden, *The Reality of God*, p. 175.
14. *Man's Vision of God and the Logic of Theism* (Chicago: Willett, Clark & Co., 1941): 174.
15. *The Divine Relativity: A Social Conception of God* (New Haven: Yale University Press, 1948): 31.
16. Ibid., p. 32.
17. Ibid., p. 36.
18. Ibid., p. 77.

Hartshorne begins to achieve some clarity in an essay written in 1956 and entitled "The Idea of God — Literal or Analogical?" Here he distinguishes between non-literal concepts, such as love and knowledge, which involve degrees and are qualitative, and literal concepts which are not matters of degree but rather express the formal status of God. He gives several examples of the latter: the necessity of the divine existence, the contingency of the divine predicates, etc.[19]

Finally, in an essay entitled "Three Strata of Meaning in Religious Discourse" published in 1962, Hartshorne achieves further clarity on the question of analogy. The three strata are symbolic or material, non-symbolic or formal, and analogical. The first stratum compares deity with a particular part of the psycho-physical universe. In the second kind of predication no one part of the universe more than any other is involved in the comparison. The third or analogous type of predication involves psychical concepts. "God is symbolically ruler, but analogicaly conscious and loving, and literally both absolute (or necessary) in existence and relative (or contingent) in actuality, that is, in the concrete modes of His existence."[20] Symbolic or material predication, however, obviously includes analogical predication. So we have really only two kinds of predication one of which has two varieties. It is not clear why Hartshorne limits analogy to psychical concepts. In this same essay Hartshorne notes the "strange sense" in which analogical concepts apply literally to God and analogically to creatures.[21] This is the sense which caused his earlier ambivalence about which are the primary and secondary analogates. So it does not seem that Hartshorne has developed a consistent logic of analogy, and his approach does not shed much light on the criticisms which have been made of the doctrine.

Ross

Since his dissertation on the theory of analogy of St. Thomas {1958), James F. Ross has devoted a lot of attention to developing a new theory of

---

19. *The Christian Scholar* 39 (1955): 135.
20. *The Logic of Perfection and Other Essays in Neoclassical Metaphysics* (LaSalle, IL: Open Court Publishing Co., 1962): 140.
21. Ibid., p. 141.

analogy. Ross understands analogy to be "meaning derivation for sets of same terms." It is a pervasive semantical feature of natural language and part of the expansion structure of the language, i.e., "those structural features by which the language is adaptable to new kinds of thoughts and transformable to express new kinds of experience."[22] The theory of analogy is an explication of such rule-governed meaning derivation.

When applied to religious and theological language the theory of analogy supplies an account of the cognitivity of religious discourse and the meaningfulness of theological statements. Since analogy is pervasive in natural language, its occurrence in religion and theology is not a problem unique to these domains. Analogy is therefore a general problem for the philosophy of language, and its application to cases where the object is not directly observable is simply a subclass of the cases to be accounted for by the general theory. Ross asserts that analogy theory is empirically based. Analogy rules are semantical rules which are followed in correct speech. They are subject to the same empirical establishment and falsification as the other rules of syntax, semantics, and pragmatics. So an analogy rule is a description of a linguistic regularity which explains the generation of meanings of some equivocal terms from one another.[23]

According to Ross, most recent writers in philosophical theology have judged the medieval theory of analogy as hopeless. This is largely because they have mistakenly interpreted the proportionality analogy on the model of a mathematical proportion and have understood it as a theory of inference (which St. Thomas did not) rather than a theory of meaning.[24] Following and elaborating on St. Thomas, Ross presents the two main analogy rules for religious language, namely, the analogy of attribution and the analogy of proper proportionality, of which the latter is more fundamental in religious discourse.[25]

---

22. "A New Theory of Analogy," in *Logical Analysis and Contemporary Theism*, ed. John Donnelly (New York: Fordham University Press, 1972): 126.

23. *Introduction to the Philosophy of Religion* (London: Macmillan Co., 1969): 155-9.

24. Ross, "Analogy," p. 468 and note.

25. Ibid., pp. 476-97; idem., *Introduction*, pp. 164-73.

Does Ross help to resolve any of the difficulties with the doctrine of analogy which have been mentioned above? He implicitly contradicts Ogden's assertion of the untenability of the classical theory. Since Ogden's point about the contradiction between positive and negative assertions about God is not very specific, it is not clear how he would respond to Ross. Ogden's main criticism is directed at classical theism and its categorial metaphysics and Ross does not consider this issue.

Since Dewart ignores the pervasive presence of analogy in natural language, his point about its being unnecessary in language about God is undercut. Furthermore, he contradicts himself by repeatedly appealing to personal analogies in elaborating his view of the divine presence.[26]

Ross speaks directly to the criticism made by Palmer and Ferré and agrees that the analogy of proportionality is uninformative in the sense of not offering any new knowledge of God. He argues that this was not the intention of St. Thomas, and that modern arguments to the contrary are mistaken. As we have seen, he asserts that analogy theory is not a theory of inference but of meaning. Thus he agrees with Palmer and Ferré that analogy theory is a way of explaining how religious language functions and of controlling its usage.

Ross does not speak directly to the point made by Ogden, Blackstone, and Neville that analogy must be based on some immediate, literal, or non-analogical knowledge of God. But his analysis of the pervasiveness of analogy in natural language implies that either this is not possible or that it is a meaningless requirement. The basis of Ross' view is found in the later Wittgenstein and the modern philosophy of language. Ogden and Neville, do not refer to these developments, and Blackstone, although he is aware of them, does not apply them to his views of analogy.

Smith and Burrell

Ross' point is that because of the pervasiveness of analogy in ordinary language, the application of terms analogically to God is not a special or unique

---

26. See, e.g., *The Future of Belief*, pp. 176-7.

case of analogy. His point can be elaborated with the help of John E. Smith and David Burrell. Smith argues that the distinction of literal and symbolic as applying to ordinary and religious language is an oversimplification.

> But if at least one of the lessons to be learned from the contemporary analysis of language is to be taken seriously, it should be clear that this so-called literal domain is a myth. The fact is that a spectrum of related but not identical meanings develops in the use of every term within the supposed literal domain itself.[27]

Also Ferré refers to "an adequate account of literal linguistic meaning" as "the yet unfinished task of more than a generation of workers in philosophy."[28]

Burrell makes a similar point. "If much of our ordinary usage is already quite 'extended,' it becomes superfluous to seek a justification of extended usage generally."[29] After mentioning "the difficulty of finding a determinate set of criteria even for univocal usage," he concludes, "and when we add to these observations the fact that ordinary usage freely employs terms generally recognized to be analogous, the distinction between ordinary and extended usage blurs considerably."[30] Burrell goes on to suggest that ordinary usage which is full of analogy is what is properly meant by univocal usage. Furthermore, metaphors are created to make particular points, but as they become domesticated they also become in effect univocal terms.[31]

Smith does allow that there is a "core" meaning of a term which is derived from direct experience. His main point is that experience is the basis of analogy, but he insists that this does not mean that other meanings of terms are invalid. He states that "the transposition of terms whose meaning is based on sensible experience to the transcendent referent of religious expressions does *not* represent

---

27. *The Analogy of Experience: An Approach to Understanding Religious Truth* (New York: Harper & Row, 1973): 46. See Palmer, *Analogy*, p. 85.
   28. "Metaphors, Models, and Religion," *Soundings* 51 (1968): 329.
   29. *Analogy and Philosophical Language* (New Haven: Yale University Press, 1973): 21-2.
   30. Ibid., p. 23.
   31. Ibid., pp. 220-2.

some special and thought-defying case, but is instead one more instance of a phenomenon to be found in every use of language."[32]

Burrell, however, is uneasy about the concept of a core meaning of a term. He argues that the main tradition on the doctrine of analogy beginning with Cajetan is in agreement in denying the presence of any common property, content, concept, or "univocal core" in the various uses of an analogical term.[33]

> For by undermining the mystique of definition as a search for an underlying common element, it [the recognition of vagueness in generic usage] helps reduce the demand for locating a core of meaning common to the varied uses of an analogous term. What *is* common to these diverse yet not unrelated uses seems to be more on the side of intent.[34]

Thus Burrell would deny Neville's requirement of a univocal foundation for analogy and assert that such a requirement is unnecessary and impossible of fulfillment.

Burrell's first thesis is that a formal characterization of analogous usage is impossible. He criticizes Ross' attempt to do this, notes his admission of the difficulties, deficiency, and unclarity of his proposal about analogy rules, and argues that this amounts to giving up the attempt at a formal characterization of analogy.[35]

Burrell's second and more fundamental thesis is that the key to understanding analogous usage is to be found in the language user, in the context of language in human life and its concerns, more especially in the intentions of a person, and most specifically in decision, assessment, and evaluation, the "demands of appraisal and judgment."[36] He takes as the paradigm case of analogy evaluative or appraisal terms and in particular the transcendentals.[37] He

---

32. Smith, *The Analogy of Experience*, p. 46.
33. Burrell, *Analogy*, pp. 14, 16, 19, 21.
34. Ibid, p. 23.
35. Ibid, pp. 15-18.
36. Ibid, p. 30, see pp. 11, 23, 31, 241-4, 257.
37. Ibid, chaps. 9-10.

notes that these terms necessarily involve the use of some standard.[38] Burrell concludes with his recurring theme:

> Decisions will not thereby be counted irrational even though they cannot be given a completely systematic warrant. This fact of life and of discourse encapsulates a recurring theme of this study of analogous uses of language: there is no method for assuring proper analogous use.[39]

But his point about a standard for the selection of analogies suggests one further issue.

Pannenberg

Burrell has argued that the use of the kind of terms which are a paradigm case of analogy involves the bringing of some standard into operation. I interpret him to be pointing to the question of the grounds on which we choose an appropriate analogy. Ferré and Palmer have pointed out that a "cognitive principle of selection" must be brought into operation in choosing what analogies are appropriate to God.[40] This is similar to Neville's point that some non-analogical knowledge of God is necessary as a ground for asserting the analogy and as a standard for determining what is to be denied of the analogy.[41] To my knowledge the only theologian who has addressed this question of the standard or principle of selection of analogies is Wolfhart Pannenberg in an essay entitled "Analogy and Doxology" (1963) which represents a continuation of work begun in his unpublished inaugural lecture, "*Analogie und Offenbarung*," of 1955.

According to Pannenberg, the doctrine of analogy deals with the problem raised by the fact that according to the Bible, for the most part the reality of God appears in the world of experience only indirectly through the mediation of other beings.[42] Pannenberg's main thesis is that whereas analogy, understood as an

---

38. Ibid, pp. 217, 227, 250.
39. Ibid, p. 242.
40. Ferré, "Analogy in Theology," p. 96a. See idem., *Language, Logic and God*, p. 75; Palmer, *Analogy*, p. 77.
41. Neville, *God the Creator*, pp. 19, 141.
42. *Basic Questions in Theology: Collected Essays* Vol. 1, trans. George H. Kehm (Philadelphia: Fortress Press, 1970): 211-2.

inference of the attributes of God from the creation, involves a common logos between God and creation, doxology or adoration of God involves the sacrifice, surrender, or release of the univocity of speech and its handing over to God himself. The obscurity of this thesis is indicated in such statements as the following: "In the act of adoration, by contrast, the one who brings his praise sacrifices his 'I' and thereby, at the same time, the conceptual univocity of his speech."[43] (It is statements like this which have inspired Palmer's elegant dictum, "Arguments of unknown meaning must be of inestimable value," and his discussion of "Loch Ness theology.")[44]

But Pannenberg's elaboration of his main thesis contains some important insights. He approaches the question of the basis of doxological statements, of how specific statements about God are to be supported at all, and asserts, "Every metaphorical use of language requires that its basis be shown by reference to a state of affairs that occasions this metaphorical use of the word in question."[45] But in analogy, according to Pannenberg's definition, the occasion for its use is of only temporary significance. "In contrast to this, the occasion for doxological speech about God is a specific experience of a divine act. On the basis of his deeds, God is praised as he who is eternally good, righteous, and faithful."[46] Because of the indirectness of our speech about God, to describe an event as an act of God requires another way of speaking than the ordinary language which sees this event by itself or only in relation to other worldly events. This is where "analogical transference" takes place, and in the biblical tradition the words used are drawn from the realm of human behavior because of the essential non-manipulability of human beings. Pannenberg interprets this transference to be based on a revelation of God understood as "an ultimate, a final self-demonstration of God."[47] "When on the basis of individual experiences, statements are made about God himself as he is from eternity to eternity — viz.,

---

43. Ibid, p. 216.
44. Palmer, *Analogy*, pp. 102-3.
45. Pannenberg, *Basic Questions*, p. 228.
46. Ibid.
47. Ibid, p. 234.

almighty, gracious, just — an ultimacy is claimed that can be justified only by the revelation of the deity of God."[48] Pannenberg concludes,

> At the place where the old doctrine of analogy asserted a correspondence of the word used to name God with God himself, there stands, in our view, the concept of revelation . . . [God] makes our metaphorical speech his own through his revelation, and thereby for the first time gives our words of praise their ultimately valid content.[49]

The importance of Pannenberg's thesis does not lie in his unnecessarily narrow view of analogy or in his contrasting it with doxology, but in his perception of the basis of language about God in revelation.[50] This, however, needs further exploration.

Revelation

I want to sketch in brief outline a view of the development of religious language and analogy. Language about the divine arose along with language about everything else and developed as a part of ordinary usage. It was no more or less extended or analogical than any other part of ordinary usage. In other words language about the divine developed through encounters with and experience of the divine which were as common and everyday as encounters with and experience of natural objects, events, and people. This is not to say that encounters with the divine did not have the kind of unique character which has been analyzed by the phenomenologists of religion, but simply that they were not unusual in the sense of being rare and occurring to only a few people. The idea that language about God must be uniquely extended arose in an age in which God was believed to be primarily transcendent and in which there was relatively less awareness of the presence of God. Thus a rich fund of ordinary language about the divine developed during the time of so-called primitive or archaic religion.

---

48. Ibid, p. 236.
49. Ibid, p. 237.
50. See also Ian T. Ramsey, *Religious Language: An Empirical Placing of Theological Phrases* (New York: Macmillan Co., 1957): chaps. 3-4.

130

In the emergence of the specifically biblical language about God we are concerned with revelation in the sense of the encounter with and experience of the God who is disclosed in the history of Israel culminating in the appearance of Jesus.[51] In recounting this history and interpreting it as the self-disclosure of God, the prophets and apostles had at their disposal the rich deposit of ordinary language about the divine which had been developed in previous religious history, especially in ancient Near Eastern religion. They presumably selected from this fund of ordinary language those terms which best expressed their encounter with and experience of God. The Old Testament language became provisionally normative for the New Testament authors, and the biblical language became provisonally normative for succeeding generations of Christians.[52]

I am suggesting that the basis of Christian language about God is to be found in the biblical testimony to revelation. Thus the question of the standard (Burrell), ground (Neville), or cognitive principle of selection (Ferré) for what analogies are to be applied to God is resolved by the appeal to the language involved in the biblical testimony to revelation. The assessment of any particular analogy will therefore involve all the complex questions of hermeneutics which are at the center of contemporary debate but which lie beyond the scope of this essay. But briefly, the assessment of an analogy will center on the question of whether it is an adequate interpretation or elaboration of one or more biblical analogies and is coherent with them.

This raises the question of how these analogies communicate meaning when the exact manner of their application to God is unknown. In Neville's terms this is the question about the "determinate distance" between the creation and God which is the basis for affirming an analogy and for perceiving what is to be denied

---

51. This generally neo-orthodox view of revelation has been under heavy attack for the last two decades. For an assessment of this attack and a reformulation of the doctrine of revelation, see my book *Introduction to Theology* (Wilton, CT: Morehouse-Barlow Co., 1983): chap. 2.

52. For an interpretation of the normative character of biblical language, see ibid., chaps. 2-3.

of it.[53] Since no non-analogical assertions about God are possible, the solution to this question can be found only in the relation between various analogies.

The metaphor of triangulation may help to indicate how a "determinate distance" is approximated. Each analogy will be based at a different point in human experience and will point in a specific direction. The "place" where a number of analogies appear to converge will indicate the "determinate distance" between the creation and God.

We may be able to get some help here from A. M. Farrer's concept of "analogical dialectic." In his book *Finite and Infinite* he takes up the question of speech about substance and the unique. He argues that analogy is the only possible way of speaking about such things. But analogy is tantalizingly inadequate. For example, we explain how an unknown X is like and unlike a known A. "We hope as we do this our hearers will jump to the recognition and isolation of the X."[54] Then we can introduce a second analogy B, and again we may hope that the jump to recognition will take place. Thus we can try a whole series of analogies, but however we pursue this "analogical dialectic" "the result must be the same at last. We shall declare that no analogy satisfies, and that several express something, and we shall try to balance and combine them."[55] After giving several examples of such "analogical dialectic" Farrer concludes, "Throughout the process, the hidden spring of movement is the character of X, which drives us from one position to another — this is the positive spring; a *negative* motive of instability is the mutual incompatibilities of the analogues. And the purpose of the whole is that the listener may grasp the underlying dynamism and jump to the apprehension of X himself."[56] This is not very precise, and this is why there is a limit to the precision of theological language. As Burrell says, "There is no method for assuring proper analogous usage."[57]

53. Neville, *God the Creator*, pp. 19, 141.
54. *Finite and Infinite: A Philosophical Essay* (Westminster: Dacre Press, 1943): 81.
55. Ibid.
56. Ibid, pp. 82-3.
57. Burrell, *Analogy*, p. 242.

Finally, the proof of the pudding is in the eating, and the language of Christian faith and theology are tested in the venture of the Christian life. Do they illuminate and inform, serve and enhance the Christian life or not? This is what T. W. Silkstone describes as the pragmatic demonstration of analogies,[58] and what Tillich calls "experiental verification."[59] It is not a simple verification, because life itself is not very simple.

58. "Analogy," *Theology* 70 (1967): 510.
59. *Systematic Theology*, 3 vols., (Chicago: University of Chicago Press, 1950-63): 1:102.

CHAPTER 7

BEING AND SOME THEOLOGIANS

Introduction

A crucial issue in contemporary theology is the doctrine of God and especially the nature of the divine reality. What kind of reality is God? How is God's reality like, unlike, and related to other kinds of reality? There are many ways to talk about the reality of God. I want to focus on one way, namely, God as being or being-itself, not because I believe that it is the best way to talk about God but because it is one of the oldest ways, because it seems to be undergoing something of a revival, and because I am baffled and intrigued by it.

In this essay I want to explore the various attitudes which some theologians in this century have taken toward the doctrine of God as being-itself. This will include various ways in which the doctrine has been affirmed and denied.

Terminology

What are the possible meanings of the term "being"? Linguistically the term is the present participle of the verb "to be," but we are not concerned with its simple participial use, e.g., "He's being funny." The linguistic form with which we are concerned is "being" as a verbal substantive. The *Oxford English Dictionary* lists four usages:

1. "Existence, the fact of belonging to the universe of things material or immaterial."
2. "Existence in some relation of place or condition."
3. "Existence viewed as a property possessed by anything."

4. "That which exists or is conceived as existing."

These can be summarized as the fact of existence, existence in relation, the property of existence, and the existent itself.

The main philosophical usages of the term "being" include the above and also others: a realm of true reality beyond the sensible world, a genus or class to which everything belongs that is. A number of other less clear philosophical usages will be considered below.

It is sometimes asserted that the doctrine of God as being-itself has been affirmed by the Greek Fathers, Augustine, and Aquinas.[1] However, this kind of generalization obscures a great complexity and even greater diversity of interpretation on this question.

The main source of this complexity is that of the Aristotelian doctrine of being or substance.[2] But this complexity is increased by the other sources of Greek patristic thought in Platonism and Stoicism. It is further increased by the differing contexts in which the terms for being or substance are used, namely, the apophatic theology and the doctrine of the Trinity. The final source of complexity is the variety of possibilities of translating the Greek terms (*einai, ousa, on, ousia*) into the Latin terms (*esse, ens, essentia, entitas*) and all of these into English terms (being, beingness, entity, substance, essence).[3]

This complexity and confusion is brought out by Michael Durrant in his study of *ousia* in Aristotle, the Greek Fathers, and the Latin equivalents in Augustine. He concludes that none of the Aristotelian or Greek patristic usages of *ousia* can be applied legitimately to the Christian God and that Augustine's usage is hopelessly confused.[4]

The diversity of possible interpretations of all this can be seen by comparing Durrant with Gilson's study which treats the issue from Plato to

---

1. See, e.g., John Macquarrie, *Principles of Christian Theology* (New York: Scribner's, 1966): 107.
2. See Joseph Owens, *The Doctrine of Being in the Aristotelian 'Metaphysics'* (Toronto: Pontifical Institute of Mediaeval Studies, 1951).
3. Ibid., 139-43.
4. *Theology and Intelligibility* (London: Routledge and Kegan Paul, 1973): xvi, 71, 110, 124.

Kierkegaard (but omits the Greek Fathers) and comes to the opposite conclusions.[5] Furthermore, Alasdair MacIntyre has dubbed Gilson's approach as the "Neo-Thomist myth of the history of philosophy," in which a doctrine of being as such is foisted on Aristotle and Aquinas and the history of philosophy is interpreted as a series of answers to the question, What is being?[6]

About all that we can conclude from this is that the doctrine of God as being-itself is obscure in the Greek Fathers, that it is affirmed but unexplored in Augustine,[7] and that it is affirmed and explored by Aquinas and not again until the Neo-Thomists and Tillich. An important sidelight is that there is a recurring theme to the effect that God transcends being, which can be found in Clement of Alexandria, perhaps the Cappadocians, Victorinus, Pseudo-Dionysius, Maximus the Confessor, John of Damascus, Erigena, and Gregory Palamas.[8]

Gilson

Roman Catholic theologians have generally identified God with being-itself since Thomas Aquinas. This is especially true of the Neo-Thomist tradition of Garrigou-Lagrange, Gilson, and Maritain. It is also true of the school of Transcendental Thomism which originated in the work of Maréchal and has been developed by Rahner, Coreth, and Lonergan. We shall look particularly at the thought of Gilson, Rahner, and Lonergan on this question.

For Gilson, the concept of being has a dual meaning. It can mean an existent thing or the act of being by which this existent is a thing. "In a 'that which is' (*id quod est*) or a 'having being' (*esse habens*), we can spontaneously emphasize either the *id quod* and the *habens* or the *esse* and the *est*." Gilson maintains that the latter meaning is primary in Thomistic philosophy. "What

---

5. Étienne Gilson, *Being and Some Philosophers* (2nd rev. ed.; Toronto: Pontifical Institute of Mediaeval Studies, 1952).

6. "Being," *The Encyclopedia of Philosophy*, ed. Paul Edwards (8 vols.; New York: Macmillan/Free Press, 1967): 1.275a.

7. See *De Trinitate* 5.2.

8. See Gilson, *Being*, chap. 1; Vladimir Lossky, *The Mystical Theology of the Eastern Church* (London: Clarke, 1957): chap. 2; A. H. Armstrong, ed., *The Cambridge History of Later Greek and Early Medieval Philosophy* (Cambridge: Cambridge University, 1967); Brooks Otis, "Nicene Orthodoxy and Fourth Century Mysticism," *Actes du XIIe Congrès International des Études Byzantines* (Geograd: 1964): 2.475-84.

characterizes Thomistic ontology thus understood is . . . the primacy of the act-of-being, not over and above being, but within it." Thus, he holds that it is preferable to translate *ens* by "being" and *esse* by "act-of-being."[9] The *esse* or act of being in a thing is its very core, its "secret energy."[10]

However, the act of being cannot be conceived or defined because it has no essence or quiddity of its own.[11] The act of being or existence per se can only be signified by a judgment which always takes the form, It is, or, It is not.

For Gilson, God is "He who is," being-itself, *esse,* the act of being. Furthermore, God as the pure act of existence is all, everything and anything, that it is possible to be, and nothing can be conceived as being which the pure act of being is not.[12]

Sometimes Gilson asserts that God has no essence, because then God would be subject to becoming and would not be a necessary being.[13] Other times he states that God's essence is identical with his existence or act of being.[14] Finally, he concludes that God is "a beyond essence." "God is the being whose essence is to be beyond essence or, in other words, God is the being whose essence it is to be."[15]

The main problem I have with Gilson's doctrine of God as being-itself or the pure act of being is the meaning of the concept, of pure act. As Sidney Hook asks, "What acts in the act of Being or existing? Certainly not possibilities, essences, or natures. The meaning of 'death' is not lethal; the notion of 'fire' burns nothing."[16] I suppose that it is possible to conceive of the existence of a

---

9. Étienne Gilson, *The Unity of Philosophical Experience* (London: Sheed and Ward, 1938): 320; see idem, *The Christian Philosophy of St. Thomas Aquinas* (trans. L. K. Shook; New York: Random House, 1956): 40.

10. *Elements of Christian Philosophy* (Garden City, NY: Doubleday, 1960): 123; idem, *The Spirit of Thomism* (New York: Harper & Row, 1964): 64, 68-9, 72; idem, *Christian Philosophy of Thomas,* 374.

11. *Spirit of Thomism,* 76; see 65-6; *Christian Philosophy of Thomas,* 44.

12. *God and Philosophy* (New Haven: Yale University, 1941): 51-2.

13. *Being,* 180; *Christian Philosophy of Thomas,* 91; *Elements,* 114, 119.

14. *Christian Philosophy of Thomas,* 91, 371; *Elements,* 126; *The Spirit of Mediaeval Philosophy* (trans. A. H. C. Downes; New York: Scribner's, 1940): 51.

15. *Elements,* 133.

16 Sidney Hook, *The Quest for Being and other Studies in Naturalism and Humanism* (New York: Dell, 1934): 154.

being as an action or activity, although this is rather odd. But to abstract from this odd notion to the idea of being in general as activity and thus to the idea of a pure act without any agent is unintelligible to me.

Gilson is very much aware of this difficulty. In his latest extended treatment of this idea, he asks,

> How did Thomas Aquinas achieve the awareness of the very possibility of this notion? It certainly results from a supreme effort of abstraction, since, in order to form it, the intellect must conceive, apart from the condition of being an existent, the act owing to which the existent finds itself in this condition. . . . It is not a notion universally evident to all human minds.[17]

Gilson concludes that Thomas learned of the notion of being as act through divine revelation in Exod 3:14:

> Moses could not learn this sublime truth from our Lord [that God's essence is His very *esse*] without at the same time learning from Him the notion of what it is to be a pure existential act. . . . In order to reach the new metaphysical notion of being, which identifies it with its very act, one has only to accept the words of Scripture at their face value.[18]

Again, what is it that Moses, Thomas, and Gilson learn from the Lord? It is something which is indefinable and inconceivable.[19] What does it mean to learn of a concept that is indefinable and inconceivable? What is Gilson really trying to say here? It seems to me that he is trying in this way to assert the transcendence of God. "When we reach the question, what is God? the time has come for our intellect to cast off its moorings and to set sail on the infinite ocean of pure *esse*, or *act*, whereby that which is actually is. Then, of course, we no longer can say where we are, because there are no landmarks where there is no land."[20]

Thus the concept of the pure act of being seems to join those of ineffability, unknowability, incomprehensibility, absoluteness, etc., in the

---

17. Gilson, *Elements*, 131.
18. Ibid., 132. Cp. Tillich's idea below, that the understanding of being requires a conversion.
19. See above, p. 135.
20. *Elements*, 134.

138

language of transcendence. This particular concept of act of being is useful in this connection in that it at the same time indicates the mode of the divine immanence. God is "innermost" in all things because "God is present in the totality of all the elements of which the substances consist as well as in all their operations, from the mere fact that he is present in the act of *esse* owing to which they are." As the pure act of being, God is the "ontological energy" that causes everything to be.[21]

Rahner

Karl Rahner's thought on this doctrine is rather confusing. At first he affirms the traditional Thomist doctrine of God as being-itself, but in his more detailed exposition of the doctrine of God, he seems to move away from this position.

Rahner begins by asserting that being can be known but is essentially indefinable. Then he states "the first proposition of a general ontology." "The essence of being is knowing and being known in an original unity, which we call the (conscious) being-present-to-itself of being." Furthermore, "the most general structures of being in general, that is, all that is attributable to being" or "the transcendental definitions of being" are as follows: "Being is being-present-to-itself. Being is knowing or luminosity. Being is self-affirmation, the will, and the good."[22]

Rahner clearly identifies being-itself with God, and all that he affirms of being-itself he affirms of God as the Absolute Being. However, a possible qualification of Rahner's identification of God and being-itself is the frequent suggestion in *Hearers of the Word* that God is *a* being possessing absolute "having-being." Rahner begins by asserting that having-being is a matter of degree. This is the basis of his interpretation of being as an analogical concept.[23] Then this distinction is applied to God. "God also in this sense may not be

---

21. *Spirit of Thomism*, 71-2.
22. Karl Rahner, *Hearers of the Word* (trans. Michael Richards; New York: Herder, 1969): 39-40, 147; see idem, *Spirit in the World* (trans. William Dych; New York: Herder, 1968): 67-9, 71; idem, *Theological Investigations* (Baltimore: Helicon, 1961): 4.50-52.
23. *Hearers*, 47; see *Spirit*, 69-72.

thought of as simply 'being,' but . . . as the existent possessing absolute 'having-being' and thereby as the existent of pure and absolute self-clarification."[24]

To be sure, this statement occurs in a footnote which has been added by J. B. Metz to the second revised edition of the work, but Metz asserts that the concept of "having-being" has the "explicit assent" of Rahner. That this is in fact Rahner's view is indicated by further statements that God is "the thing of which is affirmed absolute 'having existence'," "an existent thing of absolute 'having being'," and a "supra-mundane existent thing." He also describes God as "a free autonomous and powerful person."[25]

These statements imply that God is subordinate to being or that being is a property in which all beings, including God, participate. This interpretation is supported in turn by Rahner's assertion that the concept of being-itself is arrived at by abstraction.[26] We shall note that Tillich and Macquarrie are quite concerned to avoid the idea that God is a being, since this would make God subject to the categories and subordinate to being-itself and thus not the ultimate reality.

Perhaps we should interpret Rahner's doctrine of being-itself (mystery, horizon, etc.) as the limit of metaphysical knowledge apart from revelation. Then in the Christian revelation being-itself as mystery and horizon is perceived as the personal God, and the former concepts become no longer necessary.

Lonergan

Lonergan's approach to being is through the analysis of human cognition. As a notion, being is "the objective of the unrestricted desire to know." This includes all that is known and all that remains to be known. Being is what is to be known by the totality of true judgments, the complete set of answers to the complete set of questions. "It refers to all that can be known by intelligent grasp and reasonable affirmation."[27]

---

24. *Hearers*, 48 (note); see 50 (note).
25. Ibid., 63-4, 89, 147-9, 151-3.
26. *Spirit*, 171, 179, 408, chap. 3 *passim.*
27. Bernard J. F. Lonergan, *Insight: A Study of Human Understanding.* (New York: Philosophical Library, 1956): 348, 360.

Lonergan notes that this is a "second order" definition; i.e., it indicates not what is meant by being but how that meaning is to be determined. At another point he states that being cannot be defined but only characterized.[28]

Lonergan distinguishes proportionate and transcendent being. Proportionate being is defined as "whatever is to be known by human experience, intelligent grasp, and reasonable affirmation." Transcendent being is what may be known beyond human experience. "Being is proportionate or transcendent according as it lies within or without the domain of man's outer and inner experience."[29]

In discussing transcendent knowledge or knowledge of transcendent being, Lonergan distinguishes the idea of being from the notion of being. The idea of being is the content of an unrestricted act of understanding which grasps everything about everything. In the idea of being Lonergan distinguishes a primary component which is identical with the unrestricted act of understanding or with this act's understanding of itself, and a secondary component which consists of the unrestricted act's understanding of everything else because it understands itself.

Then Lonergan proceeds to argue on the basis of contingency and causality for the existence of such an act of unrestricted understanding which is a transcendent being, an ultimate being, an ultimate ground of the universe.[30] He develops the notion of God through further analysis of the concept of an unrestricted act of understanding. He identifies God with the primary component of the idea of being, namely, the unrestricted act of understanding itself or this act's understanding of itself.[31]

Thus Lonergan identifies God with being only in a limited sense. He cannot identify God with the notion of being, because this is defined as the objective of the unrestricted desire to know, which objective includes both transcendent and proportionate being, both God and world. Furthermore, Lonergan cannot identify God with the idea of being as such for the same reason.

---

28. Ibid., 350, 360.
29. Ibid., 391, 640.
30. Ibid., 646, 655-6.
31. Ibid., 658, 674.

For the idea of being is the content of an unrestricted act of understanding. "Content" here apparently means the object of such an act, and in the case of the notion of being, this would include proportionate as well as transcendent being.

Can Lonergan consistently identify God with the primary component of the idea of being? Sometimes he defines this primary component as the unrestricted act of understanding and sometimes as this act's understanding of itself.[32] It is not clear that these are identical concepts. In any case, since the unrestricted act of understanding is presumably an analogous concept based on the restricted human act of understanding, the question arises as to the agent of the act. If God has or engages in the unrestricted act of understanding, it is not clear how he can be identical with it. (The concept of *actus purus* is not relevant here, since it refers to the absence of potentiality rather than the absence of an agent.) Lonergan confirms this distinction between God and being in his statement, "Unrestricted understanding pertains only to God."[33] I take this to mean that God is the subject of the unrestricted act of understanding and thus is not identical with the idea of being as defined.

This leads to another difficulty in Lonergan's view of the relation of God and being. He often refers to God as *a* being, for example, as "the primary being," "a transcendent being," "the ultimate being," "a rational self-consciousness."[34] Thus Lonergan seems to overlook the "ontological difference" between being and beings. As one commentator puts it,

It would seem, then, that Fr. Lonergan is in no way interrogating Being as *different* from beings, indeed (as far as the present writer can see) there appears to be no indication that he takes account of such a difference at all. A beetle-browed Heideggerean would probably say, then, that Fr. Lonergan is a victim of the 'forgetfulness of Being' (*Seinsvergessenheit*), or, more precisely, of a 'forgetfulness of the ontological difference.'[35]

32. Ibid., 646, 648.
33. Philip McShane, ed., *Language, Truth and Meaning: Papers from the International Lonergan Conference 1970* (Dublin: Gill and Macmillan): 311.
34. *Insight*, 655, 658, 668.
35. William J. Richardson, "Being for Lonergan," in McShane, *Language, Truth and Meaning*, 277, see 283.

142

Finally, Lonergan's approach to the idea of being through the analysis of human cognition and understanding makes these latter concepts prior to that of being. "All other divine attributes follow from the notion of an unrestricted act of understanding. Moreover, since we define being by its relation to intelligence, necessarily our ultimate is not being but intelligence."[36]

Tillich

Paul Tillich is the main Protestant theologian who has affirmed the doctrine of God as being-itself in this century. His doctrine of being is extraordinarily complex. This is indicated by the fact that Tillich equates the concept of being with the power and ground of being,[37] the structure of being and reality,[38] existence itself,[39] the basis of thought,[40] and the presupposition of knowledge.[41]

It is clear that the exploration of the nature of the relationships among these concepts and the problems arising therefrom would be a task too extended for this essay. A few examples will have to suffice. Being-itself can hardly be identified with the power of being or the ground of being. If the genitives are taken in the subjective sense, it must be objected that being-itself can have no ground or power other than itself. If they are taken in the objective sense, the term "being" must refer to beings and not to being-itself.

Being-itself as the object of existential concern can hardly be identified with the structure of being, understood as the generic traits of any and all subject matters as in the Aristotelian metaphysics. The first is similar to the One of Neo-Platonism and the Absolute of Idealism, while the second is simply the proper

---

36. *Insight*, 677.
37. Paul Tillich, *Systematic Theology*, 3 vols. (Chicago: University of Chicago, 1951-63): 1.72.
38. Ibid., 1.18-20; idem, *Love, Power and Justice: Ontological Analysis and Ethical Applications* (New York: Oxford University, 1954): 19; idem, *The Protestant Era* (trans. James Luther Adams; Chicago: University of Chicago, 1948): 85.
39. *Protestant Era*, 85; *Biblical Religion and the Search for Ultimate Reality* (Chicago: University of Chicago, 1959): 6; *Systematic Theology*, 1.163.
40. *Systematic Theology*, 1.163, 2.11; *Theology of Culture* (ed. Robert C. Kimball; New York: Oxford University, 1959): 15.
41. *Systematic Theology*, 1.18.

object of free metaphysical inquiry, as carried out by Tillich in his analysis of the four levels of ontological concepts. Yet, Tillich identifies God as being-itself with the structure of being. "He *is* this structure."[42]

Finally, if being-itself is the presupposition of all thought and knowledge, it could be argued that it cannot be thought or known per se. Indeed, Tillich declares that being-itself is indefinable "since it is the presupposition of every definition." Therefore, concludes Tillich, "every assertion about being-itself is either metaphorical or symbolic."[43] This may be the root of our difficulty and the explanation of why many sympathetic philosophers are hard put to grasp the meaning of Tillich's concept of being-itself.[44]

Tillich grants that the concept of being is a difficult one for us modern people. He argues that the later medieval criticism of the ontological approach has undermined it for the larger part of Western humanity.[45]

> It is hard for the modern mind to understand the Latin *esse-ipsum*, being-itself, or the Greek *on e on*, being-insofar-as-it-is-being. We are all nominalists by birth. And as nominalists we are inclined to dissolve our world into things. But this inclination is an historical accident and not an essential necessity.[46]

In another book Tillich speaks of the necessity of conversion for understanding the ontological approach.

> Ontology presupposes a conversion, an opening of the eyes, a revelatory experience. It is not a matter of detached observation, analysis and hypothesis. Only he who is involved in ultimate reality, only he who has encountered it as a matter of existential concern, can try to speak about it meaningfully.[47]

---

42. Ibid., 1.238; see W. Kegley and Robert W. Bretall, eds., *The Theology of Paul Tillich* (New York: Macmillan, 1952): 139-40, 160-1, 335.

43. *Biblical Religion*, 19; *The Courage to Be* (New Haven: Yale University, 1952): 179; see *Love, Power and Justice*, 35.

44. See, e.g., Charles Hartshorne, "Tillich and the Other Great Tradition," *ATR* 43 (1961): 157; Dorothy Emmet, "The Ground of Being," *JTS* n.s.15 (1964): 289.

45. *Theology of Culture*, 16.

46. *Love, Power and Justice*, 18.

47. *Biblical Religion*, 65.

In his *Systematic Theology* Tillich asserts that God is being-itself and not *a* being, not even the highest or most perfect being, for if God were *a* being, he would be subordinate to being-itself and subject to the categories of finitude and thus not the answer to the existential question of human finitude. God as being-itself means that God is the ground of being or the power of being. Also, God is the ground of the structure of being. "He *is* the structure."[48] God as being-itself is not the universal essence (pantheism) but rather beyond the contrast of essential and existential being.

Tillich asserts, "The statement that God is being-itself is a non symbolic statement. It does not point beyond itself. It means what it says directly and properly." This is "the most abstract and completely unsymbolic statement which is possible." "Other assertions about God can be made theologically only on this basis."[49] This would seem to be a serious mistake. I would argue that the concept of being in its original or proper meaning has a finite reference. Thus, when it is applied to God, it is used symbolically.

In the second volume of his system, Tillich tacitly withdraws this statement and asserts that the only non-symbolic statement we can make about God is that "everything we say about God is symbolic."[50] This is indeed a non-symbolic statement, but it is not a statement about God but rather about statements about God. Then Tillich goes on to assert that the equation of God and being-itself is both symbolic and non-symbolic because it designates the boundary line at which the symbolic and the non-symbolic coincide. I have no idea at all what that means.

Tillich's claim that the identification of God and being-itself is a non-symbolic statement also contradicts his assertions in his shorter works that being-itself is indefinable and that statements about it are metaphorical or symbolic. If we can speak of two concepts only symbolically, then any statement about their relation must also be symbolic. (E.g., "The Father begets the Son.") It would

---

48. *Systematic Theology*, 1.238; see 1.235-37.
49. Ibid., 1.238-39.
50. Ibid., 2.9.

seem that consistency requires Tillich to hold that all statements about God, being-itself, and their relations are symbolic or analogous.

Tillich's concept of being is highly ambiguous and diffuse. As we have seen, he identifies being-itself with the power, ground, and structure of being, with existence, the basis of thought, and the presupposition of knowledge. It is very difficult to get one's head around a concept which does all these jobs. The vagueness of Tillich's doctrine of God as being-itself seems to derive from the interplay of two concepts which are equally diffuse in Tillich's writings. In particular, the vagueness of the concept of being seems to be derived from the influence of the traditional doctrine of God rather than vice versa. Thus, being-itself is indefinable, transcendent, can be spoken of only symbolically, and can be understood only through a turning or conversion. If this is the case, then it is not surprising that the concept of being turns out to be very little help in clarifying the doctrine of God.

Macquarrie

John Macquarrie is one of the few theologians who has made extensive use of Heidegger's doctrine of being in connection with the doctrine of God.[51] He believes that theology has shared in the "forgetting of being" with which Heidegger charges philosophy. The forgetting of being can take place in two ways. Being can be considered more and more transcendent until it is forgotten, or it can be considered more and more immanent until it is fragmented and absorbed into the beings. Macquarrie is also able to define sin as the forgetting of being, as the turning away from being to the beings. Thus, theology too must be recalled to being and to the fight against the forgetting of being.[52]

Macquarrie begins his doctrine of being by stating what being is not. Being is not a being, a property, a class, or genus, a substance or substratum, or

---

51. For another attempt to make use of Heidegger's doctrine of being in the doctrine of God, see Heinrich Ott, *Denken and Sein: Der Weg Martin Heideggers and der Weg der Theologie* (Zollikon: Evangelischer Verlag, 1959): 139-52. He concludes that if one is to speak of God and being in Heidegger's terms, God must be understood as *a* being.

52. *Principles*, 106, 150-1, 238, 288.

the absolute understood as the all-inclusive being or the totality or sum of beings. Being is not "some invisible, intangible realm that is supposed to lie back of the appearances, as a world of "things-in-themselves." Furthermore, being is to be distinguished from nothing, becoming, appearance, and the ideal.[53]

The direct definition of the concept of being is difficult because it does not fall under any of our usual categories. It is incomparable. It is a *transcendens* which must remain mysterious. (*Transcendens* is Heidegger's term for the scholastic *transcendentia* or universally applicable characters.) Macquarrie has two main characterizations of the concept of being. One is that being is the prior condition that anything may be or that there may be anything whatsoever. The other is that being is the dynamic letting-be of beings in the sense of enabling to be, empowering to be, bringing into being. Being is present and manifest in every being.[54]

Macquarrie points out that the terms "God" and "being" are not synonymous. Some people experience being as indifferent or alien. "God" is synonymous with "holy being" or being understood as gracious.[55]

There are certain difficulties in Macquarrie's doctrine of God as being. First, if being is not a being, a property, a class, a substratum, the totality of being, or the all-inclusive being, it is not clear what it is. His two key terms are condition and letting-be. By "condition" he apparently means prerequisite, but the prerequisite of beings is the source of beings. This points to the idea of letting-be which he also defines as the source of beings. However, it is not clear why a source of beings must be or can be being-itself and not, e.g., God understood analogously as a being. Macquarrie's only response to this is that "such a being would not be an ultimate because we could still ask about *his* being."[56] This seems to be a begging of the question. Similarly, we could say to Macquarrie, if being is ultimate reality, we can still ask about the reality of being.

---

53. Ibid., 102; see pp. 98-101.
54. John Macquarrie, *Studies in Christian Existentialism* (Philadelphia: Westminster, 1965): 89, 255; *Principles,* 87, 99, 103-6, 132, 183, 186, 194.
55. *Principles,* 79, 95, 105-6; *Existentialism,* 11.
56. *Principles,* 106; see 103, 183.

However, there is a more serious difficulty in Macquarrie's doctrine of God as being. On the one hand, he asserts that "being is nothing apart from its appearances"; "there is no being apart from beings"; "apart from the beings, Being would become indistinguishable from nothing."[57] On the other hand, he asserts that being is the *transcendens*, the transcendent which is distinct from the beings, beyond every possible being.[58] It is not clear how these statements can be held together. Furthermore, it is also not at all clear how the first set of assertions is coherent with the independence or aseity of God, which Macquarrie also wants to affirm.

Neville

Robert C. Neville is the third main protestant thinker who identifies God and being-itself, but he writes on this issue as a philosopher. One of Neville's definitions of being-itself is "that of which the determinations of being are determinations." "Being-itself is the being that [things] have considered in abstraction from them."[59]

His second definition is that being-itself is the ontological one for the many, that which unifies the diversity of the world, the ground of the most comprehensive unity. But this requires that the concept of being-itself be used univocally. "For if the concept of being is applied to different things only analogically, then being-itself is not sufficiently unified in its relations to the many determinations of being to unify them."[60]

The main thesis of Neville's book is that in order for being-itself to be the ontological one, it must be indeterminate. The argument runs as follows: If being-itself is construed as determinate, then it must have a determinate contrast term to be meaningful. However, according to "the principle of the ontological equality of reciprocal contrasts," being-itself cannot have a contrast term because

---

57. Ibid., 102, 109, 126; see 287.
58. Ibid., 103, 109, 126, 187.
59. Robert C. Neville, *God the Creator* (Chicago: University of Chicago, 1968): 12, 15; see 40, 91.
60. Ibid., 12.

it is the ontological one, and there is nothing on the same ontological level with it or nothing outside of it to contrast with it. Therefore, being-itself must be indeterminate. Put more simply, since being-itself is ubiquitous, it must be present in or apply to the significant contrast to any determinate characterization of being-itself as well as to the determinate characterization itself, which is contradictory. Thus, being-itself is indeterminate.[61]

Next Neville argues that if being-itself is indeterminate, it must transcend the determinations of being in the sense of "being outside of" the determinations. Then using a form of the cosmological argument, he concludes that being-itself is the creator of the determinations of being and that this justifies the identification of being-itself with God.[62]

It is further argued that God as being-itself is one, real, infinite, mysterious, and unintelligible. The latter two terms are attributed to God because as being-itself he is indeterminate.

> What the creator is apart from all such connections [with the determinations] is a mystery. Furthermore, it is a mystery in the philosophically acceptable sense of that word. A mystery is unacceptable to philosophy when it means that we do not understand something well enough. But a mystery is quite proper when it means that there is nothing to understand. If the creator is indeterminate, then any alleged understanding of it in those indeterminate respects would be in error.[63]

Being-itself is unintelligible because it is not determinate. As creator of the determinations, "God is prior to intelligibility, for only what is determinate can be intelligible in any ordinary sense." Hence, God is "essentially unintelligible."[64]

Neville's claim that God as being-itself is indeterminate leads him into some difficulties because he also wants to assert that God is personal, has intentions, creates, acts providentially, forgives, etc. It would seem impossible to affirm that the God to whom these things can be attributed is indeterminate.

---

61. Ibid., 28, 40-1, 91.
62. Ibid., 60-1, 64.
63. Ibid., 76.
64. Ibid., 99; see 84.

Neville attempts to solve this problem by means of a distinction between essential and conditional features in God.

All determinations of being have essential and conditional or non-essential features. The essential feature of a determination is what it is apart from its relations to any other determination. The conditional features derive from the real distinctions that pertain between the determination and that with respect to which it is determinate. Thus, Neville describes the above-mentioned attributes of God as conditional features. God as being-itself has no essential features, and there are no real distinctions between God and the world, because God as being-itself is indeterminate. Therefore, God's conditional features are different from those of determinations of being in that they arise from God himself as creator and not from the created determinations.[65]

The problem becomes acute when Neville asserts that "being-itself gives itself [its conditional] features in creating the determinations of being."[66] But what is it that gives to God as being itself its conditional features of creator? Neville's only answer can be that God as being-itself creates its conditional feature of God as creator, but this would seem to lead to an infinite regress.

Neville claims that an infinite regress is avoided by the indeterminate character of being-itself and thus by the heterogeneity of being-itself with respect to the determinations of being or the created order. "It is in virtue of the heterogeneity that the procession of explanations is halted, for there is nothing in the indeterminate transcendent, such as *de facto* unity, that allows the explanation to move out of the transcendent term."[67]

But then it is not clear how the procession of explanations gets *to* the transcendent term. If God as being-itself *gives himself* his conditional feature of creator, then God as being-itself is determinate. If God as being-itself does not give himself his conditional feature of being creator, then he is not creator. If the fact that God as being-itself gives himself his conditional feature of being creator

---

65. Ibid., 45-6, 97-8.
66. Ibid., 97; see 75, 100, 104.
67. Ibid., 135; see 102.

is a conditional feature of God, then we have an infinite regress of conditional features, and we do not arrive at the transcendent term.

Although God as being-itself is indeterminate and therefore has no essential features, Neville wants to affirm his essential character and reality in some sense.

> That being-itself has conditional features would seem to imply that it has essential features. . . . Although being-itself does not have essential features, there is still a contrast between essential and conditional, for it is the character of the conditional features, in their very determinateness and hence contingency to bespeak their dependence on what is essential. There would be no conditionals without the essential.[68]

Furthermore, although we cannot say that being-itself "is," we can say that it is real. "Part of the meaning of being creator is that God must *also* have reality apart from that determinate connection [with the creation] and that this other reality is prior to his reality as creator."[69] Thus, Neville is forced to claim that while God as being-itself is in some sense real and has something like an essential character and is creator, etc., yet he is also absolutely indeterminate and cannot be said to be.

Neville runs into similar difficulties in regard to the question of the unity of God as being-itself. Although God as being-itself is the ontological one for the many and constitutes itself as the one by creating the many, in no sense can he be called one or unified because he is indeterminate.[70]

Another difficulty arising from the indeterminate character of God as being-itself is the problem of his relation to the determinations of being. On the one hand, Neville asserts that God as being-itself is present in all the determinations of being, that all the determinations participate in being-itself, that being-itself is the being which all the determinations of being have, and that therefore God as being-itself is closer to the determinations than they are to

---

68. Ibid., 97-8.
69. Ibid., 99; see 76, 93.
70. Ibid., 60, 86, 71.

themselves.[71]   On the other hand, because God as being-itself is absolutely indeterminate, he is "unconditioned by any relation to the determinations of being."[72] Presumably this apparent contradiction is overcome by the distinction between essential and conditional features, but this simply moves the difficulty to the next stage. Neville would have to say that there is no relation between the conditional features and that which is essential in God as being-itself. But then it is not clear in what way the conditional features are features of God as being-itself.

Another odd result of the indeterminate character of God as being-itself is that the distinction between creator and creature tends to dissolve. On the one hand, because God as being-itself must be indeterminate, God's "character as creator is an actual part of the created product." On the other hand, "insofar as the created realm is a conditional feature of God . . . it can be called divine." "We have found every determinate thing to be the creative presence of God; there is nothing whose whole being is not the immanence of God."[73] This is the result of identifying God with being-itself, for then God must be defined as that of which the determinations of being are determinations, the being that things have in abstraction from them, and that which all things have in common.[74]

Finally, we must raise the question of the status of indeterminateness in God. Does the alleged indeterminate character of God as being-itself refer to the reality of God in himself or only to our knowledge of God? Is God actually indeterminate in himself, or can we think of him only as indeterminate? Neville seems to mean the latter.

That the creator is indeterminate . . . is an analytic component of the feature of being creator. Its referent is what the creator must be in order to be creator. It does not refer to any fuzziness or chaos in the creator's essential nature. Rather it points out that the contingent fact that the creator is indeed the creator entails a contradiction in the attribution of a determinate nature to the

---

71. Ibid., 116, 91, 15, 200.
72. Ibid., 85.
73. Ibid., 100, 110, 119.
74. Ibid., 12, 15, 91.

creator apart from all connection with the determinations. . . . What
the creator is apart from all such connections is a mystery.[75]

Here Neville seems to be playing down the significance of his assertion of
the indeterminate character of God as being-itself. His description of it as an
"analytic component" and a "contingent fact" and as not referring to the creator's
essential nature implies that it does not refer to indeterminacy in the creator but
rather to an incidental implication of the form of the argument and thus simply to
the character of our knowledge of God. "What the creator is in itself we do not
know: and we have argued that it cannot be known." "Even the category of
being-itself is not a conception of what God essentially is but is only a conception
arising from his relation to us that guides our approach to him." Does this mean
that God transcends being-itself?[76]

Given the many difficulties cited above which are involved in the
conception of God as being-itself and as indeterminate, it can be argued that the
alternate view has fewer difficulties. This would consist of the argument that the
analogy of being and the determinate character of God involve fewer difficulties
than the univocity of being and the indeterminate character of God. Neville
states, "To say that the creator is indeterminate is merely to deny of it the
character that the determinations have, that is, determinate being."[77] Now Neville
is not willing to deny of the creator all of the characteristics which the
determinations have, e.g., reality and something essential corresponding to their
conditional features. So why not simply deny of the creator the character of *finite*
determinate being? We have noted his arguments against such a view. I am only
suggesting that it can be argued that it involves fewer difficulties than his own
approach.

Dewart

The most influential Roman Catholic theologian who denies the identity of
God and being is Leslie Dewart. He attempts a reconstruction of the doctrine of

---

75. Ibid., 76.
76. Ibid., 77, 195; see 194.
77. Ibid., 73.

God which can be integrated with contemporary experience. His main thesis is that the Greek-scholastic metaphysical tradition which affirms the identity of reality and being must be transcended. This tradition is based on the linguistic structure of Indo-European languages and upon the Parmenidean metaphysical presupposition of the identity of thought and being.[78] This tradition assumes that its way of thinking is the universal human way of thinking. But Dewart argues that this is not the case and offers the example of classical Chinese language and thought.[79]

Therefore, philosophy must transcend its metaphysical stage and initiate what Dewart calls its meta-metaphysical stage. Theology likewise must develop a meta-metaphysical doctrine of God.[80] This means primarily the overcoming of the identification of reality and being or the reduction of reality to being.

Dewart defines being as that which is or that which exists. It is absolutely contingent, and therefore "necessary being" is a contradiction in terms. Being is what is empirically given; it is the sort of reality which is revealed in experience.[81]

Dewart's main concepts for God are "reality" and "presence." Religious experience discloses God not as a transcendent being or as being-itself but as a reality *beyond* being.[82] Dewart describes God as "that which we experience as the open background of consciousness and being." "To be sure, the Christian experience of God *can* be cast in the concept of being. It can also be cast, however, in the concept of reality, as the presence of that which (though not itself being) manifests itself in and through being, that-which-is."[83]

Dewart defines reality as "whatever the self can have real relations towards" and as "*that in relation to which* absolute contingencies can be absolutely contingent upon." Thus God is a reality which transcends being but

---

78. Leslie Dewart, *The Foundations of Belief* (New York: Herder, 1969): 402-13.
79. *Foundations*, 413-20.
80. Ibid., 19, 361, 391.
81. Ibid., 397, 399, 422, 431, 492.
82. Leslie Dewart, *The Future of Belief. Theism in a World Come of Age* (New York: Herder, 1966): 173, 175.
83. Ibid., 176, 180.

154

which is immanent in being and which is manifest in and through being as present to being.[84]

> Among the various ways in which we may conceptualize positively that reality which transcends being, 'presence' seems to me particularly apt. . . . I have suggested, therefore, that God is better conceived as a reality which is *present to* being than as a reality which *is* being, that God's reality should be conceived in terms of *real presence* rather than in terms of *real being*.[85]

It now becomes clear that for Dewart being means the totality of being or existence, the world, or the creature. He states, "God creates being."[86] Although Dewart's definition of being is that of the older Neo-Thomism generally ("that which is"), his interpretation of this definition is unique among the theologians we have considered.

Duméry

A position similar to that of Dewart is presented by the French Roman Catholic philosopher, Henry Duméry. Duméry adopts the three-fold reduction of Husserl (eidetic, phenomenological, and transcendental) in order to test the act of faith, but he believes that this is incomplete and must be supplemented by a fourth which he calls the henological reduction.

This leads Duméry to a doctrine of God as the One who is trans-ordinal, trans-categorical, beyond all determinations, and beyond essence and existence.[87] He explicitly follows the apophatic tradition of Plotinus and Pseudo-Dionysius in asserting that God as the One is not being but is beyond being and can be called Super-Being or Nothing.[88]

God as the One is the source of the being which proceeds from him but does not receive a part of him or participate in him. Being appears only at the

---

84. *Foundations,* 399, 493; see 385, 387, 444, 470; *Future,* 177.
85. *Foundations,* 442 and note.
86. Ibid., 386; see *Future,* 195.
87. Henry Duméry, *The Problem of God in the Philosophy of Religion: A Critical Examination of the Category of the Absolute and the Scheme of Transcendence* (tr. Charles Courtney, Evanston: Northwestern University, 1964): 49-50, 52 (note), 54, 85-6, 94, 99, 109, 128.
88. Ibid., 50, 86, 88 (note), 101.

155

level of the created. Thus Duméry asserts that there is a clear opposition between a participationist ontology and a processionist ontology which he calls henology. He defines them as follows: "The first holds that the inferior borrows a part of what it is from the superior; the second holds that the inferior receives from the superior the means to be what the superior is not."[89]

Duméry argues that the henology of God as the One more rigorously preserves the transcendence of God than does the ontology of God as being. "The super-being God, that of Plotinus and Pseudo-Dionysius . . . is, so to say, more absolute (the only absolute) than the Being-God, who can be placed above the determinations only by means of supplementary correctives."[90]

Neo-Orthodoxy and Process Theology

Protestant neo-orthodox and existentialist theology generally rejects the doctrine of God as being-itself, Tillich being the main exception. Karl Barth resists "the threatened absorption of the doctrine of God into a doctrine of being." The principle to be followed here is *esse sequitur operari* and not the reverse.[91] This is closely connected with Barth's rejection of the *analogia entis* throughout his works.[92]

Emil Brunner sees the identification of God with being as a Neo-Platonist speculative concept which has nothing to do with the Biblical concept of God.[93] From the point of view of an existentialist historicism, Carl Michalson criticizes Heinrich Ott's attempt to use the doctrine of being of the later Heidegger as a basis for systematic theology.

> History is not one among several areas but the horizon of every area of investigation. . . . History is an horizon so inescapable that being itself is a derivative of history. . . . In the eschatological faith

89. Ibid., 89, see 85-6.
90. Ibid., 88 (note); see 128.
91. Karl Barth, *Church Dogmatics,* vol. 2: *The Doctrine of God* (ed. G. W. Bromiley and T. F. Torrance; Edinburgh: Clark, 1957): 1.260; see 83, 261.
92. See my article, "Barth on Non-Christian Knowledge of God," *ATR* 46 (1964): 268-71.
93. Emil Brunner, *The Christian Doctrine of God* (Philadelphia: Westminster, 1950): 248-9.

of the New Testament, being cannot qualify history because it is history which qualifies being, giving it its end.[94]

Theologians influenced by process philosophy reject the doctrine of God as being-itself because they believe that it implies the changelessness and unrelatedness of God, the immutability and. absoluteness of God. This in turn makes incomprehensible either God's knowledge of and presence in the world or the reality of change in the world. Schubert M. Ogden argues that the starting point for a genuinely new theistic conception is what Whitehead calls "the reformed subjectivist principle." This requires that we take as the experiential basis of all our most fundamental concepts the primal phenomenon of our own existence as experiencing subjects or selves. The result is a complete revolution of classical metaphysics. "In consequence the chief category for finally interpreting anything real can no longer be 'substance' or 'being' (as traditionally understood) but must be 'process' or 'creative becoming,' construed as that which is in principle social and temporal. . . . God, too, must be conceived as a genuinely temporal and social reality."[95]

Arguing along similar lines, Charles Hartshorne affirms the priority of becoming to being.

> In general, all attempts to explain becoming as a special case of being, novelty as a special case of permanence, have failed. . . . We shall see that, by contrast, being can very well be explicated as an aspect of novelty.[96]

Conclusion

The theologians who affirm the doctrine of God as being-itself fall into two main groups, neither of which is successful in maintaining this identification.

94. Carl Michalson, *Worldly Theology: The Hermeneutical Focus of an Historical Faith* (New York: Scribner's, 1976): 104-5. For a summary of these and similar views, see Ronald Gregor Smith, *The Doctrine of God*, ed. K. Gregor Smith and A. D. Galloway (Philadelphia: Westminster, 1970): chap. 3.

95. Schubert M. Ogden, *The Reality of God and Other Essays* (New York: Harper & Row, 1963): 58; see also Delwyn Brown, Ralph E. James, Jr., and Gene Reeves, eds., *Process Philosophy and Christian Thought* (Indianapolis: Bobbs-Merrill, 1974): 179-81.

96. Charles Hartshorne, "Introduction: The Development of Process Philosophy," in *Philosophers of Process*, Douglas Browning, ed. (New York: Random House, 1965): xiv.

The first group defines God as the one who has being in the highest degree in the sense of self-knowledge. For example, Rahner defines being as knowing and being known or being present to oneself, and he asserts that God possesses absolute having-being in this sense. Lonergan defines the idea of being as the unrestricted act of understanding of itself and asserts that this pertains only to God. Neither achieves the identification of God and being-itself, for in both cases God is the subject of a predicate which is distinct from the subject.

The second group asserts that God as being-itself is the act or power of being in everything (Gilson, Tillich), or the dynamic empowering of the being of beings (Macquarrie). This involves either the use of the term "being" in two different senses or the definition of being in terms of itself, neither of which is very clear or satisfactory.

Neville's approach does not fall into either group. His preliminary definition of being-itself is clear enough, namely, the being that things have considered in abstraction from them. However, the identification of God and being-itself in this sense would make God simply an abstraction or universal property in spite of Neville's denial. The insurmountable problems involved in his further assertion that God as being-itself is indeterminate have been noted.

This situation leads one to ask why anyone would want to use the concept of being in his theology. What are the possible motives for the assertion of the doctrine of God as being-itself?

1. Because it is a central element in a canonized tradition which needs reinterpretation (Gilson, Rahner, Lonergan).

2. Because it is the fundamental and unavoidable concept in any philosophy or theology (Tillich, Neville).

3. Because it is the fundamental concept of the most important contemporary philosophy (Macquarrie).

4. Because it is useful or helpful in elaborating the doctrine of God.

No. 1 is not decisive for me because this doctrine is not canonized in the tradition in which I stand. I am not persuaded that no. 2 is the case. In regard to no. 3, I would agree that Heidegger's philosophy is one of the most influential in this century and therefore that the interpretation of the doctrine of God in its terms will be an important means of elaborating and communicating the meaning of Christian faith. However, this is qualified by the fact that Heidegger's doctrine of being seems to be more obscure than the received doctrine of God which is being interpreted. Thus the interpretation of the latter in terms of the former may shed light on the doctrine of being but not on the doctrine of God. No. 4 would be decisive if it were the case, but in all the examples we have investigated it seems to me that the doctrine of being is too obscure or problematic to be useful in elaborating the doctrine of God.

This is not surprising in light of the fact that all the theologians who affirm that God is being-itself also state that being-itself is indefinable, inconceivable, and unintelligible. A concept which can be characterized in this way is not going to be very helpful in clarifying the doctrine of God. If it is argued that the appreciation of the concept of being requires revelation or conversion (Tillich, Gilson), I would respond that while concepts may require revelation or conversion for their affirmation, they should not require it for their intelligibility. It is asserted by some of these theologians that the very inconceivability of the concept of being points to the transcendence of God, but this is to confuse unintelligibility with transcendence.

As a matter of fact, one of the main problems in the identification of God with being-itself is the tendency to pantheism. For Gilson, God is the act of being in all things; God is everything that it is possible to be. For Tillich God is the power and structure of all being. For Macquarrie God as being is nothing apart from the beings. For Neville there is nothing whose whole being is not the immanence of God. Duméry notes that God as being-itself can be placed above the determinations of being only by means of "supplementary correctives."

Furthermore, the reasons given for the indefinability, inconceivability, and unintelligibility of being-itself are logical rather than theological. Being-itself cannot be conceived or defined because it has no essence or quiddity of its own (Gilson). It is indefinable because it is the antecedent of knowing and being known (Rahner) or because it underpins and transcends the content of every definition (Tillich, Lonergan) or because it does not fall under our usual categories of thought (Macquarrie). It is unintelligible because it is indeterminate and prior to intelligibility (Neville).

However, it can be argued that the transcendence of God is not a logical matter but rather a theological one. The transcendence of God is manifest in the character of his presence in the contingencies of history, in his free activity. Early Christian theology should "have been able to understand the otherness of God more radically than philosophy as not only the incomprehensibility of the world-ground but as the otherness of the freedom of God precisely in his acts which cut across and surpass all expectations and planning."[97] It can also be argued that the incomprehensibility of God is not a logical matter but rather the mysteriousness of God which emerges through his self-disclosure on the analogy of human personal self-disclosure.[98]

Thus I conclude that if the doctrine of being is to be used at all in Christian theology, it should be used in the doctrine of the world or the creation (Dewart, Duméry). Then being would be defined as that which is, or as the totality of existence. Being or some aspect of being could be attributed to God analogically, and the ways in which the being of God is like and unlike the being of the creature could be specified. Thus I would associate myself with the tradition which asserts that God transcends being and is the creator of being.[99] To be sure, this involves many other problems. But that should be the subject of another essay.

---

97. Wolfhart Pannenberg, *Basic Questions in Theology* (Collected Essays, tr. George H. Kehm; Philadelphia: Fortress, 1971): 2.181.

98. See Karl Rahner, "The Concept of Mystery in Catholic Theology," *Investigations*, 4.36, 73.

99. See above, pp. 154-5.

CHAPTER 8

RECENT THOUGHT ON DIVINE AGENCY

Theologians continue to talk a great deal about God's activity in the world, and there continue to be only a very few who pause to consider some of the many problems involved in such talk. So the issues raised in my book *God's Activity in the World* continue to be pressing ones.[1]

In this chapter I shall offer an assessment of the current state of the discussion on this question, referring first to the books and essays which have appeared since 1982.[2] Then I will add some comments on the questions which still surround the nature of divine activity in the world.

Tracy, Jantzen and Thiemann

A promising development of what I have called the personal action view of God's activity in the world has appeared in two books. I refer to Thomas F. Tracy's *God, Action and Embodiment* and Ronald F. Thiemann's *Revelation and Theology: The Gospel as Narrated Promise.*[3] Both authors develop the theme of God as personal agent and explore the question of double agency. Neither,

---

1. O. C. Thomas, *God's Activity in the World: The Contemporary Problem* (Chico: Scholars Press, 1983).

2. One book on which I will not comment further is M. Wiles, *God's Action in the World: The Bampton Lectures for 1986* (London: SCM Press, 1986). In these lectures, Wiles elaborates the view which was outlined in his essay in *God's Activity in the World* and which I characterized as the Uniform Action approach. God's action in the world is uniform and in no sense particular or specific, the appearance of particularity being given by varying human response to the unchanging divine action. But in this book Wiles does not develop his view significantly beyond the original essay. See my review in *The Anglican Theological Review* 69, no. 4 (October, 1987): 401-3.

3. T. P. Tracy, *God, Action and Embodiment* (Grand Rapids: William B. Eerdmans Publishing Company, 1984): 22. R. F. Thiemann, *Revelation and Theology: The Gospel as Narrated Promise* (Notre Dame: University of Notre Dame Press, 1985).

however, focuses on the issue of the relation of divine activity to creaturely activity.

Tracy's purpose in his book is to explore the theological possibilities and problems involved in conceiving God as one who acts, as an agent, the bearer of a personal identity made manifest in action. He agrees with the way in which Gilkey has posed the issue of divine activity, but he is critical of the ways in which Ogden and Kaufman have responded to it. Both, he believes, have drawn back from asserting that God does in fact act in history, and both have traded on a mind-body dualism.[4]

In the first part of his book Tracy argues that in order to ascribe traits of character to God, such as love or justice, we must be able to identify enduring patterns in God's intentional action. In the second part he explores Descartes' mind-body dualism and the consequences for theology of rejecting such dualism. In the final part Tracy develops a non-Cartesian understanding of the human agent and explores and criticizes the view that God is embodied in the world (Hartshorne). His own proposal is that God is not so embodied but represents the perfection of agency in being self-created, fully unified as an agent and all-powerful.[5] He believes that this constitutes a new path between classical and neoclassical theism.

What contribution does Tracy make to the question of understanding God's activity in the world in relation to finite activity? In a chapter on "Embodiment and Identification" he argues that "God might be identified by indicating a unique relation that he has to our shared world of objects and events located in space and time. If we think of God as an agent, might we identify God from those events in our experience that are taken to be his acts?"[6] Then he raises all the difficult questions about this which have been explored in my book, and especially those raised by Gilkey about the Exodus events. But it does not appear

---

4. Tracy, xii-xvi.
5. Tracy, 126.
6. Tracy, 77.

to me that he gives any indication about how he would go about resolving any of these questions.

One problem Tracy does explore further is whether the act-agent relation always points to a single agent. He states that it does not, that a single act description may be exemplified by two agents simultaneously in a single identifiable event, for example, two people pulling on a rope to ring a bell. But certain features of the context of an action or characteristics of the agent can rule out ascribing a single instance of an action to more than one agent. For example, the theistic story is stubbornly monotheistic. Also the action in question can be such that admits of only one agent, for example, creation. Finally, any instance of a basic action, that is, an action without any instrumental substructure, can in principle be ascribed to only one agent. However, in actions in which there is such an instrumental substructure, two agents can be involved in bringing about a single event. This raises the question of whether God's actions in the world are basic actions or involve instrumental substructures. This depends, states Tracy, on the way the theologian formulates the theistic story.[7] Thus the issue of the relation of divine and finite agency is not engaged.

In the chapter exploring whether God can be considered to be a fully embodied agent, a cosmic organism, Tracy returns to the double agency question as a difficulty in this view.

> Can a single event be an action in precisely the same sense for both the sub-individuals and the super-individual? If so, can they be distinct agents? Are the actions of sub-individuals to be understood as enactments of the super-individual's intentions? If so, are the sub-individuals agents in their own right at all? Is the action of the super-individual simply the accumulated effect of the actions of many sub-individuals? If so, is the super-individual an agent in any significant sense? Does the super-individual act by somehow influencing the actions of the many sub-individuals? If so, is the super-individual surreptitiously being treated as a distinct entity that acts upon the society of many sub-individuals?[8]

---

7. Tracy, 80-3.
8. Tracy, 115.

On the basis of these and other problems Tracy dismisses this view. Yet the same problems arise in connection with his own approach, but he does not treat them there.

Mention should also be made at this point of Grace Jantzen's book *God's World, God's Body* in which she argues that God is embodied in the world.[9] God's relation to the world is analogous to a person's relation to his or her body when this relation is interpreted holistically. She argues further that the idea of God's action in the world makes more sense on the model that the world is God's body than on the traditional model. In the former view any action of God on the world is a direct or basic action not mediated by anything else. Furthermore, unlike persons' relations to their bodies, God is in control of all parts of the world. Indeed, all events in the world are God's basic actions.[10] However, Jantzen does not explore the nature of the resulting relation between divine and finite activity.

This leads us to Thiemann's book, which is a defense of the doctrine of revelation against recent criticisms and as the necessary basis for the affirmation of God's prevenience. He argues that the fatal flaw of modern doctrines of revelation has been their basis in epistemological foundationalism, and that contemporary theologians, such as Schubert Ogden and David Tracy, attempt to avoid a doctrine of revelation by similarly flawed transcendental and foundational moves. In their place he offers a nonfoundational view of theology and revelation using the category of narrated promise.

This approach focuses attention on the centrality of God's agency and self-characterization through divine acts in the biblical narrative. (Here Thiemann is dependent upon Tracy's argument discussed above.) Thiemann notes that although God is the main character in Scripture, direct divine actions are only rarely described, and the divine agency is most often depicted through the description of the acts of other agents. "Those acts which occur through human

---

9. G. Jantzen, *God's World, God's Body* (Philadelphia: Westminster Press, 1984).
10. Jantzen, 85-93.

agents are, insofar as they move toward a *telos* retrospectively discerned, the very acts of God."[11]

In exploring the intelligibility of belief in God's prevenience Thiemann inquires whether it is possible to identify God as the agent of scriptural and liturgical promises. He asserts that a liturgical pardon or absolution is a form of double agency.

> Though the speaker in the liturgical act is the presiding minister, the speaker who is committed to action is *God*. . . . These words are to be taken as the speech of God every time they are spoken. Is this notion of double agency intelligible?
>
> That the utterance of one speaker should be taken as the enacted intention of another presents no particular logical problem. Such complex speech-acts are a common occurrence in ordinary experience. Consider the following examples: A sister calls to her brother, 'Mom says, it's time for dinner!'; a town crier reads a royal decree in the public square; a minister reads a Presidential proclamation from the pulpit on Thanksgiving morning. In every case one speaker speaks on behalf of another agent and enacts the agent's intention to 'call,' 'decree,' or 'proclaim.' All that is required for intelligibility is that the context and/or content of the address make clear the situation of double agency. The liturgical pardon does that in its content-reference to the primary agency of Father, Son, and Spirit or in its representative mode of speech ('by [Christ's] authority I declare to you . . .')[12]

Thiemann concludes that this notion of double agency is intelligible "provided there are available procedures for identifying and distinguishing the acts and intentions of the two agents."[13] The liturgical and scriptural contexts constitute a narrative identification of God as the one who gives and fulfills promises.

Then Thiemann devotes a chapter to the literary and theological interpretation of the Gospel of Matthew to demonstrate that it involves a narrative identification of God. "That description locates God as an agent of intentional action both within the scriptural text and within our common world of

---

11. Thiemann, 90.
12. Thiemann, 106.
13. Thiemann, 106f.

experience."[14] "God is thereby identified as the one whose promises are fulfilled in the mission of the Son of God and who enacts his intention to save in the raising of Jesus from the dead."[15] It should be noted that in this interpretation the gospel story is taken as it stands without any historical critical interpretation. That is, it is at least implied that God does everything that the author of Matthew says God does.

The main area in which Tracy and Thiemann may have made a contribution is that of double agency, and I will return to this later.

(Since the original presentation of this paper, I have learned of another important explication of the personal action view which has appeared in a book by Vernon White entitled *The Fall of a Sparrow: A Concept of Special Divine Action*.[16] After describing the demands of revelation and criticizing the views of Wiles, Ogden, Baelz and process theologians, White presents an approach in which "God acts personally, universally, with priority and sovereign efficacy; he acts in relation to particular events."[17] He holds that divine action is thoroughly analogous to human action, which is defined by intention, and that God acts in nature as well as in history and human lives. It should also be noted that White agrees with Farrer that the "causal joint" between divine and creaturely actions, the "how" of double agency, is beyond our understanding.)

McLain and Alston

Two recent essays make similar suggestions as to how we may understand a special act of God. In an important essay which is included in this volume[18] F. Michael McLain offers an incisive analysis of the way in which Gilkey poses the problem and a critique of the ways in which Ogden and Kaufman have responded. He argues that incorporeality is no barrier to thinking of God literally as an agent.

---

14. Thiemann, 108.
15. Thiemann, 113.
16. V. White, *The Fall of a Sparrow: A Concept of Special Divine Action* (Exeter: Paternoster Press, 1985).
17. White, 55.
18. McLain's essay may be found in *Divine Action*, edited by B. Hebblethwaite and E. H. Henderson (Edinburgh: T and T Clark, 1990).

He judges that Ogden and Kaufman have not succeeded in working out a concept of a particular special action of God. He concludes that Austin Farrer has offered the most fruitful suggestion for understanding such an action, namely, someone's perception of more than usual of the divine purpose in a particular event. Although he regularly refers to "God acting in and through the actions of finite agents," he does not suggest how this double agency might be understood.

In an essay entitled "God's Action in the World" William P. Alston takes up the problem of divine agency in a rather different way from Tracy, Thiemann and McLain.[19] Although he holds God to be literally a personal agent, his approach to divine agency is closer to the primary cause view of Thomas than to the personal action theory.

In the first part of his essay Alston argues that almost all events in the world, including those due to natural causes, can be understood as intentional actions of God. Assuming a causal determinism in the natural order, God as creator and sustainer is the agent of all events in this order. This, however, does not remove the reality of created agency, since an event in the natural order involves different roles for the divine and finite agents.

A question arises at this point. Can the results of the action of creation and preservation be properly considered the intentional acts of God? Action theory seems to imply a closer relation between agent and event than there is here. However, I suppose that Voyager II photographing the moons of Uranus in January 1986 can be considered the intentional act of the engineer who planned, designed, programmed and executed the launch of Voyager eight years before.

Then Alston inquires whether God can be said to perform the actions of autonomous agents, if they are assumed not to be causally determined in accordance with the libertarian view, and he concludes negatively. In this connection, I wonder what Alston would make of Thiemann's case of liturgical pardon and similar examples in the Bible, which are asserted to be cases of double agency. I will return to this later.

---

19. W. P. Alston, "God's Action in the World," in *Evolution and Creation*, edited by E. McMullin (Notre Dame: University of Notre Dame Press, 1985): 197-220.

Alston also notes that the libertarian position greatly complicates the case for divine agency even of causally determined happenings, since especially today human actions have affected most events on or near the surface of the earth. What is the role of divine agency in those causally determined events which are affected by human volition? He explores the possibility of God's determination on the basis of foreknowledge but rejects it. Alston concludes that although God partly determines events influenced by human volition, God is not their agent completely.

In the second part of his essay Alston takes up the question of whether some events are actions of God in a special sense. He argues that miracles or God's direct action can be considered such special actions and cannot be ruled out by any of the arguments which have been proposed against them. However, he wants to explore the possibility of special acts of God other than miracles, such as God's guiding and strengthening people and God's providential care. Direct divine intervention is not required for this, since "God is still intentionally doing everything done by the natural order He creates."[20] Following a suggestion by Tillich and Macquarrie, Alston proposes that an event in which someone can see the divine purpose or more of the divine purpose is a special act of God for that person. Thus the specialness is derived from the perception of the action and not from the action itself.

You will recall that David Griffin takes up a closely related question in his essay in *God's Activity in the World*. He argues that apart from miracles the claim that certain events are special acts of God is totally a function of their being perceived as special, and that there is nothing about the event in itself which makes the perception of it as special appropriate. This, he believes, leads to a relativism in regard to the revelation of the purpose of God.[21] I am curious to know what Alston would make of this objection.

---

20. Alston, 214.
21. D. Griffin, "Relativism, Divine Causation, and Biblical Theology," in *God's Activity in the World: The Contemporary Problem*, edited by O. C. Thomas (Chico: Scholars Press, 1983): 117-36.

Dulles, Polanyi and Rahner

Another contribution to the understanding of God's activity in the world has been suggested to me by conversations and correspondence with Fr. Avery Dulles of Catholic University. During the preparation of *God's Activity in the World* he sent me an outline of his interpretation of divine agency. I was not able to persuade him to expand this into an essay for inclusion in the book, so I will try to elaborate his ideas myself.

Dulles's approach consists of an expansion and reinterpretation of the primary cause view with some help from Michael Polanyi and Karl Rahner. His outline of God's activity in the world consists of three parts: God acting simply as first cause, God bringing about a particular effect in its specificity, and God's action by grace as quasi-formal cause. I will concentrate, as he does, on the latter two.

1. God's acting as first cause contributes the *esse*, the real existence, of the effect, not its specific nature. God's relation to the world in this connection is one of intimate presence to each thing which is perhaps better brought out by the participation categories of Platonic metaphysics.

2. God's bringing about a particular effect in its specificity can be compared to the effect of the mind on the body, except that God exists independently of the world, whereas the mind apparently does not exist independently of the body. The mind can be understood to act on the body not efficiently but by directing the powers that come from material nature. Likewise God can be interpreted to affect the world not by supplying a new force but by directing forces already in the world. In this fashion God may be thought to direct the world providentially.

Thus, as Rahner suggests, special divine activity in the world does not necessarily involve suspension of the laws of nature, because "every determined level and order of being is from the very start open towards a higher level and order and can be incorporated into it, without its own laws thereby having to be suspended." He notes that the laws of two-dimensional space are not suspended

170

in three-dimensional space, and the laws of inorganic matter are not suspended in biology. "Similarly, the world in its material context must be conceived as open from the outset to the reality of the spirit . . . and must be conceived as open to the reality of God."[22]

Rahner discusses this point in more detail in an exploration of the relation of the creation of the human soul and the theory of evolution. He argues that the divine special act of the creation of the individual soul is one in which God actively enables the biological processes of human bodies to transcend themselves without changing their essences and without divine causality replacing finite causality or inserting itself into the causal series. The ontological basis of this position is found in the basic theses of Rahner's transcendental Thomism.

The fundamental paradigm of a being is found in the being who knows and acts. The real nature of causal operation and becoming is primarily manifested in the sphere of mind and spirit. In any occasion of finite knowledge a human being is intrinsically oriented toward absolute being or God as the ground and goal of this movement of the mind. All other efficient causes are deficient modes of this causality. Therefore, any agent is able to transcent itself on the basis of the presence of God as the ground of this self-movement. This self-transcendence does not cease to be self-movement but attains its own proper nature thereby. Thus Rahner affirms the evolutionary development of matter towards spirit and concludes that the parents beget a human being and not just a human body. This, he states, exemplifies the relation between the primary cause and secondary causes.[23]

Dulles suggests the same point in a somewhat different way with the help of Polanyi's concept of "boundary control." Polanyi asserts that a number of different principles can control a comprehensive entity at different levels, for example, the laws of mechanics, the principles of physiology, or the principles of

22. K. Rahner, *Theological Investigations*, vol. 5 (Baltimore: Helicon Press, 1966): 467. See also K. Rahner, *Foundations of Christian Faith: An Introduction to the Idea of Christianity* (New York: Seabury Press, 1978): 259.

23. K. Rahner, *Hominisation: The Evolutionary Origin of Man as a Theological Problem* (New York: Herder and Herder, 1965): 62-93. I considered using this passage in *God's Activity in the World.*

artifacts, such as a vocabulary or the rules of chess. The range of application of such principles is limited by boundary conditions which are controlled by higher principles.

> Thus the boundary conditions of the laws of mechanics may be controlled by the operational principles which define a machine; the boundary conditions of a muscular action may be controlled by a pattern of purposive behaviour, like that of going for a walk; the boundary conditions of a vocabulary are usually controlled by the rules of grammar; and the conditions left open by the rules of chess are controlled by the stratagems of the players. And so we find that machines, purposive action, grammatical sentences, and games of chess, are all entities subject to dual control. Such is the stratified structure of comprehensive entities. They embody a combination of two principles, a higher and a lower.[24]

Thus the operation of a machine relies upon the laws of mechanics and the operation of an organism relies upon the laws of physics and chemistry. These operations transcend and direct these laws but do not violate them. Likewise the special action of God in the world can be understood as one which transcends and directs the laws of finite causality without violating them.[25]

3. God's action in grace can be understood by Rahner's concept of quasi-formal cause. Rahner's departure from the traditional scholastic doctrine is his emphasis that grace is the actual self-communication of God to human beings. This is not to be understood as the giving of a created and finite reality (for example, infused habitual grace) to human beings by efficient causality, but the giving of the divine reality itself by means of what he calls quasi-formal causality.[26]

In his *Foundations of Christian Faith* Rahner drops the "quasi" but makes his essential point about the divine self-giving as formal causality more clearly.

---

24. M. Polanyi, *Knowing and Being: Essays by Michael Polanyi*, edited by Marjorie Grene (Chicago: University of Chicago Press, 1969): 217.

25. See A. Dulles, "Faith, Church and God: Insights from Michael Polanyi," *Theological Studies* 45, no. 3 (September, 1984): 548-50; A. Dulles, *Models of Revelation* (Garden City: Doubleday and Company, 1983): 146f.

26. See K. Rahner, "Christology Within an Evolutionary View of the World," in *Theological Investigations*, vol. 4 (Baltimore: Helicon Press, 1966): 15, 96; *Theological Investigations*, vol. 5 (Baltimore: Helicon Press, 1966): 205.

"Man is the event of a free, unmerited and forgiving and absolute self-communication of God. . . . God in his most proper reality makes himself the innermost constitutive element of man. We are dealing, then with an *ontological* self-communication of God."[27] This, he says, has "divinising" effects in human beings without their ceasing to be finite and without God ceasing to be infinite. Therefore, "this can and must be understood as analogous to a causality in which the 'cause' becomes an intrinsic, constitutive principle of the effect itself." This is a "relationship of *formal* causality as distinguished from efficient causality."[28]

Dulles comments:

The best created analogy is the form-matter relationship which occurs, for instance, when the soul animates the body, making it into a human body. This causality is not in the efficient but in the formal order. In the case of God's supernatural gift of grace, God may be called quasi-formal cause since when he communicates his personal life he remains self-subsistent and does not enter into composition with the creature. Although grace is in the order of being, not action, it affects the way the graced creature acts, so that the results may be attributed to God as something more than first cause.[29]

Conclusion

In conclusion I want to summarize some of the main points in the literature we have surveyed. I believe that the best way to do this is to focus on the question of double agency since I am persuaded that this is the key issue in the general problem in God's activity in the world.

I noted in *God's Activity in the World* that double agency was asserted in the primary cause view represented by Thomas Aquinas, Protestant orthodoxy and Barth, and implied in the approach of liberal theology represented by Schleiermacher, Bultmann and Kaufman, and also by Farrer and Gilson as followers of Thomas.

---

27. Rahner, *Foundations of Christian Faith*, 116.
28. Rahner, *Foundations of Christian Faith*, 120f.
29. A. Dulles, personal correspondence.

What is affirmed in double agency, as I understand it, is that in one event both the divine and creaturely agents are fully active. God has not overwhelmed the finite agent so that it is merely a passive instrument, and God is not simply the creator and sustainer who allows the creaturely agent to act independently of divine agency. Furthermore, the divine and finite agents are not merely complementary, that is, they do not contribute distinct parts to the one event. As many authors have put it, God acts in and through the finite agent which also acts in the event.

Now what progress has been made in the literature we have considered on this issue of double agency? Is it an intelligible and coherent concept or not? Our authors have assumed that it is intelligible and they have suggested various analogies and examples of divine-creaturely double agency. Let us assess them in the light of the foregoing definition, and let us look first at the analogies.

Tracy's analogy of two people pulling on a rope to ring a bell is clearly not a case of double agency, since each agent contributes part of the action. The same applies, I believe, to Thiemann's analogies of the sister passing on the mother's message about dinner, the town crier reading the royal decree and the minister reading the presidential proclamation. In each case the agents are performing distinct actions or distinct parts of one action. They would be valid analogies of double agency only if the passing on or reading were in fact the very occasion on which the message, decree, or proclamation became a reality or became effective, such that there was an identity of the actions of the two agents. For example, in the case of the royal decree, if the context were such that it actually became effective in an official proclamation, say, by a magistrate before the parliament, then this might be a fairly good analogy of divine-human double agency. Both agents, the crown and the magistrate, would be active in the one event of the proclamation of the decree.

Furthermore, Rahner's analogies (two and three dimensional space, the laws of inorganic matter and biology) and some of Polanyi's analogies (the laws of mechanics and machines, vocabulary and grammar) are also not analogies of double agency since no intentional action is involved. However, Polanyi's other analogies (physiology and purposive action, the rules of chess and the player's strategies) are possible analogies of divine-creaturely double agency. But they are analogies of double-agency between God and sub-human agents rather than between God and autonomous agents. They are analogies of the way in which divine agency causes lower levels of being to transcend themselves without being disrupted.[30]

This leaves us with the two examples of divine-creaturely double agency, as distinct from analogies, namely, Thiemann's example of liturgical pardon and Dulles's and Rahner's example of grace as quasi-formal cause. Both seem to fulfill the conditions of double agency, and they also offer examples of two distinct types of divine-creaturely double agency which I shall call promissory and gracious, respectively.

In liturgical pardon the minister relying on the promise of God absolves the penitent in the name of God.[31] Thiemann quotes the Lutheran Book of Worship: "As a called and ordained minister of the church of God, and by his authority, I therefore declare to you the entire forgiveness of all your sins, in the name of the Father, and of the Son, and of the Holy Spirit."[32] Here the divine and human agents are fully active in the one event of pardon. I am surprised that the Lutheran Thiemann did not also use the example of Christian preaching in which the hearer, relying on the promise of God, trusts that the human word becomes the vehicle of the word of God.[33]

Dulles and Rahner could have given many specific examples of the action of grace as quasi-formal cause. I will mention two possibilities. God inspires the prophet who says, "Thus says the Lord . . ." God speaks to Israel in and through the words of the prophet. This is close to the example of preaching, but it is more an example of the gracious divine presence than of trusting in a divine promise.

---

30. It should be noted that in the book mentioned above, Vernon White offers as analogies of double agency the following: human interpersonal influence, the relation of human agency to physical systems and the relation of three to two dimensional space. See *The Fall of a Sparrow*, 110, 115, 118f.

31. See Matthew 16:19, Matthew 18:18; John 20:23.

32. Thiemann, 106.

33. See Luke 10:16, 1 Thessalonians 2:13, and the Reformation principle, *Praedicatio verbi Dei est verbum Dei* (Second Helvetic Confession, 1566).

Another example is the Christian acting in love of the neighbor by the inspiration of God.[34] God loves the neighbor in and through the action of the Christian who is inspired by the divine love.

This gracious type of double agency has been central in Christian experience and reflection from the beginning, because it is based on the fundamental Christian paradigm of incarnation. The interpretation of Jesus' relation to God and more specifically the relation of Jesus' actions to God's actions has always been the basic pattern or model of the God-world relation and of divine-creaturely double agency. I referred to this in the final chapter of *God's Activity in the World*, and I want to return to it now.

In many passages of the New Testament Jesus is described as doing the works of God. Jesus is the very word of God become flesh.[35] It is by the Spirit of God that Jesus casts out demons.[36] The words and works of Jesus are the words and works of God.[37] Jesus is the power and wisdom of God in action.[38] I have expanded on this theme following the suggestions from John Hick and W. R. Matthews to develop a Christology whose main assertion that the love manifest in Jesus' actions is numerically identical with the love of God.[39]

Since Jesus has usually been regarded as the prototype of the Christian life, we can expect to find similar testimonies from Christian experience. And this is exactly what we do find beginning with the New Testament and especially Paul. "By the grace of God I am what I am. . . . I worked harder than any of them, though it was not I, but the grace of God which is with me."[40] "It is no longer I who live, but Christ who lives in me; and the life I now live in the flesh I live by faith in the Son of God."[41] Then Augustine: "Even if we do good things which pertain to God's service, it is God that brings it about that we do what God

---

34. See Romans 5:5, etc.
35. John 1:14.
36. Matthew 12:28.
37. John 5:19, John 19:10, etc.
38. 1 Corinthians 1:24.
39. See O. C. Thomas, *Introduction to Theology*, rev. ed. (Wilton: Morehouse-Barlow Co., 1983): 152-5.
40. 1 Corinthians 15:10.
41. Galatians 2:20.

commanded?"[42] And Anselm: "Whatever our heart rightly wills, it is of God's gift." Finally, there are many assertions in the Reformation confessions that our good works are all by grace and the Holy Spirit.[43] We should note that these are all examples of divine-human double agency and that no valid analogies of it have been proposed with the possible exception of my interpretation of Thiemann's analogy of the reading of the royal decree.

Now is this concept of double agency intelligible or not? In *God's Activity in the World* David Griffin argues that it is not. He states the primary-secondary cause version of double agency assumes the sufficiency of each cause and that the idea of two sufficient causes for one event is self-contradictory.[44] He expands on this in an extended criticism of the philosophical theology of James F. Ross.[45]

Another critique of the primary cause view of double agency is made by Frank Dilley in *God's Activity in the World.* He holds that in double agency either the freedom of one of the agents is denied or the action must be divided between them. If there *is* genuine unity of action, there is no duality of causes, and if there is duality of causes, there is no unity of action, no single event.[46]

One solution to this problem is to loosen the definition of double agency and follow the lead of process theology. Then neither the divine nor the creaturely agent is a sufficient cause of the event. There is duality of causes, but no unity of action. The two causes are complementary, and each contributes a distinct part to the event.

---

42. Augustine, *On the Predestination of the Saints [De Prædestinatione Sanctorum]*, chap. 19, in *Nicene and Post-Nicene Fathers of the Christian Church. Volume 4: Saint Augustine: Anti Pelagian Writings*, edited by P. Schaff (New York: Charles Scribner's Sons, 1902).

43. See D. M. Baillie, *God Was in Christ* (New York: Charles Scribner's Sons, 1978): chap. 5, for these references and the development of this theme.

44. D. Griffin, "Relativism, Divine Causation, and Biblical Theology," 117-23.

45. J. F. Ross, *God, Power and Evil: A Process Theodicy* (Philadelphia: Westminster, 1976): chap. 14. See also L. Ford, *The Lure of God* (Philadelphia: Fortress Press, 1978): 19.

46. F. Dilley, "Does the 'God Who Acts' Really Act?" in *God's Activity in the World*, edited by O. C. Thomas (Chico: Scholar's Press, 1983): 55-7.

The other solution is to affirm double agency but also to assert that it is mysterious in character or with Farrer that the "causal joint" is by hypothesis outside of our knowledge, even as the mind-body relation is unintelligible to us.[47]

Is there another solution to the problem of double agency? I have not yet heard it. And so I suggest that this question should be a major focus of future discussions.

---

47. See Thomas, *God's Activity in the World*, 197-9, 201, 211.

PART III

APPLICATIONS

CHAPTER 9

INTERIORITY AND CHRISTIAN SPIRITUALITY

In the tradition of writing about the Christian life or spirituality, commonly known as ascetical theology,[1] down to the present burgeoning of this literature, a pervasive emphasis and focus has been on the inner or interior life as distinct from the outer, bodily, and communal life. For example, in the "Preface to the Series" in each of the twenty-five volumes entitled *World Spirituality*, the general editor, Ewert Cousins, states, "This series focuses on that inner dimension of the person called by certain traditions 'the spirit.' This spiritual core is the deepest center of the person."[2] Also, Thomas Merton, in a circular letter to his friends in 1968 shortly before his death, wrote: "Our real journey is interior; it is a matter of growth, deepening, and an ever greater surrender to the creative action of love and grace in our hearts."[3] Finally, in a recent study, Michael Downey comments on contemporary currents in Christian spirituality as follows: "The common perception is still that spirituality is primarily concerned with the life of the soul, the inner life, one's prayer life, one's spiritual life, as a separate compartment of the Christian life. The tendency to equate the spiritual life with the interior life is particularly prevalent in our own day."[4]

A closely related development emerges in recent studies of attitudes toward spirituality and religion. A sharp distinction is made between them with

---

1. I will be arguing that these terms should be used synonymously as is increasingly the case today. See any recent dictionary of theology or spirituality.

2. Ewert Cousins, ed., *World Spirituality: An Encyclopedic History of the Religious Quest*, 25 vols. (New York: Crossroad, 1985-).

3. Quoted in William A. Shannon, *Silent Lamp: The Thomas Merton Story* (New York: Crossroad, 1992): 2.

4. Michael Downey, *Understanding Christian Spirituality* (New York: Paulist, 1992): 105.

182

the result that religion tends to be denigrated and spirituality honored.[5] In response to an essay in which I suggested that "spirituality" and "religion" are synonymous, a former student and the founder and director of one of the oldest and largest centers for spiritual formation communicated to me that we should "see religion as the container [or] platform for the spiritual life, which in its essence may be qualitatively different from the container; as the heart is from the skeleton." Along with this honorific/pejorative distinction goes the assumption that whereas religion deals with the outer life, that is, institutions, traditions, practices, doctrines, and moral codes, spirituality treats the inner life, which thus tends to be individualized and privatized.

Many other examples of this emphasis on the inner life could be given both from the primary literature as well as from secondary commentary. One thinks, for example, of *The Interior Castle* of Teresa of Avila and of Thomas à Kempis's *The Imitation of Christ* in which book 2 is entitled "Suggestions Drawing Us toward the Inner Life." Now there are a few signs that this emphasis may be beginning to change. Note this statement in a dictionary of spirituality: "Christian spirituality is not simply for the 'interior life' or the inward person, but as much for the body as the soul, and is directed to the implementation of both the commandments of God, to love God and our neighbour."[6] But such ideas are quite rare, and the emphasis in the tradition and the contemporary consensus is on the centrality of the interior life.

My thesis in this chapter is that this emphasis is mistaken philosophically, theologically, and ethically and that it needs to be redressed not only to a more balanced view of the inner/outer relation but also to an emphasis on the outer as

---

5. See Wade Clark Roof, *A Generation of Seekers: The Spiritual Journey of the Baby Boom Generation* (San Francisco: Harper, 1993): 76-9; Downey, pp. 23-5.

6. Gordon S. Wakefield, "Spirituality," in *The Westminster Dictionary of Christian Spirituality*, ed. Gordon S. Wakefield (Philadelphia: Westminster, 1983): 362a. But in another dictionary essay on spirituality published the same year, Wakefield does not make this point about the outer (see his "Spirituality," in *The Westminster Dictionary of Christian Theology*, ed. Alan Richardson and John Bowden [Philadelphia: Westminster, 1983]: 549-50a). See also Downey, pp. 40, 61-2, 105; and Michael Cooper, "Ignatian Spirituality: Unitative Action with Christ on Mission," *Presence: An International Journal of Spiritual Direction* 2, no. 3 (September 1996): 25-39, in which he argues that while Dominican and Franciscan spirituality follow an inner/outer/inner dynamic, Ignatian spirituality follows an outer/inner/outer dynamic.

primary and as a major source of the inner. I will also raise the question of the very intelligibility of the inner/outer distinction.

The philosopher Charles Taylor argues that this inner/outer distinction, which seems to us so natural and universal, is in fact a product of Western culture and that "our modern notions of inner and outer are indeed strange and without precedent in other cultures and times":[7]

> In our language of self-understanding, the opposition 'inside-outside' plays an important role. We think of our thoughts, ideas, or feelings as being 'within' us, while the objects in the world which these mental states bear on are 'without.'. . . But strong as this partitioning of the world appears to us, as solid as this localization may seem, and anchored in the very nature of the human agent, it is in large part a feature of our world, the world of modern, Western people. The localization is not a universal one, which human beings recognize as a matter of course, as they do for instance that their heads are above their torsos. Rather it is a function of a historically limited mode of self-interpretation, one which has become dominant in the modern West and which may indeed spread thence to other parts of the globe, but which had a beginning in time and space and may have an end.[8]

Taylor's thesis that interiority is a uniquely Western construct is contested and confirmed in different ways by Karl Jaspers, Denys Turner, Peter Berger, and Stephen Sykes. Jaspers claims that one of the characteristics of the axial period, which was centered around 500 B.C.E. and which included "all men on earth," was the emergence of selfhood and interiority. "[Man] experienced absoluteness in the depths of selfhood. . . . He discovered within himself the origin from which to raise himself above his own self and the world."[9] But Jaspers also sees inwardness as one of the typical features of Western development. "The *conscious inwardness of personal selfhood* achieved, in Jewish prophets, Greek philosophers and Roman statesmen, a perennially decisive absoluteness."[10] (It is interesting to note that Ewert Cousins, in pursuing Jaspers's theme, claims that

---

7. Charles Taylor, *Sources of the Self: The Making of the Modern Identity* (Cambridge, MA: Harvard University Press, 1989): 114.

8. Ibid., p. 111.

9. Karl Jaspers, *The Origin and Goal of History* (New Haven, CT: Yale University Press, 1953): 2-3.

10. Ibid., p. 63.

"from the time of the Axial Period, the spiritual path tended to lead away from the earth and towards the heavenly realms above," and that in the Second Axial Period, which has now begun, there will be [should be?] a reverse in this direction involving the rediscovery of themes of the pre-Axial Period, namely, "a collective and cosmic [consciousness] rooted in the earth and the life cycles."[11] It is not clear how this change of emphasis is related to Cousins's focus on interiority, which has been noted above.)

This universality of the emphasis on interiority is affirmed in a different way by Turner in his study of medieval mysticism. He holds that the inner/outer distinction is

> so primitive as perhaps to be rooted in a physical fact of the greatest generality about the human body. . . . Inevitably our ways of perceiving ourselves are governed by *some* contrast between 'inner' and 'outer' and by the inevitable allocation of that which is most to do with ourselves as conscious, intending beings, to the inner. . . . It seems inconceivable that human beings could perceive of themselves otherwise than in terms of the priority of the 'inner' over the 'outer.' Human beings must experience themselves in terms of *some* contrast between them. . . . It is as near to being a 'pre-cultural' and 'natural' fact of human cognitivity as any is.[12]

Berger, however, sees the world religions as divided between two great types: those of Asia, which are marked by interiority, and those of the West, which are marked by confrontation. Thus interiority is not the main characteristic of religions of the West but rather those of the East. In the interiority type of the East, "the divine does not confront man from the outside but is to be sought within himself as the divine ground of his own being and of the cosmos. The divine here is metapersonal and beyond all attributes, including those of will and speech. Once the divine ground of being is grasped, both man and cosmos pale

---

11. Ewert Cousins, "A Spirituality for the New Axial Period," *Christian Spirituality Bulletin* 2, no. 2 (Fall 1994): 15b.

12. Denys Turner, *The Darkness of God: Negativity in Christian Mysticism* (Cambridge: Cambridge University Press, 1995): 90-1.

into insignificance or even illusiveness. Individuality is not sharpened but absorbed, and both history and morality are radically relativized."[13]

Finally, Sykes, in his study of the essence, identity, and continuity of Christianity, argues that Christianity has both an "inwardness tradition" and an "externality tradition," which are related by "dialectical tradition," and that Christian history shows an oscillation of emphasis between the two.[14]

Although Taylor's thesis about the uniqueness of the Western emphasis on interiority is contested and confirmed in these ways, I will not pursue it further since it is not central to the argument of this chapter. But in the rest of this chapter, I will pursue his claim that this emphasis is a construct and perhaps an aberration, and I will argue further that the outer should be considered primary and a major source of the inner.

Now what is the origin of this emphasis on interiority? First of all, it should be emphasized that the discovery of interiority came late in human development and constituted a major human achievement. Its beginnings, at least in the West, can be seen in Homer and in the Hebrew scriptures, among other places. Taylor claims that in its developed form, the emphasis on the inner life derives from Augustine, who was influenced at this point by Plotinust[15] and, I would add, the Stoics, especially Marcus Aurelius.[16] The Platonic distinctions of "spirit/matter, higher/lower, eternal/temporal, immutable/changing is described by Augustine, not just occasionally and peripherally, but centrally and essentially in terms of inner/outer."[17] And the reason is that the inner is the road to God. "Do not go outward; return within yourself. In the inward person dwells the truth":[18]

---

13. Peter Berger, *The Heretical Imperative: Contemporary Possibilities of Religious Affirmation* (Garden City, NY: Anchor, 1979): 147.

14. Stephen Sykes, *The Identity of Christianity: Theologians and the Essence of Christianity from Schleiermacher to Barth* (Philadelphia: Fortress, 1984): chap. 2, esp. pp. 230-8.

15. For the influence of Plotinus on Augustine in regard to interiority, see Turner, *The Darkness of God*, pp. 75-9. For Plotinus on interiority, see *The Cambridge Companion to Plotinus*, ed. Lloyd P. Gerson (Cambridge: Cambridge University Press, 1996): 276, 289, 306-7. But see *Enneads* 4.3.20, where Plotinus explains that we say that the soul is in the body only because the soul is invisible and the body visible.

16. See, e.g., Marcus Aurelius, *Meditations* 4.3, 7.28, 33, 59.

17. Taylor (n.7 above, pp. 128-9).

18. Augustine, *De vera religione* 39.72.

Augustine's turn to the self was a turn to radical reflexivity, and that is what made the language of inwardness irresistible. The inner light is the one which shines in our presence to ourselves; it is the one inseparable from our being creatures with a first-person standpoint. What differentiates it from the outer light is just what makes the image of inwardness so compelling, that it illuminates the space where I am present to myself. It is hardly an exaggeration to say that it was Augustine who introduced the inwardness of radical reflexivity and bequeathed it to the Western tradition of thought. The step was a fateful one, because we have certainly made a big thing of the first-person standpoint. The modern epistemological tradition from Descartes, and all that flowed from it in modern culture, has made this standpoint fundamental — to the point of aberration, one might think. It has gone as far as generating the view that there is a special domain of 'inner' objects available only from this standpoint; or the notion that the vantage point of the 'I think' is somehow outside the world of things we experience.[19]

Turner offers a much more detailed analysis of Augustine on interiority. Augustine turns away from the outer and toward the inner not only because the inner is the place where he finds his true self and God but also because the outer is mutable and mortal, since it is bodily and material, whereas the inner is immutable and immortal.

Turner suggests that Augustine uses the basic distinction of what is inside and outside the body as a metaphor for a more specialized distinction of consciousness and its objects. In the latter "the boundary between the inner and the outer falls not between the mind and the body but between that part of the mind which is intrinsically dependent on the body for the exercise of its powers (the 'outer') and the part of the mind which is not so dependent (the 'inner')."[20] Thus reason is inner, and sensation, imagination, and memory are outer.

Turner also suggests that Augustine's language about interiority is self-subverting, since "the more 'interior' we are the more our interiority opens out to that which is inaccessibly 'above' and beyond it."[21] Turner also pursues this theme in discussing Meister Eckhart and *The Cloud of Unknowing*, and I will

---

19. Taylor, p. 131.
20. Turner, *The Darkness of God*, p. 90; cf. Augustine *e Trinitate* 12.1.
21. Turner, *The Darkness of God* (n. 12 above): 69.

return to it later. Moreover, Margaret Miles points out that for Augustine, the processes of the soul are known only in the movements of the body: "If he is accurately to represent the soul's progress, Augustine must rigorously observe the body's movements — its reactions and responses. His vehicle for characterizing inner movements is physical change. . . . Because the soul's fluctuations are discernible only as physical events, the body must be painstakingly scrutinized for knowledge of the soul."[22]

It was Descartes who confirmed and elaborated the centrality of inwardness for the modern period with his emphasis on thought as distinguished from extension, *res cogitans* from *res extensa*. Finally, Locke completed the modern development with a radically subjectivized view of the person in which consciousness is clearly distinguished from, even detached from, its embodiment. Thus the objects of knowledge are objectified, and consciousness is disengaged from them. Needless to say, Taylor is uneasy about this development and holds that the self (and its ideas) can be understood only in the context of its embodiment and practices.

Taylor's argument is confirmed by the careful analysis of the concept of the person by P. E. Strawson, who concludes that a person is "a type of entity such that *both* predicates ascribing states of consciousness *and* predicates ascribing corporeal characteristics, a physical situation, etc. are equally applicable to a single individual of that single type. . . . So the concept of the pure individual consciousness — the pure ego — is a concept that cannot exist."[23] In elaborating Strawson's point, F. Michael McLain states: "The connection between conscious state and physical behavior is frequently so tight knit that the basis for ascribing the former is precisely the latter. . . . We persistently view human behavior as

---

22. Margaret R. Miles, *Desire and Delight: A New Reading of Augustine's Confessions* (New York: Crossroad, 1992): 14; see also p. 62.
23. P. F. Strawson, *Individuals: An Essay in Descriptive Metaphysics* (London: Methuen, 1959): 102.

expressive of, and imbued with, thoughts, feelings, and intentions, and we are right in doing so; it is a logically adequate criterion of the 'inner side'."[24]

The main source, however, of this philosophical critique and revision of the Augustinian-Cartesian inner/outer distinction and emphasis on the inner is found in the later writings of Ludwig Wittgenstein, who influenced both Strawson and Taylor. One of the main achievements of Wittgenstein in his *Philosophical Investigations* and other later writings was to reverse the Cartesian view of human beings and to argue that the outer side of human life, namely, the body, actions, customs, practices, community, and tradition, is primary and the foundation of everything inner.

Interpreting Wittgenstein, however, is made difficult by his idiosyncratic and enigmatic style, which is full of rhetorical questions, irony, and aphorisms. But a few examples can help us to perceive the drift of his argument:

> This simile of 'inside' or 'outside' the mind is pernicious.[25]

> One of the most dangerous ideas philosophically is, oddly enough, the idea that thinking takes place with, or in, our heads.[26]

> Nothing is more wrong-headed than calling meaning a mental activity.[27]

> An 'inner process' stands in need of outer criteria.[28]

> Thinking is not an incorporeal process which lends life and sense to speaking, and which it would be possible to detach from speaking.[29]

> The human body is the best picture of the human soul.[30]

> In what sense are my sensations private? . . . . Other people very often know when I am in pain.[31]

---

24. F. Michael McLain, "On Theological Models," *Harvard Theological Review* 62 (1969): 165ff.

25. Ludwig Wittgenstein, *Wittgenstein's Lectures: Cambridge, 1930-1932*, ed. Desmond Lee (Oxford: Blackwell, 1980): 25. I am indebted to Fergus Kerr (*Theology after Wittgenstein* [Oxford: Blackwell, 1986]) and to my friend Gordon Kaufman for many of these references.

26. Ludwig Wittgenstein, *Philosophical Grammar*, ed. Rush Rhees, trans. A. J. P. Kenny (Oxford: Blackwell, 1974): 100.

27. Ludwig Wittgenstein, *Philosophical Investigations*, trans. G. E. M. Anscombe, 3rd ed. (New York: Macmillan, 1958): § 693.

28. Ibid., § 580.

29. Ibid., § 339.

30. Ibid., p. 178.

A doctor asks: "How is he feeling?" The nurse says: "He is groaning." A report on his behaviour.[32]

How should we counter [someone] if he said that with him knowing how to play chess was an inner process? — We should say that when we want to know if he can play chess we aren't interested in anything that goes on inside of him. — And if he replies that this is in fact just what we are interested in, that is, we are interested in whether he can play chess — then we shall have to draw his attention to the criteria which would demonstrate his capacity, and on the other hand to the criteria for the 'inner states!'[33]

'But you surely cannot deny that, for example, in remembering, an inner process takes place.' — What gives the impression that we want to deny anything? . . . The impression that we want to deny something arises from our setting our faces against the picture of the 'inner process.' What we deny is that the picture of the inner process gives us the correct idea of the word 'to remember.'[34]

There are innumerable passages like these in the later writings of Wittgenstein, all focusing on the inner/outer distinction that he believes is so misleading. But why the odd style? I believe that it is the result of the fact that the inner/outer distinction with an emphasis on the inner is so deeply seated in our ways of thinking in the West that Wittgenstein despairs of getting at it directly or in any other way than by this subtle, teasing, joking, storytelling manner that is calculated to shake us out of our deeply grounded, customary way of thinking and talking.

Wittgenstein's beginning point is biological: "I want to regard man here as an animal; as a primitive being to which one grants instinct but not ratiocination. . . . Language did not emerge from some kind of ratiocination."[35] All language begins with our natural responses as animal organisms to external stimuli: cries of pain, joy, and fear, as well as smiles, frowns, and other gestures. The infant learns words for these natural expressions. Socialization leads to

31. Ibid., § 246.
32. Ibid., p. 179.
33. Ibid., p. 181.
34. Ibid., § 305
35. Ludwig Wittgenstein, *On Certainty*, ed. G. E. M. Anscombe and G. H. von Wright, trans. Denis Paul and G. E. M. Anscombe (Oxford: Blackwell, 1969): § 475.

elaboration and differentiation of language, including reference to the self and others. Gordon Kaufinan interprets this as follows: "Thus, there is no originary [i.e., originating] 'inwardness' in human beings; we naturally respond in *external* and visible ways to what is happening to us (to the 'sensations' we receive), and our inwardness is only gradually built up as language develops. . . . If 'inwardness' is a linguistic construction, it will, thus, vary greatly in different cultural and linguistic settings. . . . Thus inwardness is not a kind of 'inner chamber' accessible only to the self. It is, rather, the range of possibilities of *action* and *speech* that becomes open to the child."[36]

It is important to note that there is considerable disagreement among interpreters of Wittgenstein about his intention in regard to the inner/outer distinction. Some hold that Wittgenstein is a behaviorist who wants to deny the reality of interiority. Others claim that Wittgenstein's intention is rather to deny that inner experiences refer to objects to which we have privileged access and to which we can refer with a private language. I believe that the latter interpretation is more persuasive. Jacques Bouveresse, for example, argues that Wittgenstein's thesis about the "myth of interiority" does not involve behaviorism.[37]

Wittgenstein's discussion of private language is not only the most controversial part of his philosophy but also its central argument, the focus of his attack on Cartesianism, and the basis of his critique of the ideas of inner experience, inner process, and interiority in general. Wittgenstein claims that we cannot imagine or invent an absolutely private language and that no existing language could function if it were private. The central point of the argument is that it is not possible to refer to inner experiences as objects. To make this point, he returns again and again to the experience of pain. He asserts that if the word "pain" referred only to people's private experience, it would have no common meaning at all. The word "pain" is a learned form of "pain-behavior":

---

36. Gordon Kaufman, "Reading Wittgenstein: Notes for Constructive Theologians," *Journal of Religion* 79, no. 3 (July 1999): 414-5.
37. Jacques Bouveresse, *Le mythe de l'intériorité: Expérience, signification et langage privé chez Wittgenstein* (Paris: Les Éditions de Minuit, 1976): 25.

Words are connected with the primitive, the natural, expression of the sensation and used in their place. A child has hurt himself and he cries; and then adults talk to him and teach him exclamations and, later, sentences. They teach the child new pain-behavior.

'So you are saying that the word 'pain' really means crying?'— On the contrary: the verbal expression of pain replaces crying and does not describe it.[38]

One interpreter concludes:

Wittgenstein's position is that our own inner sensations, states and feelings are not *private objects* 'known' only to the person who 'has' them. This is not, of course, to deny the 'reality' of these inner sensations, states and feelings. Nor is it to maintain that they are only 'real' if they are public. It is only to insist that the words *object* and *know* are misused in this case and give rise to (and are produced by) a thoroughly misleading picture. The 'inner façade' which I alone observe is, for Wittgenstein, an illusion. But this is not to say that there are no *inner sensations* or *inner states*, for these terms do not lose their usefulness for being thought of in a different way. It is the *private* object and the picture of the *inner process* which Wittgenstein wishes to dissolve, and not the reality or importance of the 'inner life.'[39]

This interpretation of Wittgenstein suggests that there are two distinct ways of looking at the inner/outer relation, which may be called the genetic and the structural. The genetic addresses the question of how the inner life arises from the outer in the development of a child. The structural refers to the resulting relation of inner and outer in the normal adult. Although the genetic view illuminates the relationship of inner and outer, Wittgenstein's focus is on the structural, and that is our concern in this chapter.

A theological critique of the inner/outer distinction and the emphasis on the outer is presented by Fergus Kerr in his book *Theology after Wittgenstein*.[40] He argues that Wittgenstein's main purpose in his later writings is to overcome the grand theological and metaphysical tradition that began with Augustine and was elaborated by Descartes and that looks upon the self or soul as an

---

38. Wittgenstein, *Philosophical Investigations* (n. 27 above), § 244.

39. Henry Le Roy Finch, *Wittgenstein — the Later Philosophy: An Exposition of the "Philosophical Investigations"* (Atlantic Highlands, NJ: Humanities Press, 1977): 127.

40. Kerr (n. 25 above).

autonomous, rational, invisible, inner reality essentially independent of the body, the community, and the culture with its language and practices.

Moreover, Kerr interprets this tradition as deriving originally from the Orphic and Gnostic myth of the soul that has fallen into exile in the body and the natural world and that seeks to free itself and transcend these prisons in order to achieve spiritual purity and true knowledge. He could well have referred to Paul Ricoeur's treatment of "the myth of the exiled soul," which "presided, if not over the birth, at least over the growth of Greek philosophy. . . . In this awareness, in this awakening to itself of the exiled soul, all 'philosophy' of the Platonic and Neo-Platonic type is contained."[41] Kerr sees modern Christian theology and spirituality as deeply infected by this dualistic religious and philosophical tradition, and he offers examples from the writings of Karl Rahner, Hans Kung, Schubert Ogden, Donald Cupitt, and others: "Spiritual writers in the last three centuries or so have driven many devout people into believing that the only real prayer is silent, wordless, 'private.' . . . It is amazing how often devout people think that liturgical worship is not really prayer unless they have been injecting special 'meaning' to make the words work. The inclination is to say that participation consists in private goings-on inside the head. . . . There is . . . a central strain in modern Christian piety which puts all the emphasis on people's secret thoughts and hidden sins."[42] Then he quotes Wittgenstein: "Only God sees the most secret thoughts. But why should these be all that important?"[43]

According to Kerr, Wittgenstein's method of undercutting this pervasive theological tradition is to point out in his idiosyncratic manner the manifold ways in which all human language and thought derive from and are dependent on what is really the given, the primary, the ultimate background of all human thought and consciousness, namely, what Wittgenstein calls the "facts of living" or the "forms of life," that is, the various complex activities and practices of everyday life involving the body, the family, and the community with its customs and

---

41. Paul Ricoeur, *The Symbolism of Evil* (New York: Harper & Row, 1967): 174, 300.
42. Kerr, pp. 172-73.
43. Ibid., p. 173. The quote is from Ludwig Wittgenstein, *Zettel,* ed. G. E. M. Anscombe and G. H. von Wright, trans. G. E. M. Anscombe (Oxford: Blackwell, 1967): § 560.

traditions. This led to Wittgenstein's being accused of being a behaviorist.[44] But he denied this because he was trying to find a way between the false mentalism of the tradition and the false behaviorism that denies the inner entirely.

A pervasive emphasis of Kerr's book is that Wittgenstein was a deeply religious person and that theological concerns were of great importance to him. This is documented in detail in Ray Monk's biography in which he states that Wittgenstein "lived a devoutly religious life."[45] It was these concerns that lay behind Wittgenstein's commitment to reverse the theological tradition of the primacy of the inner over the outer. Kerr clearly implies that someone standing in the Christian tradition of the doctrines of creation, incarnation, and the resurrection of the body would understand the importance and primacy of the outer.[46]

Here we come on one of the great paradoxes of Christian history. On the one hand, the biblical tradition seems to emphasize the primacy of the outer — the body, speech, and action — while, on the other hand, the Christian tradition under the influence of Stoicism and Neoplatonism via Augustine and Dionysius, among others, tends to emphasize the inner.

This does not mean that the biblical authors do not know of the inner/ outer distinction and its importance. In the Hebrew scriptures, the inner was focused on the "heart," which R. C. Dentan describes as "the inner-most spring of individual life, the ultimate source of all of its physical, intellectual, emotional, and volitional energies, and consequently the part of man through which he normally achieved contact with the divine."[47] Jesus' teaching includes this

---

44 . Wittgenstein, *Philosophical Investigations*, §§ 305-8.

45. Ray Monk, *Ludwig Wittgenstein: The Duty of Genius* (New York: Free Press, 1990): 580. Also see his index under "Christianity" and "religion."

46. Kerr, pp. 140, 185-7. Many of Kerr's points had been made many years earlier by Dietrich Bonhoeffer and more recently by Rowan Williams (see Dietrich Bonhoeffer, *Letters and Papers from Prison: The Enlarged Edition*, ed. Eberhard Bethge [New York: Macmillan, 1971]: 344-6, and *Ethics*, ed. Eberhard Bethge [New York: Macmillan, 1955]: 200; Rowan Williams, "The Suspicion of Suspicion: Wittgenstein and Bonhoeffer," in *The Grammar of the Heart: New Essays in Moral Philosophy and Theology*, ed. Richard H. Bell [San Francisco: Harper & Row, 1988]: esp. 36-9, 41-4, and "Interiority and Epiphany: A Reading in New Testament Ethics," *Modern Theology* 13, no. 1 [January 1997]: esp. 29-31, 46, 50).

47. R. C. Dentan, "Heart," in *Interpreter's Dictionary of the Bible*, ed. George Arthur Buttrick et al., 4 vols. (New York: Abingdon, 1967): 2:549b. See also 1 Sam. 16:7.

distinction: "It is from within, from the human heart, that evil intentions come" (Matt. 7:18; see Matt. 7:21, 23:27; Mark 7:18, 21; Luke 11:39). The inner/outer distinction is most fully developed by Paul. He often points to the contrast between the inner man (*eso anthropos*) and the outer man (*exo anthropos*) (see, e.g., Rom. 7:22; 2 Cor. 4:16). About the inner man, John Knox says that it is "what could be called 'mind,' 'heart, 'spirit'."[48]

In regard to Paul, however, several commentators note the influence of Hellenistic philosophy at this point. Victor Paul Furnish states: "The contrasting expressions are doubtless influenced by the widespread anthropological dualism of the Hellenistic world."[49] Markus Barth notes that other commentators refer to the anthropology of Hellenistic dualism, Gnostic sources, Platonic thought, and so forth. But he argues that "under Paul's hands [the] pagan meaning [of the inner man] was either lost or so altered that the original dualistic anthropological sense is no longer in the foreground."[50]

In general, however; from the call of Abraham and Moses to the Decalogue of the Sinai covenant, the covenant with David, the preaching of the eighth-century prophets, and Jesus' teaching about the reign of God, the biblical emphasis is on the outer: faith manifest and visible in obedience, sacrifice, and just action; repentance shown in the rending of garments and weeping; thanksgiving seen in dancing, singing, and feasting; and the reign of God perceived in preaching and healing and compared to buying a pearl, sowing seed, and holding a feast.

It should be noted that Jewish spirituality stands in this biblical tradition. Arthur Green defines Jewish spirituality as "life in the presence of God" and continues: "Spirituality in the Western sense, inevitably opposed in some degree to 'corporeality' or 'worldliness' (all apologies to the contrary notwithstanding), is unknown to the religious world view of ancient Judaism. Defining spirituality

---

48. John Knox, *Romans*, vol.. 9 of *Interpreter's Bible*, ed. George Arthur Buttrick et al. (New York: Abingdon, 1954): p. 502; see also Victor Paul Furnish, *II Corinthians*, vol. 32A of *The Anchor Bible* (Garden City, NY: Doubleday, 1984): 289.

49. Furnish, p. 261.

50. Markus Barth, *Ephesians*, vol. 34 of *The Anchor Bible* (Garden City, NY: Doubleday, 1974): 390.

as the cultivation and appreciation of the 'inward' religious life, we find both assent and demurral in the sources of Judaism. At the same time, concern is aroused lest the inner be praised at the expense of the outer."[51]

In the Christian tradition, the emphasis tended to shift to a focus on the inner life, to the development of the theological and cardinal virtues, and to the progress in grace through the purgative, illuminative, and unitive ways. This tendency is seen in many details as well as in broad tendencies. It appears, for example, in the tendency to interpret *entos in* Luke 17:21 ("The kingdom of God is among you") as "within" rather than "among,"[52] whereas the overwhelming majority of exegetes agree that it means "among."[53]

I am obviously using a very broad brush here, and there are many exceptions, especially in some Reformation traditions. An early exception is Irenaeus, who interprets references to the inner man to be an essential theme of Gnosticism. He states that the Gnostics interpret redemption in such a way that "knowledge is the redemption of the inner man [*interioris hominis, endon anthropon*]" and that "the inner man may ascend on high in an invisible manner, as if their body were left among created things in this world."[54] Although the desert ascetics of the fourth and fifth centuries commonly referred to the inner/outer distinction, they understood the soul to be manifest most clearly in the actions of the body. Margaret Miles states that "the ascetics of the Egyptian desert believed that minute observation of physical symptoms revealed the state of one's soul more accurately than introspection."[55]

Also, as I noted above, Turner discovers the self-subverting character of the language of interiority in Eckhart and *The Cloud of Unknowing*. In Eckhart, he finds the assertion that true detachment, which is the fundamental virtue,

---

51. Arthur Green, "Introduction," in *Jewish Spirituality*, vol. 1, *From the Bible through the Middle Ages,* ed. Arthur Green, *World Spirituality*, vol. 13 (New York: Crossroad, 1986): xiv.

52. See, e.g., Thomas à Kempis *The Imitation of Christ* 2.1.

53. See the extended discussion of this question by Joseph A. Fitzmyer, *The Gospel According to Luke, X-XXIV* vol. 28 of *The Anchor Bible* (Garden City, NY: Doubleday, 1985): 1160-62.

54. Irenaeus *Against Heresies* 1.21.4-5; Alexander Roberts and James Donaldson, eds., *Ante-Nicene Fathers* (Buffalo, NY: Christian Literature Publishing, 1885): 346b.

55. Margaret R. Miles, *Plotinus on Body and Beauty* (London: Blackwell, 1999): 135. Quote is in reference to Palladius *Lausiac History* VI.

involves letting go of the desire to seek self and God in interiority: "For the truly detached person, there can be no such distinction [of interiority and exteriority]."[56] He also notes that Eckhart's doctrine of detachment has "the potential for the critique of an ego-serving spirituality, a spirituality of 'ways to God'. . . . This is not so much a spirituality as the critique of spirituality."[57]

Turner explores these themes further in a chapter entitled *"The Cloud of Unknowing* and the Critique of Interiority."[58] *The Cloud of Unknowing* author uses the inner/outer distinction only to transcend it. This distinction is a construct of the imagination from the outer world of spatial relations. *The Cloud of Unknowing* author warns against this language, because it conceives of the inner life as a quasi-physical, quasi-psychological place inside consciousness. But in the perspective of the truly spiritual person, there is no distinction of inner and outer: "See that in no sense you withdraw into yourself. And, briefly, I do not want you to be outside or above, behind or beside yourself either!"[59]

It is only for the outer self that the duality of inner and outer persists. The inner self knows that there is no inner as against outer. Turner states: "The *Cloud* Author's interiority' . . . is the achievement whereby we become detached from, that is, liberated from, the very dualism itself between interiority and exteriority in theory and practice. . . . To see them as opposed, . . . to actively seek interiority is to lack interiority. It is to be attached to what the *Cloud* author sees as a 'spirituality' . . . [with] all its spiritual strategies of prayer; self-denial, repentance and the like; and all its spiritual by-products of a self-absorbed, interiorist piety."[60]

In spite of these exceptions, however, it seems clear that the main emphasis in Christian history has been on the centrality of the interior life. Recent historians of Christian spirituality (Louis Bouyer, Urban T. Holmes, Richard Woods, Bradley Holt, Bernard McGinn, et al.) have not focused on the

---

56. Turner, *The Darkness of God* (n. 12 above): 184.
57. Ibid., p. 185.
58. Ibid., pp. 186-210.
59. Clifton Wolters, ed. and trans., *The Cloud of Unknowing* (New York: Penguin, 1961): chap. 68, p. 142.
60. Turner, *The Darkness of God*, pp. 209-10.

inner/outer distinction. My reading of this history, however, has led me to the judgment that when this distinction is employed, the emphasis has almost always been on the centrality of the interior life at the expense of the outer life. My judgment has been confirmed in a recent and well-researched study by Michael Downey. He argues that whereas in the early centuries, the Christian tradition of spirituality continued in the biblical tradition and can be described as holistic and integrated, it gradually became more and more narrow. It tended to be elitist, other-worldly, and focused on the interior life, the way of perfection, and the mystical graces, which were pursued mainly by the monks and the clergy.[61]

This leads directly to the final element of the critique. I believe that the focus in Christian spirituality on the inner life has been a mistake ethically. On the basis of the emphasis on the interior life, the mainline Christian traditions have understood the goal of the moral life to be essentially the moral perfection of the soul, sanctification, and growth in the virtues. Some of some of the virtues obviously involve outward action toward the neighbor, but this has usually been interpreted as a means to the end of the perfection of the soul. Augustine, for example, teaches that love of the neighbor is really loving God in the neighbor, which brings us closer to God.[62]   In general, under the influence of the Neoplatonic tradition, the inner direction of the Christian life has been metaphorically upward, an ascent out of the concerns of the world to God.

Alasdair MacIntyre, in his discussion of medieval ethics in *After Virtue*, has criticized this development. He refers to Abelard's essentially Stoic emphasis on will and law as the "interiorization of the moral life."[63] Here, physical, social, and political circumstances are essentially irrelevant to morality. Ideas of the common goal of communal human life are also irrelevant: "Abelard's retreat into interiority is . . . a refusal to face the [social and political] tasks" of his day. For Abelard, "the external social world was merely a set of contingent and accidental

---

61. See Downey (n. 4 above): pp. 58-62.
62. Augustine *In evangelium Joannis* 65.2.
63. Alasdair MacIntyre, *After Virtue: A Study in Moral Theory* (Notre Dame, IN: University of Notre Dame Press, 1984): 168.

circumstances."[64]   MacIntyre summarizes: "For the Platonist, as later for the
Cartesian, the soul, preceding all bodily and social existence, must indeed possess
an identity prior to all social roles; but for the Catholic Christian, as earlier for the
Aristotelian, the body and the soul are not two linked substances. I am my body
and my body is social, born to those parents in this community with a specific
social identity."[65]

This tendency in traditional moral theology has been widely criticized by
various forms of political and liberation theology that have emphasized the
centrality of the outer actions of seeking justice and serving neighbors for their
own sake. From the beginning, Latin American liberation theology has made the
moral critique of traditional spiritual or ascetical theology, but this critique was
not made in terms of the inner/outer dialectic except by implication.[66]

This moral critique by liberation theology has been appropriately based on
Scripture, where the pervasive emphasis is on action for the well-being of the
neighbor. For example, in the servant poems of the second Isaiah, God pours out
the divine Spirit upon the servant so that he will "establish justice in the earth;"
act as "a covenant to the people, a light to the nations, to open the eyes that are
blind, to bring out the prisoners from the dungeon" (Isaiah 42, 49). In a similar
manner, in the passage of Isaiah chosen by the Jesus of Luke for his first
preaching, the Spirit of God empowers the preacher "to bring good news to the
poor, . . . to proclaim release to the captives and recovery of sight to the blind, to
let the oppressed go free" (Luke 4:18-19).

Finally, when the disciplines of John the Baptist ask Jesus if he is the
Messiah, Jesus responds: "Go and tell John what you have seen and heard: the
blind receive their sight, the lame walk, the lepers are cleansed, the deaf hear, and
the poor have good news brought them" (Luke 7:22; Matt. 11:5). These themes
are repeated and confirmed in the teaching of Jesus about the reign of God. The

---

64. Ibid., p. 170.
65. Ibid., p. 172. Williams also asserts that a rhetoric of interiority has been morally
"corrupting" and has led to the "disempowerment of the moral agent" ("Interiority and Epiphany"
[n. 46 above], p. 46).
66. See Gustavo Gutierez, *A Theology of Liberation: History, Politics and Salvation*, ed. and
trans. Sister Caridad Inda and John Eagleson (Maryknoll, NY: Orbis, 1973): 4-7, 203-8, 287-8.

struggle against injustice, disease, and other forms of evil is at the forefront in the calling to the Christian life. This struggle is not one that goes on in the privacy of the mind or spirit but one that goes on in public action informed by public worship. In conclusion, we need to get clearer on the meaning of the inner/outer distinction and then suggest some implications for the theory and practice of Christian spirituality.

Wittgenstein argues that the inner/outer distinction is essentially a linguistic construction. He states in one of his fundamental propositions that philosophical problems "are solved . . . by looking into the workings of our language, and that in such a way as to make us recognize those workings: *in despite of* an urge to misunderstand them. The problems are solved, not by giving new information, but by arranging what we have always known. Philosophy is a battle against bewitchment of our intelligence by means of language."[67]

Is the use of the inner/outer distinction itself an example of this kind of bewitchment? Wittgenstein is at least suggesting that we need to be more conscious and cautious in our language here. The first step is to be clear that interiority is a spatial metaphor for something that is nonspatial. It is a metaphor; it makes no sense to say that the self, consciousness, mind, or spirit is literally inside the body. But the referent of interiority, while nonspatial, is localized. It is somehow related to the body and not entirely apart from the body, although the theological and philosophical traditions are divided on this issue.

Stanley Cavell raises a further problem in the concept of interiority and the inner/outer distinction in his comments on Wittgenstein's claim that "an 'inner process' stands in need of outward criteria." He notes that the philosophical tradition has tended to regard the inner/outer distinction as obvious, which it is not. He interprets Wittgenstein to mean that "until you produce criteria on the basis of which, in a particular case, you count something as an 'inner process,' you have said nothing. . . . Once you produce the criteria, you will see that they are merely outward, and so the very thing they are supposed to show . . . is threatened. . . . Whatever the criteria tell by way of identifying the other's [inner]

---

67. Wittgenstein, *Philosophical Investigations* (n. 27 above): §§ 108-9.

200

state (or process, etc.), they are still *outward*. — Outward as opposed to what? . . .
One tries to make the remark [of Wittgenstein] into a thesis, and one starts
babbling."[68]

Would another metaphor avoid this problem? It would depend on the
metaphor, and there are no obvious alternatives available to us from the tradition.
The only modern alternative of which I know is the mathematical concept of
multiple spaces developed by G. F. B. Riemann and employed by Karl Heim.[69]
According to Heim, the nonobjective space of the ego and the I-thou relation are
distinct from the space-time system of modern physics and related to it as the
third dimension is related to two-dimensional space. The third dimension
impinges at every point in two-dimensional space, yet it is not in two-dimensional
space. Thus the inner might be spoken of metaphorically as present at every point
in the outer yet not in the space inhabited by the outer. In this chapter, however, I
will focus only on the metaphor of interiority.

So by interiority we mean not physically inner but psychologically or
spiritually inner such that the self or soul is inner and the facial expression and
gesture are outer; such that the mind is inner and the brain outer; and such that the
will or intention is inner and the bodily action and speech are outer. And we may
want to add the further distinctions that Turner found in Augustine, namely, that
sensation, imagination, and memory are outer.

In this connection, Turner suggests a "fantastical thought experiment, that
our vital organs of perception and thought were exposed in transparent bubbles on
the surface of our skins, and so 'outside.' Then perhaps, we would metaphorize
our 'selfhood' and 'outer.'"[70] Turner makes this point, however, only to
underscore the inevitability of the traditional inner/outer distinction. But Turner's
suggestion serves to alert us to the ways in which the self is in fact outer and to
the possibilities of radically revising the distinction.

68. Stanley Cavell, *The Claim of Reason: Wittgenstein, Skepticism, Morality, and
Tragedy* (New York: Oxford University Press, 1979): 96, 99.
69. See G. F. B. Riemann, *Über die Hypothesen, welche de Geometrie zu Grunde liegen*
(Berlin: Springer, 1923); and Karl Heim, *Christian Faith and Natural Science* (New York:
Harper & Brothers, 1953).
70. Turner, *The Darkness of God* (n. 12 above): 91.

Wittgenstein's statement that "the human body is the best picture of the human soul" suggests that we might consider the soul as spread out over the surface of the body and thus outer. Whitehead, unique among modern philosophers, offers an alternative. His concept of the soul, which includes the mind as the body includes the brain, is that it is composed of "actual occasions" of experience that have "physical poles" and "mental poles" that live in the interstices of the actual occasions that constitute the brain.[71] Thus the soul is as "outer" as the brain.

The question that Wittgenstein is raising is, Why is it appropriate to refer to the self, soul, mind, will, and intention as inner while all expressions of these in gesture, speech, facial expression, and action are outer? His point is that the former are known mainly in and through the latter, not only to an observer but also to the subject.

I believe that on this point there are some clues in our experience. Action often precedes conscious thought. I often discover what I think by speaking with others or by writing something out. This is exemplified in Kerr's statement that "worship is not the result but the precondition of believing in God."[72] This verges on behaviorism, the view that all mental terms can be analyzed in terms of behavior, that the inner is an epiphenomenon of the outer. But we do not have to adopt behaviorism in order to make the point that the inner is often or usually produced and informed by the outer.

After we get clearer about the meaning of "inner" and "outer," we must decide on where we stand on the relationship between the two concepts. Here we are confronted with a spectrum of views that can be outlined as follows:[73]

> 1. There is no inner; all is outer. Talk of the inner is illusory (behaviorism, materialism).

---

71. For a detailed exposition, see John B. Cobb, Jr., *A Christian Natural Theology Based on the Thought of Alfred North Whitehead* (Philadelphia: Westminster, 1965): chap. 2

72. Kerr (n. 25 above): 183.

73. I am indebted to Philip Clayton for some suggestions on this spectrum as well as other comments on a draft of this article.

2. The outer is primary and the sole source of the inner. The inner is an epiphenomenon of the outer (Wittgenstein?).

3. The outer is primary and the major, but not the sole, source of the inner (Wittgenstein?).

4. The inner and the outer are equiprimordial. There is inner as well as outer causality, mutual influence, and reciprocity (Strawson).

5. The inner is primary and the major, but not the sole, source of the outer (Christian tradition).

6. The inner is primary and the sole source of the outer. The outer is an epiphenomenon of the inner (idealism).

7. There is no outer; all is inner. All we know is our own experience (solipsism).

The argument of this chapter leads me to the third view, which is one possible interpretation of Wittgenstein. I will conclude with three implications of this view for the theory and practice of Christian spirituality or ascetical theology.

The first implication is the necessity of a renewed emphasis on the body and the material, social, political, and historical world rather than an exclusive focus on the soul or interior life in Christian spirituality. This emphasis is founded on the centrality in Christian faith of the themes of creation, incarnation, and the resurrection of the body. In spite of common contemporary claims to the contrary, the Christian tradition has been generally affirmative about the body and the material world. Miles asserts that in spite of "the assumption that we have received an overwhelmingly negative view of the body from Christian history," "Christian authors were not only intensely interested in but also *overwhelmingly affirming* of the body as an integral and permanent aspect of human being."[74]

This positive emphasis on the body and the material world has been reaffirmed by many Christian thinkers in the past century, perhaps most strikingly by William Temple in his statement that Christianity is "the most avowedly materialist of all the great religions. . . . Its own most central saying is: 'The

---

74. Margaret R. Miles, *Fullness of Life: Historical Foundations for a New Asceticism* (Philadelphia: Westminster, 1981): 10, 8; emphasis added.

Word was made flesh,' where the last term was, no doubt, chosen because of its specifically materialist associations. By the very nature of its central doctrine Christianity is committed to a belief in the ultimate significance of the historical process, and in the reality of matter and its place in the divine scheme."[75] This will mean that in Christian formation, more attention should be paid to responsibility for the outer world of the body and the community, including the material, economic, social, political, and historical world.

A second implication of a reversal of the traditional emphasis on the inner life over the outer is that the theme of the reign of God must become central again in Christian spirituality.[76] The reign of God is the fundamental theme of Jesus' mission — its breaking in and manifestation in Jesus' presence, healing, and teaching. To be a follower of Jesus means to repent and to open oneself to the presence of this reign, to look for and point to signs of the reign, to participate in this reign by manifesting its signs in active love of neighbor and the struggle for justice and peace.

The presence of the reign of God is a matter primarily of outward signs and actions rather than the progress and perfection of the inner life. The focus of the reign of God is primarily on public, communal, political, economic, and historical life rather than on private interior life. The traditional emphasis in Christian ascetical theology on interiority has led the Church in its mission to focus primarily on private, emotional, and family life to the exclusion of public, work, and political life. This should be reversed.[77]

A third implication of a reversal of the traditional focus on interiority is that there must be a primary emphasis on practice in Christian formation. The priority of practice in the Christian life has a long history. The Johannine Christ teaches that they who do the truth will know the truth.

---

75. William Temple, *Nature, Man and God* (London: Macmillan, 1934): 478. See also Colleen McDonnell, *Material Christianity: Religion and Popular Culture in America* (New Haven, CT: Yale University Press, 1995): 4.

76. For an elaboration of this point, see Jon Sobrino, *Spirituality of Liberation: Toward Political Holiness* (Maryknoll, NY: Orbis, 1988): chap. 7.

77. See Owen C. Thomas, "Parish Ministry: A Theologian's Perspective," *Sewanee Theological Review* 40:4 (1997): 444-56.

The Matthean Christ teaches that we will be judged on the basis of how we have responded to those in need. It has usually been a principle of Catholic theology that it is the practice of the Christian life that leads to the understanding of the Christian faith rather than the other way around.

The priority of practice is part of a general tendency today in a number of disciplines, including history, linguistics, literary criticism, sociology, and anthropology."[78] George Lindbeck has applied the priority of practice to the relation of inner and outer in religion. He argues that a religion, including Christianity, is like "a set of acquired skills. . . . Like a culture or a language, it is a communal phenomenon that shapes the subjectivities of individuals rather than being primarily a manifestation of those subjectivities. . . . In the interplay between 'inner' experience and 'external' religious and cultural factors, the latter can be viewed as the leading partners." This view "reverses the relation of the inner and the outer. Instead of deriving external features of a religion from inner experience, it is the inner experiences which are viewed as derivative"[79]

The priority of practice suggests that formation in the Christian life should focus on the practices of the outer life, such as public worship, the building up of the community, the service of those in need, and participation in the struggle for justice and peace, rather than on the disciplines of the inner life, such as silence, meditation, and contemplation. It is not that these traditional disciplines should be excluded but that they should take second place to communal and public practice.

If the argument of this chapter is valid, ascetical theologians face a major task of reformulating much of the theory and practice of Christian spirituality. This will involve an emphasis on the outer life as the major source of the inner life and, thus, a renewed stress on the body and communal and public life as well as a renewed focus on participation in the reign of God as the center of the

---

78. For a more extended discussion, see Owen C. Thomas, "On Stepping Twice into the Same Church: Essence, Development, and Pluralism," *Anglican Theological Review* 70, no. 4 (October 1988): esp. 299-302.

79. George A. Lindbeck, *The Nature of Doctrine: Religion and Theology in a Postliberal Age* (Philadelphia: Westminster; 1984): 33-4.

Christian life, including a renewed emphasis on moral and liturgical practice in Christian formation. Some of this work has already begun, but it has coexisted with a widespread focus on the inner life. Only renewed attention to this issue can bring to the theory and practice of Christian spirituality a new coherence.

CHAPTER 10

THOUGHT AND LIFE:
THE CASES OF HEIDEGGER AND TILLICH

In 1973 I was lecturing on Tillich's *Systematic Theology* at the Gregorian University in Rome. One day a student showed me a copy of *Time* magazine with a story about Hannah Tillich's new book *From Time to Time*. It recounted Tillich's infidelities, his exploitive relations with women, and his fascination with sadism and pornography. The student asked me how this would affect my assessment of Tillich's theology. It was a good question, an important and very complex question, and I have been thinking about it off and on ever since. It is most broadly the question of the relation of thought and moral life, and more specifically the relevance of the moral life of the thinker for the assessment of the thinker's work.

It has been common in the modern West especially since the Romantic movement to assume that the assessment of the works of artistic and scientific geniuses transcended philistine moral concerns. It has generally been assumed that the moral life of the artist, philosopher or scientist was entirely irrelevant to the assessment of the work. This view has been underscored by the New Critics who argued that biography was irrelevant even to the interpretation of a work, and by the postmodern critics who claim that we have no authors, only texts. One author has recently referred critically to the "biographical fallacy" which is defined as bringing to bear what a person did on what that person wrote.[1]

---

1. Page DuBois, "Subjected Bodies, Science, and The State: Francis Bacon, Torturer," in *Body Politics: Disease, Desire, and the Family*, ed. Michael Ryan and Avery Gordon (Boulder, CO: Westview Press, 1994): 188.

Many commentators have noted the muckraking tendency of recent biographies but have generally discounted the significance of what is revealed. One states, "Such unsavory stuff is predictable fare in recent biographies. But in the cases of, say, Frost, Plath, Jean Stafford, and, most recently, Philip Larkin, *immense talent proves a strong deodorant:* the petty human personality ends up second, appropriately, to the monumental work."[2]

Martin Amis criticizes Andrew Motion's biography of Philip Larkin that strongly highlights and criticizes his virulent racism. Amis comments, "None of this matters, because only the poems matter." He notes that Motion has retracted some in a recent column in the *Observer* in which he states that the "conflation of life and art" does not understand that "art exists at a crucial distance from its creator." This conflation "rests on the assumption that art is merely a convulsive expression of personality. Sometimes in its purest lyric moments, it may be. More generally, it is a suppression of personality . . . an adaptation, an enlargement."[3]

Also George Steiner in a review of Humphrey Carpenter's biography of Benjamin Britten asks, "Why should we have biographies of composers?," and considers the analogous cases of abstract painters and mathematicians. He concludes, "In both cases the relations that count, that can be made intelligible, are internal." He suggests, however, that among musicians there are some exceptions, such as Wagner, and agrees with Humphrey that "the case of Britten is one in which biographical knowledge is indispensable. . . . We simply cannot make sense of many of his works "without a dispassionate but closely informed awareness of Britten's homosexuality."[4] I note, however, that Humphrey's point refers to interpretation rather than assessment.

Robert Stewart in a recent review of the first volume of the Freud-Ferenczi correspondence states, "Surely there is more to be gained by taking as our starting point the separation of the *biographical* in the evolution of psychoanalysis from

---

2. Carol Neske in a review of a biography of Laura Riding, *New York Times Book Review*, November 28, 1993, p. 14. For a more extended analysis of this phenomenon, see Michiko Kakutani, "Biography Becomes a Blood Sport," *New York Times*, Friday, May 20, 1994, pp. C1, 24.

3. *New Yorker* 69:21 (July 12, 1993): 76.

4. *New Yorker* 69:20 (July 5, 1993): 86.

the system of thought itself . . . [Ferenczi's] works should be evaluated solely on their theoretical and clinical merits, and I am reminded here of Karl Popper's relevant remark that 'theories, and the conduct of their protagonists, belong to two entirely separate worlds."[5]

In the United States in recent decades the relation of the sexual behavior of politicians to their ability to carry out their responsibilities has become a major issue. But Anthony Lewis has stated, "As the record of great figures in history shows, the correlation between a politician's sexual fidelity and his or her contribution to mankind is zero."[6] Richard Rorty makes the same point in rejecting "the notion that learning about a philosopher's moral character helps one evaluate his philosophy. It does not, any more than our knowledge of Einstein's character helps us evaluate his physics. You can be a great, original, and profound artist or thinker, and also a complete bastard."[7]

The same has been true of the tradition of Western philosophy. In a study of Martin Heidegger and his relation to Nazism Tom Rockmore and Joseph Margolis state, "A persistent dogma of the philosophical tradition blocks the resolution of this inquiry: philosophy, it is said, is *in* but not *of* time. . . . The profound question Heidegger raises which we in turn must raise about Heidegger's own life and thought, the question of the relation between thought and time or between thought and context, cannot even be rightly posed in the grand tradition of philosophy that views itself ahistorically."[8] Although they include Plato in this assessment, they do not consider his thesis that moral discipline and virtue are necessary to the practice of philosophy.[9]

Now if there is a universal consensus that the life is irrelevant to the assessment of the thought, why is it that so many critics think they must make this point? Why does it even occur to us that the life might be relevant to the

---

5. *New York Times Book Review*, March 6, 1994, p. 23b.
6. *New York Times*, December 24, 1993, p. A27.
7. Richard Rorty, "Taking Philosophy Seriously," *New Republic* 198:15 (April 11, 1988): 32c.
8. *The Heidegger Case: On Philosophy and Politics*, ed. Tom Rockmore and Joseph Margolis (Philadelphia: Temple University Press, 1992): 3.
9. E. g., *Republic* 6, 746-51 (Jowett).

assessment of the thought? I believe that it derives from an obscure conviction about the intrinsic linkage between truth and goodness and about the value of the integrity of a human life. I think that we, at least in the West, have an ideal of the unity of life, of the integrity of life and thought which derives from the origins of the Western religious traditions in figures such as Moses and Jesus and from the origins of the Western philosophical tradition in figures such as Socrates and Marcus Aurelius. This came to a clear formulation in the medieval theory of the unity of the transcendentals, the true and the good.

Robert Bernasconi has explored the tradition of the nobility of the philosophical life from its beginnings in Greek philosophy. He claims that it is still widely prevalent today, although he believes that it is an illusion. As an example of its contemporary prevalence he refers to a quip attributed to Gilbert Ryle: "Heidegger. Can't be a good philosopher. Wasn't a good man."[10] Bernasconi's main point is that although Heidegger himself apparently affirmed this tradition, it was his life which has thoroughly undercut it. Bernasconi continues: "Heidegger's failings, which extend beyond the political and the moral to thinking itself, reflect not just on him, or on a school of philosophy, but on the very ideal of the Western philosophical tradition as a way of life. . . . Here is an end of philosophy, of philosophy's self-conception. . . . He enacted it in his own life and works by showing what for too long had gone unsuspected, that great thoughts, under the mask of nobility, can lead us astray."[11] Bernasconi does not pursue the obvious question about this apparent disjunction between the true and the good, about how thoughts can be great if they lead us astray.

In Christian history heterodoxy was often assumed to imply immorality, but I do not know of any cases in the history of Christian theology in which the moral life of the theologian was considered relevant to the assessment of the theology. In a related context, however, the eighteenth century pietists argued against the orthodox that if the theologian were not regenerate as evidenced in the

---

10. Robert Bernasconi, *Heidegger in Question: The Art of Existing* (Atlantic Highlands, NJ: Humanities Press, 1993): 57.
11. Ibid., p. 73.

experience of conversion, the theology could not, be true (*theologia irregeneratorum*). Although Plato's (and St. John's) point was made frequently that in order to know the good one must do the good,[12] I am unaware of any reverse arguments that since X did not do the good, X obviously cannot know the good (or the true).[13] I believe, however, that this has begun to change since the Holocaust. In 1963 on sabbatical leave in Basel I recall conversations with students from Germany who were discussing the degrees of *Braunheit* of various German theologians, an issue about which I was at that time largely unaware.

A couple of recent books have discussed the cases of the *braun* theologians, Paul Althaus, Friedrich Gogarten, Emmanuel Hirsch, and Gerhard Kittel, and their degrees of support for Hitler and the German Christian movement.[14] Althaus supported Hitler and the Nazis in 1933 but fell silent in 1937. The same applies to Gogarten who also joined the German Christian Movement in support of Hitler. Hirsch was a strong supporter of the Nazis from beginning to end, joined the German Christian movement, and never recanted. Kittel published many strongly anti-Semitic essays during the Nazi regime and also publicly supported it throughout his life. These books, however, do not explore the question of the relevance of the moral/political life for the assessment of the thought.

Nazism and the Holocaust have certainly become the occasion for the reassessment of Martin Heidegger. I would like to examine the case of Heidegger, since it has been explored the most thoroughly, then consider the case of Tillich, and finally explore theoretically the question of the relevance of the life to the assessment of the thought. The importance of the Heidegger case derives from the fact he is probably the most creative and influential philosopher of this

---

12. See, for example, *The First Theological Oration* of Gregory of Nazianzus.
13. See however, Maimonides: "A rabbi who does not walk along the good path, even though he be an extraordinary scholar and the entire nation is in need of him — [we may nonetheless] learn nothing from him until he returns to goodness." Quoted in *Tainted Greatness: Antisemitism and Cultural Heroes*, ed. Nancy A. Harrowitz (Philadelphia: Temple University Press, 1994): 281.
14. Robert P. Erickson, *Theologians Under Hitler: Gerhard Kittel, Paul Althaus, and Emmanuel Hirsch* (New Haven: Yale University Press, 1985); and Jack Forstman, *Christian Faith in Dark Times: Theological Conflicts in the Shadow of Hitler* (Louisville, KY: Westminster/John Knox, 1992).

212

century and certainly the one who has most deeply influenced Christian theology, witness Bultmann, Tillich, Rahner, Ott, and Macquarrie, among others.

The main facts about Heidegger's relation to Nazism have been fairly well known in Germany since the mid-forties, but they were not widely discussed outside of Germany. For example, in the collection of essays entitled *The Later Heidegger and Theology* and published in 1963 there is not one word about Heidegger's relation to Nazism. A year later a colloquium was held at Drew University on the relevance of Heidegger to theology. The opening address at the colloquium was an eloquent and powerful attack by Hans Jonas on Heidegger as a great danger to Christian theology because of "the profoundly pagan character of Heidegger's thought" which was manifested in his Nazism.[15] A report on the colloquium by Robert Funk mentioned Jonas' references to Heidegger's Nazism but noted that apart from some defenses of Heidegger, the attack was received with "striking indifference."[16]

This came to an abrupt end in 1987 with the publication of *Heidegger et le nazisme* in France by Victor Farias, a Chilean who was teaching in Berlin. Farias' book is a wholesale denunciation of Heidegger as a committed Nazi written in a journalistic style. It produced a wild debate in France, where Heidegger's influence has been the greatest, and also in Germany and the U. S. with a flood of articles, books and conferences.

What are the facts on which there is general agreement? First of all, Heidegger was a dues-paying member of the Nazi party from 1933 to 1945. Second, he made many strong affirmations of support for Hitler and Nazism. Third, he secretly denounced to the authorities many of his friends, colleagues, and students for their liberal democratic or pacifist views or their association with Jews. Fourth, he occasionally made it clear that he saw an essential connection between his thought and his support of Nazism. Fifth, he never recanted his views, although he tried to hide or change the record and frequently lied about it.

---

15. "Heidegger and Theology," in Hans Jonas, *The Phenomenon of Life: Toward a Philosophical Biology* (New York: Harper & Row, 1966): 248.
16. *Christian Century* 81:39 (September 23, 1964): 1175c.

Finally, he never commented on the Holocaust except to compare it to agricultural technology. It should be added that there is evidence that Heidegger soon realized that the Nazis were not going to fulfill his hopes for Germany and Western civilization. Yet he maintained his commitment to what can be called an ideal Nazism throughout his life.[17]

Some of these facts need to be fleshed out to give a clearer sense of Heidegger's involvement with Nazism. In his inaugural address as Rector of the University of Freiburg Heidegger celebrated the banishing of academic freedom and praised the "greatness and glory" of the Nazi revolution. Later the same year he persuaded Hitler to appoint him the Führer of the University of Freiburg as the first step in his goal of becoming the Führer of all German education and intellectual life. Then he proceeded to apply the Nazi "cleansing" laws to the student body. Already in 1929 he had written a letter denouncing what he called the "Jewification of the German Spirit," (*die Verjüdung des deutschen Geistes*). *Verjüdung* is a vulgar term which is not found in dictionaries but which is found in Hitler's *Mein Kampf*.[18] He told his students at Freiburg "Let not theories or 'ideas' be the rules of your being. The Führer himself and he alone is German reality and its law, today and for the future. . . . Heil Hitler." (This is a passage which Jonas quoted in his address.) In lectures in 1935 he defended "the inner truth and greatness of National Socialism." In 1953 he published these lectures in a book entitled *An Introduction to Metaphysics* and changed this phrase to "the inner truth and greatness of this movement (namely, the encounter between global technology and modern man)."[19] Then in a 1976 interview in *Der Spiegel* he denied that the text had been changed. Moreover, in the Heidegger archives at Marbach that page of the original handwritten manuscript is missing.[20]

---

17. For a brief summary of these facts see Thomas Sheehan, "Heidegger and the Nazis," *New York Review of Books* 35:10 (June 16, 1988): 38-47.

18. See Tom Rockmore, *On Heidegger's Philosophy and Nazism* (Berkeley: University of California Press, 1992): 111 and note 114.

19. Martin Heidegger, *Introduction to Metaphysics* (Garden City, NY: Doubleday, 1961): 166.

20. See Sheehan, Heidegger and the Nazis," and Jürgen Habermas, "Work and Weltanschauung: The Heidegger Controversy from a German Perspective," *Critical Inquiry* (Winter, 1989): 431-56.

Finally, in a 1998 biography of Heidegger, Rüdiger Safranski offers further details which underscore Heidegger's early, passionate, and philosophical commitment to Hitler and National Socialism. He became "intoxicated" by Nazism and "bewitched" by Hitler." The Nazi revolution became for him a "*Dasein*-controlling event, one that would penetrate his philosophy to the core." He saw the Nazi seizure of power as "a new act in the history of Being, the beginning of a new epoch."[21]

Now what are we to make of all this? Should Heidegger's relation to Nazism affect: our assessment of his philosophy? The various responses which have been made to this question lie on a spectrum from the Heidegger supporters who argue that his biography is irrelevant to the assessment of his thought to the Heidegger critics who claim that it is fully relevant and decisive.

A common position, which is close to the latter view and is represented by Jürgen Habermas, Theodor Adorno, and Thomas Sheehan, holds that in Sheehan's words, "Heidegger's engagement with Nazism was a public enactment of some of his deepest, and most questionable philosophical convictions."[22] Karl Löwith reported that when he suggested to Heidegger in 1936 that his support of Nazism seemed to come from the very essence of his philosophy, "Heidegger agreed with me without reservations and spelled out for me that his concept of 'historicity' was the basis of his political 'engagement.'"[23] In 1959, however, in a conversation with Heinrich Petzet Heidegger denied that his life was relevant to his thought.[24] Sheehan concludes his essay by stating that in order to sift Heidegger's works for what might still be of value, "One must read his works . . . with strict attention to the political movement with which Heidegger chose to link his ideas."[25]

Habermas' view of this issue is more complex. On the one hand, he speaks of the "autonomy of thought," "the legitimate distinction between person

---

21. Rüdiger Safranski, *Martin Heidegger: Between Good and Evil* (Cambridge, MA: Harvard University Press, 1998): 227-8, 231-2.

22. Sheehan, "Heidegger and the Nazis," p. 38.

23. Ibid.

24. See Rockmore and Margolis, *The Heidegger Case*, p. 19.

25. Sheehan, "Heidegger and the Nazis," p. 47.

and work," and argues that Heidegger's political conduct "cannot and should not serve the purpose of a global depreciation of his thought," that "Heidegger's work has long since detached itself from his person," that "it is simply foolish to think that the substance of the work could be discredited, more than five decades later, by political assessments of Heidegger's fascist commitments," that "one cannot bring the truth-content of a philosophy into discredit by associating it with something external to it," and that "Heidegger's philosophical work owes its autonomy, as does every such work, to the strength of its arguments."[26]

On the other hand, Habermas does not "deny all internal connection between philosophical works and the biographical contexts from which they come," and he states that "we learn from Heidegger to take into account the internal relations that exist between his political engagement and the changes in his attitude toward fascism, on the one hand, and the arguments of his critique of reason, which was also politically motivated, on the other."[27]

Habermas argues that the structure of *Being and Time* (1927) made it possible for ideological motifs to enter into Heidegger's thinking beginning in 1929. These motifs were typical of the German mandarins of the twenties and included an elitist self-understanding, idolatry of the mother tongue, the complete absence of sociological approaches, and more specifically the "pathos of heroic nihilism" typical of the Young Conservatives, such as Spengler, the Jüngers and Schmitt. These motifs combined with the influence of Hölderlin and Nietzsche paved the way for neopagan themes all interpreted by the new theory of the history of Being and led to Heidegger's deep attachment to National Socialism.[28]

Rockmore and Margolis pursue another version of this general position. We have noted their judgment that "philosophy is notoriously desultory in its discussion of the issues raised" by the Heidegger case. They trace this theme in Plato, Aristotle, Descartes, Leibniz, Kant and Husserl. They note that this "atemporal vision" has been the main cause of the emergence of all the

---

26. Habermas, "Work and Weltanschauung," pp. 431, 433-6, 455.
27. Ibid., pp. 433, 455.
28. Ibid., pp. 438-40.

historicisms and contextualisms of the last two and a half centuries which have been aimed at various foundationalisms, claims of epistemological privilege, and presumptions of invariant knowledge.[29]

They claim that Heidegger has been the major twentieth century figure in the reaction against this atemporal vision. His historicizing of being requires that his thought be understood in relation to the life context in which it emerged. Heidegger made this explicit in a letter to Karl Löwith in 1921: "I work concretely and factically out of my own 'I am,' out of my intellectual and wholly factic origin, milieu, life-contexts, and whatever is available to me from these as a vital experience in which I live."[30]

The French debate about Heidegger has been much more widespread and intense than anywhere else because of his pervasive influence on French philosophy, literary criticism, and social thought. Tom Rockmore summarizes the various stages of this debate. The first phase that began in1946 was calm and scholarly. The second that began in 1948 became increasingly heated as Heidegger's philosophy as well as his personal reputation were at risk. The third phase opened with the publication of Farias' book in 1987 and made the previous stages seem mild by comparison. Sheehan puts it this way in a recent review essay: "In 1987 Victor Farias' *Heidegger et le nazisme* dropped like a bomb on the quiet chapel where Heidegger's disciples were gathered, and blew it to bits."[31] There was a huge outpouring of essays, and in six months six book-length studies appeared.

Rockmore describes the two main French readings of Heidegger's Nazism as the necessitarian and the contingentist. The necessitarians argue that Heidegger's involvement in Nazism was permanent, morally reprehensible, and a necessary consequence of his philosophical position. The contingentists claim that it was temporary and regrettable but unmotivated by his basic philosophy.[32]

---

29. Rockmore and Margolis, *The Heidegger Case*, p. 3.
30. Ibid., p. 24.
31. Thomas Sheehan, A Normal Nazi," *New York Review of Books* 40:1&2 (January 14, 1993): 30a.
32. Rockmore and Margolis, *The Heidegger Case*, pp. 375-7.

Joseph Margolis in the concluding essay in their volume describes the central issue in the Heidegger debate as the relation between philosophy and politics. He claims that there is a wide consensus on the issue but not on the solution. The consensus on the linking of philosophy and politics includes the denial of the disjunction of theoretical and practical reasoning, the denial of the disjunction of the discovery of truth and the exercise of power, and the denial of the possibility of eliminating the political structure of science and philosophy. Margolis notes the irony of the fact that Heidegger is the most influential source of this consensus today, namely, that "all conceptual work is historically perspectived, horizoned, interested, prejudiced, contexted, resourceful, and transient."[33] Margolis claims that this puts us in a serious bind. If we are all infected by these Heideggerian themes, then how can we possibly disengage what is conceptually acceptable in Heidegger from what we must reject as his philosophical Nazism? So the supreme problem that Heidegger poses is how to shape a coherent and plausible view of theoretical and practical reason under the condition of a radical historicity.

Margolis states that there are three contemporary and unsatisfactory solutions to this problem. First, there is what he calls archism which claims that reason can discern the invariant principles of thought and action in a way which escapes the flux of history (Habermas, Gadamer, MacIntyre). Second, there is a reactivism or opportunism which is at first anarchic and then finally liberal or humane (Foucault, Lyotard). Finally, there is a quietism which is the "principled fatigue" of those who can only fall back to the "local" (Rorty).[34]

He concludes, however, that "they are all conceptual and political failures. No one has a convincing reconciliation of philosophy and politics to offer." But "we cannot comprehend [this issue] *in the way we do now* without Heidegger's magisterial influence." Thus, "the explication of the legitimated relationship

---

33. Ibid., p. 409.
34. Ibid., pp. 417f.

218

between philosophy and politics is in a way the supreme philosophical puzzle of our age."[35]

Tom. Rockmore in a separate study has carried the analysis somewhat further. He funds six main lines of analysis of the relation of Heidegger's philosophy and his Nazism. First, the view that everything that Heidegger ever did or said is Nazi to the core (Adomo). Second, the denial of the historical reality of Nazism (Beaufret). Third, Heidegger is not responsible for the political consequences of Nazism which could not be foreseen (Fedier). Fourth, Heidegger's Nazism was an insignificant moment in his life and unrelated to his thought (Habermas, Rorty). Fifth, Heidegger's early thought led to Nazism, but his later thought led away from it (Derrida, Lacoue-Labarthe). And sixth, Heidegger's philosophical thought and his Nazism are inseparable (Löwith, Bourdieu, Wolin, et al.).[36]

Mention of Derrida reminds one of his recent successful attempt through lawsuits to suppress a book by Richard Wolin because of its criticism of Heidegger and Derrida's defense of him. This is the latest battle in what Sheehan calls the "Heidegger wars."[37]

Now in addition to the six views mentioned by Rockmore we have that of Ernst Nolte, the conservative German historian, in his recent biography of Heidegger. Sheehan notes that Nolte's book "reads like a company biography of Henry Ford."[38] Nolte argues that Heidegger's decision to support Hitler was not only the result of Heidegger's philosophy but was also clearly the right decision in the face of communism, liberalism, and what he calls pragmatic pluralism. Nolte also absolves Heidegger of the charge of anti-Semitism. He defends an extremely anti-Semitic seventeenth century Catholic priest from Heidegger's home town whom Heidegger always admired, and adds that "to require that Christianity should not be 'anti-Semitic' is the same as demanding that

---

35. Ibid., pp. 418-9.
36. Rockmore, On Heidegger's Nazism, pp. 282f.
37. Sheehan, "A Normal Nazi," p. 30.
38. Ibid., p. 33a.

Christianity should not have come into existence."[39] Sheehan comments, "With friends like Nolte, Heidegger may not need enemies."[40]

Now back to Rockmore who affirms the sixth view mentioned which holds that Heidegger's philosophical thought and his Nazism are inseparable. He calls this the organic analysis. It asserts an intrinsic and essential link between Heidegger's philosophy, especially his concept of being, and his Nazism. "Heidegger's effort to awaken the long-forgotten question of Being leads seamlessly to Nazism."[41] This is a striking way to put it and I will return to it later. Other authors us the term "integral." For example, Joseph Polak states, "Surely, if anti-Semitism is integral to his works, then those works are rooted in falsehood and evil. If it is not integral, then why can we not, together with the deconstructionists, separate the writings from the man?"[42]

As to his conclusions about the relation of thought and action, however, Rockmore is rather ambivalent. On the one hand, he asserts that Heidegger's philosophy led directly to his Nazism, and states, "Theory and practice are never wholly separate and hence cannot be disjoined. At least implicitly, practice of any kind always reflects a theoretical perspective. In all cases, action follows from, and is on occasion justified by, an attitude, a reason, an intention, an aim, or even a passion."[43]

On the other hand, he agrees with Margolis that the relation between philosophy and action is obscure. "As part of our inability to understand the relation between thought and action, we do not comprehend the link between Heidegger the man and Heidegger the thinker. Any effort to elucidate this connection is forced to develop its own way of going about things, since there is no well-established procedure or even a firm idea of what that would look like."[44]

He does conclude, however, that philosophy has no advantage in the human search for the true and the good. "Despite the flattering image of their

---

39. Ibid., p. 33c.
40. Ibid., p. 32a.
41. Rockmore, *On Heidegger's Nazism*, p. 287.
42. Joseph Polak in *Tainted Greatness*, ed. Nancy A. Harrowitz, p. 278.
43. Rockmore, *On Heidegger's Nazism*, p. 287.
44. Ibid., p. 299.

discipline which philosophers have long presented, it is not in itself a source of perfect knowledge, nor is it intrinsically linked to virtue. It is merely one way among others, with no particular cognitive privilege of any obvious kind, to contribute to the truth and perhaps to serve the good."[45]

Rockmore along with other philosophers has seen a relation between Heidegger's theory of Being and his commitment to Nazism, but none of them refers to what I believe is the first critique of Heidegger on this point by Hans Jonas. In the lecture and essay mentioned earlier Jonas attacks the "profoundly pagan" character of Heidegger's thought which is manifest in his idea of historical fate, his divinizing of the world, and his gnostic speculations, all based on his theory of the history of Being. Jonas' purpose is to warn theologians against the use of Heidegger.

A similar line is taken in a critique of Heidegger by John Caputo. In his book *Demythologizing Heidegger* Caputo attempts the "disrupting of the myth of Being with the myth of justice."[46] He argues that in *Being and Time* Heidegger's main sources are Aristotle and the Christian tradition, although the biblical concept of "heart" is omitted. In the thirties, however, Heidegger began to exclude the Christian sources and to develop a myth of the Great Beginning of the history of Being among the Greeks to which the Germans are the sole heirs. This developed into a "pagan mythic world of mundane gods and divinized cosmic powers" which led him into Nazism. To this Caputo, borrowing a term from Joyce via Derrida, wants to oppose the "jewgreek myth of justice."[47]

What can we conclude from the case of Heidegger about our question concerning the relevance of the moral/political life of the thinker for the assessment of the thought? Certain clear-cut positions have emerged. First, there is the traditional view which has been called contingentist or archism which holds that the life of the thinker is not relevant to the assessment of the thought. Then there is the contemporary view, the necessitarian, that since the moral/political

---

45. Ibid., p. 293.
46. John D. Caputo, *Demythologizing Heidegger* (Bloomington, IN: Indiana University Press, 1993): 3.
47. Ibid., pp. 181, 6.

life of the thinker flows from the thought, it is directly relevant if not decisive for the assessment of the thought. There are also approaches that fall between these views.

Now let us turn to Tillich. Here the focus is not on public politics but rather on what might be called private politics, namely, Tillich's relations with women. In the patriarchal academy this shift will be greeted with ridicule and will be seen as a move from the momentous to the trivial. If this is your response, I suggest that you consult your women colleagues, the tenured ones, that is, if you have any, about the cultural connections between racism, sexism, and oppression.

Hannah Tillich's book *From Time to Time* is the place to begin. The picture we get here is of Tillich as a compulsive womanizer, adulterer, and exploiter of innumerable women, one who lavished love, time, attention, letters, and poems on other women but not on his wife. He demanded secrecy from his women friends for fear that his reputation might be ruined. The exploitation was in the use of the energy Tillich needed and received from the women to carry on his work, energy which he transmuted into his ideas. Added to this was his fascination with sadism and pornography that Hannah describes as "the obscene signs of the real life that he had transformed into the gold of abstraction — King Midas of the spirit."[48]

All this devastated Hannah and filled her with suffering, rage, and despair. "I was nothing but a piece of bleeding, tortured womanhood seeking my peace from the seesaw of suffering and hate." "Our marriage had been broken into small pieces by the relentless assault of the many women."[49] She wanted to get a divorce, but Tillich implored her not to, because again he said that it would ruin his reputation. It should be added that in reaction to Tillich's infidelities Hannah also had affairs with men and women. Finally, toward the end of his life they achieved a measure of peace and harmony together.

Needless to say Hannah's book produced much fluttering in the Tillichean dovecotes. John Carey summarized his view of the discussion some years later.

---

48. Hannah Tillich, *From Time to Time* (New York: Stein and Day, 1973): 241.
49. Ibid., pp 240-1.

222

"I remain convinced that no good has come to anyone as a result of Hannah Tillich's angry book."[50]   When Rollo May failed to persuade Hannah not to publish her book, he quickly published his own book the same year in order to give a different picture. He grants that "Paulus' own emotional and ontological needs were great, and he demanded from women . . . that they meet these needs."[51]   May states that there occurred what he calls sensual seduction of other women but implies that there was no adultery. He interprets Tillich's demands for secrecy about his erotic life as deriving from his relation to his mother rather than from concern about his reputation. He interprets Tillich's psychological withdrawal from Hannah as required by the necessary autonomy for his work.

May does grant that "a truly daimonic [demonic?] element was involved in his attitudes and behavior toward women. . . . We know that when people worship other human beings there must be a balancing negation. . . . If a person worships women, he cannot help sometimes also destroying them. The feelings of need for revenge are present in Paulus . . . He could give [women] individuality but he could also heap them into a nameless mass. He could distinguish them and also extinguish them."[52]   Also "with women he could not reach in other ways, there came out in Paulus' behavior a sadistic tendency. . . . His sadism was a desperate attempt to reach someone deeply."[53]

Finally, however, May tends to let Tillich off the hook. He concludes that sexual libido "did not figure predominantly in his aims. . . . The sexual urge . . . was in the service of another aim which I call, in its strict sense, eros. . . . His relationships were always a pull toward a higher state."[54]   May reports that Tillich in a letter asks one of his women friends, "Was my erotic life a failure or was it a daring way of opening up new human possibilities?" May states, "I have no

50. John J. Carey, "Response to Alexander C. Irwin's *Eros Toward the World, Papers from the Annual Meeting of the North American Paul Tillich Society*, San Francisco, CA, November, 1992 (Charlottesville: Department of Religious Studies, University of Virginia, 1993): 11.
51. Rollo May, *Paulus: Reminiscences of a Friendship* (New York: Harper & Row, 1973): 53.
52. Ibid., p. 60f.
53. Ibid., p. 62f.
54. Ibid., p. 52.

hesitation in stating my own conclusion: it was clearly the latter."[55] To others, however, it may sound like a self-serving rhetorical question fully expecting a positive answer.

Ann Belford Ulanov offers a Jungian interpretation of Tillich's erotic life. Tillich's "exaggerated need" for women showed his deep need for connection with being. "Tillich was clearly fed by the women who carried his own feminine side. Their receptions of being fed his abstract thought. He used women to make explicit his intuitions and attractions to being."[56]

Ulanov wonders, Why so many women? "His terror of getting trapped was always apparent in his relations with women. Perhaps that accounts for the number. He was involved each time but never permanently. He played with being in a joyous and undifferentiated way without getting pinned down in one relationship."[57] But the question persists. Ulanov continues: "From a woman's point of view, the question looms, why so many women? For it is certainly more risky and dangerous, to go down deep into the depths with one person. Then one no longer avoids the dread of mortality, symbolized in the fear of fully exhausting relationship with one person. I think Tillich defended against that threat by sheer multiplication of the number of the relationships."[58]

Ulanov, however, ends on a positive note and stresses Tillich's heroic courage and faith in facing his demons. "Tillich nonetheless went courageously into his fear of being and his accompanying fear of the devouring feminine. He risked. He went with openness. He suffered his demons and the breaking of conventions."[59] And what of the women? They "felt affirmed by Tillich, felt they were taken seriously." They felt "overwhelming gratitude and love."[60]

In their biography the Paucks give a different picture. They note that many women were offended by Tillich's advances, "hurt by his power, indeed

---

55. Ibid., p. 52.
56. Ann Belford Ulanov, "Between Anxiety and Faith: The Role of the Feminine in Tillich's Theological Thought," in *Paul Tillich on Creativity*, ed. Jacquelyn Ann K. Kegley (Lanham, MD: University Press of America, 1989): 141.
57. Ibid., p. 138.
58. Ibid., p. 143.
59. Ibid., p. 144.
60. Ibid., p. 141f.

overwhelmed by it."[61] The Paucks also make clear Tillich's attitude toward love and marriage. He held that a life vow was impossible and that love and marriage are incompatible. "Fulfilled love is, at the same time, extreme happiness and the end of happiness. The separation is overcome. But without the separation there is no love and no life."[62] (This verges on the myth of romantic love as explicated by Denis de Rougemont in his book *Love in the Western World*.) The Paucks also note that Tillich's relations with women caused him great feelings of guilt, in relation both to the women and to the moral code. They conclude that his obsessive erotic compulsion became a "new law" for him, and that Tillich himself concluded that love was tragic and marriage sad.[63]

In a 1985 biography of Reinhold Niebuhr, Richard Fox writing about the relation of Niebuhr and Tillich gives the following summary of Tillich's erotic life based on interviews with various people including the Paucks: "Tillich had for years been engaged in a succession of sexual escapades. He was not just unfaithful to his wife, Hannah; he was exuberantly, compulsively promiscuous. Niebuhr once sent one of his female students to see Tillich during his office hours. He welcomed her warmly, closed the door, and began fondling her. She reported the episode to Niebuhr who never forgave Tillich."[64] I have heard from a person in a position to know that Tillich's philandering "destroyed some marriages." Seward Hiltner suggests that proposals at the University of Chicago to appoint Tillich to the faculty in the forties were rejected because of his relations with women.[65]

Finally, we have the view of Donald MacKinnon, who argues that "a thinker's intellectual achievement must be judged damaged by grave moral faults in the man." He concludes that "deep corruption," "fraud," and "hypocrisy"

---

61. Wilhelm and Marion Pauck, *Paul Tillich: His Life and Thought, Volume 1: Life* (New York: Harper & Row, 1976): 89.

62. Ibid., p. 88; quoting from Paul Tillich, *Love, Power, and Justice* (New York: Oxford University Press, 1954): 27.

63. Ibid., p. 92.

64. Richard Wightman Fox, *Reinhold Niebuhr: A Biography* (New York: Pantheon Books, 1985): 257.

65. Raymond J. Lawrence, Jr., *The Poisoning of Eros: Sexual Values in Conflict* (New York: Augustine Moore Press, 1989): 227.

"inevitably infect the texture of [Tillich' s] oeuvre."[66] However, no theoretical basis is given for this judgment other than some references to Plato's *Republic*.

Tillich himself offered perhaps unknowingly a theological interpretation of his erotic life. In his Systematic Theology he states that the three marks of estrangement are unbelief, concupiscence, and hubris. Tillich was a living example of concupiscence, which he defines as "the unlimited desire to draw the whole of reality into one's self."[67] This is perfectly illustrated in his delighted cry at a fancy-dress ball that Berlin represented for him "the freedom of '10,000 women's legs.'"[68]

So far as I know, apart from MacKinnon, only one of the commentators on Tillich's erotic life has asserted its relevance to the assessment of his thought, namely, Alexander Irwin in his book *Eros Toward the World: Paul Tillich and the Theology of the Erotic*. In this book Irwin explores the place of the erotic in Tillich's thought and compares it with feminist and womanist approaches to the erotic. He also devotes a chapter to Tillich's erotic life and it implications for his thought.

In this chapter, however, Irwin is not at all clear about the nature of the relevance of Tillich's erotic life to the assessment of his thought. He states that Tillich's erotic life cannot be ignored or avoided in the attempt to evaluate his theory of the erotic, but he does not explain why this is so. Then he notes that the relationship between thought and life is complex, and that searching for correlations is a "delicate and uncertain enterprise," but he does not explore this complexity.[69]

Next Irwin points out that a knowledge of Tillich's erotic life is important for grasping, understanding, appropriating, and interpreting Tillich's theory of the

---

66. Donald MacKinnon, *Explorations in Theology*, 5 (London: SCM Press, 1979): 130, 134.
67. Tillich, *Systematic Theology*, 3 vols. (Chicago: University of Chicago Press, 1951-63): 2:52.
68. Hannah Tillich, *From Time to Time*, p. 115.
69. Alexander Irwin, *Eros Toward the World: Paul Tillich and the Theology of the Erotic* (Minneapolis: Fortress Press, 1991): 103, see pp. 100f.

erotic.[70] He states that Tillich's erotic life may "reinforce certain aspects of the theologian's theories about eros, and point to places where those theories are highly problematic" or "seriously flawed."[71] He concludes that Tillich's moral failure in relation to his wife "points to grave inadequacies in his understanding of erotic dynamics" and "points to a rupture in the theologian's intellectual vision of the erotic," namely, between erotic power and just action.[72]

Thus, the record of Tillich's erotic life "confirms important aspects of his theoretical understanding of eros as a life-affirming creative force," yet it also indicates "the destructive incompleteness of this understanding."[73] "The failure of justice in Tillich's erotic life shows clearly the need to move beyond the limited concept of the erotic that he was able to shape."[74] Irwin concludes that "the conduct of Tillich's personal life shows that his way of constructing connections between life-affirming eros and just action in relationships was destructively flawed."[75] It should be noted, however, that in an earlier section Irwin has made clear the centrality of justice in Tillich's ethics. "Tillich points convincingly to the need to correlate justice and right action with the dynamics of human passion."[76]

The strongest language that Irwin employs in regard to the relevance of Tillich's life to the assessment of his thought is "assess," "evaluate," "reinforce," and "confirm." Then there is the weaker language of "indicates" and "points to." But there is no explanation of the rationale for this relevance, the theory behind these assertions. Would he have been able to criticize Tillich's theory of the erotic without any knowledge of his life? His treatment of feminist and womanist thought implies that he would have been able to do this. Or did the record of Tillich's erotic life draw Irwin's attention to potential problems in the theory that he then found confirmed in the writings? Finally, is the relevance of Tillich's

---

70. Ibid., pp. 101, 103-4, 115.
71. Ibid., pp. 100, 104.
72. Ibid., pp. 115, 118.
73. Ibid., p. 119.
74. Ibid., p. 120.
75. Ibid., p. 144; see also p. 147.
76. Ibid., p. 68; see also pp. 64-6.

erotic life limited to the assessment of his theory of the erotic or does it extend beyond that to other areas of his thought?

Furthermore, Irwin does not consider the possibility that Tillich was simply unable or unwilling to live up to the moral implications of his theory of the erotic. This possibility is certainly intelligible and coherent with Tillich's concept of estrangement and sin, since he stood squarely in the Pauline, Augustinian, Lutheran tradition of the corruption of the will. It is also suggested by the testimony to Tillich's strong sense of guilt about his erotic life.

Finally, if Irwin is correct that flaws in Tillich's moral life point to correlative flaws in his theory of the erotic, why should it not be concluded that Tillich's moral life is coherent with his theory of the erotic? This is the conclusion of John Carey and Raymond Lawrence.[77] This raises again the question that arose in connection with Heidegger. In assessing the moral life of a thinker, whose moral perspective is assumed, that of the assessor or that of the thinker? Irwin is clearly employing his own moral perspective in judging Tillich's moral life.

In summary, although Irwin's work on this issue is an important beginning, it does not indicate the theoretical basis of his argument or move toward the development of a theory of the relevance of the life for the assessment of the thought.

What is clear is that apparently no one has approached this issue formally, systematically, or theoretically. The one theoretical question that has been explored at length in all the debates about the new historicisms and contextualisms is whether or not reason or conceptual thought can transcend its personal, social, cultural, historical context. The implication is that if it can, then the moral/political life of the thinker may not be relevant to the assessment or perhaps even the interpretation of the thought, and vice versa. But it is not at all clear that either of these implications follows. Furthermore, if thought can

---

77. John J. Carey, "Life on the Boundary: The Paradoxical Models of Tillich and Pike," *Duke Divinity School Review* 42:3 (Fall, 1977): 160; Lawrence, *The Poisoning of Eros*, p. 226.

transcend context, can it do so always, sometimes, or rarely? And how can we know when and in what instances?

Furthermore, the two main opposing views on Heidegger and Tillich raise important theoretical questions that have not been explored. In regard to the contemporary view that the moral/political life is directly relevant to the assessment of the thought, what is the theoretical basis of this claim? Is it based on the necessitarian thesis that the moral/political implications of the thought are directly manifest in the life of the thinker? Habermas notes that in his critical report to the denazification committee investigating Heidegger in 1945 Karl Jaspers was "guided by the strict maxim that whatever truth a philosophical doctrine contains must be mirrored in the mentality and lifestyle of the philosopher."[78] But this assumes, does it not, that the thinker's life is perfectly coherent, that the thought and the life form an integrated unity. Is this often, sometimes, or ever the case? And again how can we know? In a post-Freudian age we must ask what psychology is implied by such a thesis. Does it imply a psyche in which the unconscious has become entirely conscious, for example? A more moderate version of the contemporary view is that the moral/political life of the thinker may alert us to problems in the thought that we might otherwise overlook. But this is a quite attenuated sense of the idea that the life is relevant to the assessment of the thought, and we are concerned with a stronger sense.

Another version of the necessitarian thesis is Rockmore's assertion that Heidegger's theory of being "leads seamlessly to Nazism."[79] This sounds like strict logical entailment between metaphysical beliefs and not only ethics but also conduct. This, however, is a highly debatable claim and would be very difficult to sustain.

In a 1992 study Kathryn Tanner explores the question of the relation between beliefs and practices and comes to a quite different conclusion.

> There is a logical gap between beliefs, on the one hand, and the actions and attitudes with which they are conjoined, on the other. . . .

---

78. Habermas, "Work and Weltanschauung," p. 433.
79. See note 41.

First, no specific course of action or attitude is entailed by beliefs about what is the case. . . . Second, no single account of what is the case is a necessary presupposition for a particular attitude or action. One cannot deduce, therefore, any particular belief as a logical presupposition for a given form of action or attitude. Specific beliefs will be able to rule our or preclude certain forms of attitude or action. The logical relation by which a belief suggests, positively, the propriety of certain attitudes and actions is not, however, of this strict sort. It is not one of logical necessity but one of mere consistence or compatibility.[80]

Tanner goes on to develop a theory about how this logical gap is filled. Using a sociocultural approach she argues that four general kinds of factors fill this gap between beliefs and actions: the interpretation of the meaning of the belief, other beliefs with which it is combined, the life situation of the one affirming the beliefs, and the scope of application or reference of the belief.[81] Tanner elaborates this theoretical perspective in specific examples from the history of Christian thought.

In contemporary thought the ideas of the unity of thought, the unity of the person, and the unity of thought, person, and conduct have been sharply challenged especially by the deconstructionists and those influenced by them. In the discussion of his paper presented in Berkeley in 1989 Hans Sluga describes the doctrine of the unity of thought as "a deeply philosophical and pervasive doctrine that has dominated Western thought for so long."[82] He is, however, dubious even about logical consequence, about any proposition following from any other. He argues that there is no possible logical connection between or inference from speculative to political philosophy or between political philosophy and concrete political judgments, since they involve different discourses.

Furthermore, according to Sluga there is no logical connection between beliefs and actions. His distrust of the concepts of the unity of the person and the unity of thought, knowledge, and belief leads him to "see both persons and belief

---

80. Kathryn Tanner, *The Politics of God: Christian Theologies and Social Justice* (Minneapolis: Fortress Press, 1992): 17f.

81. Ibid., pp. 19-22.

82. Hans Sluga, *The Break: Habermas, Heidegger, and the Nazis* (San Anselmo, CA: Center for Hermeneutical Studies, 1992): 30f.

systems as being disrupted, as involving breaks and discontinuities at all points."[83]   Following Foucault he wants to explore the relations between philosophical and political discourses by means of mediating discourses or what he calls metadiscourses.

In a later work, however, Sluga comes to a skeptical conclusion about such an enterprise. He analyzes the complex relations between philosophy and politics in Germany from 1918 to 1945 in terms of the notions of crisis, nation, leadership, and order, focusing on Heidegger.   He rejects the views of the Marxists and Pierre Bourdieu that reduce philosophy to the material conditions of the lives of the philosophers. He also rejects the opposite type of reductionism by idealist philosophers. Finally, he rejects the view of Hannah Arendt that there is an unbridgeable gulf between philosophy and politics. But he is finally skeptical about the possibility of relating philosophy and politics, of relating thought and life. "One begins to suspect that no theoretical framework would ever account for the tangle of facts that has concerned us. This suggests a skeptical conclusion. It is that the relation between philosophy and politics cannot be described once and for all by means of any grand scheme, that their relation is intrinsically historical and understandable only in its narrative uniqueness."[84]

This is a radical departure from the traditional view at least of the unity of thought. Paul Tillich, for example, standing in the Platonic and idealist traditions and speaking of theology and implicitly philosophy, states, "In each fragment a system is implied. . . . A fragment is an implicit system; a system is an explicit fragment."[85]   In regard to ethics and implicitly political philosophy he asserts, "The ethical element is a necessary — and often predominant — element in every theological statement."[86]   It is clear that the questions about the unity of the person, the unity of thought, and the unity of metaphysics, ethics, political philosophy and conduct are critical for this investigation.

---

83. Ibid., p. 26.
84. Hans Sluga, *Heidegger's Crisis: Philosophy and Politics in Nazi Germany* (Cambridge: Harvard University Press, 1993): 253.
85. Paul Tillich, *Systematic Theology*, 1:58.
86. Ibid., p. 31.

Another question which must be raised at this point is the possible anachronism in the assessment of the moral/political life of a thinker. Our sensitivity to particular moral issues varies with culture, race, class, sex, and time. Can our contemporary context-specific moral principles and convictions be validly applied to the moral/political life of a thinker in a quite different time and culture? If not, what is the alternative? Put differently, what moral community is it whose norms should be used in the assessment of the moral/political life of Heidegger or Tillich? That of the early twentieth century nationalistic conservative Catholics of Messkirch? That of academic bohemian Weimar Berlin? Or that of late twentieth century mainline Protestantism or Judaism? The complexity of this question has been explored by Steven Beller in a study of the anti-Semitism of Herzl and Wagner.[87]

There would seem to be a universal consensus today (with the exception of the Neo-Nazis, Holocaust deniers, and so forth) that Nazism and the Holocaust are the greatest evils of our time. But on the question of the subordination and exploitation of women, although there has been a major change in the last three decades at least in some cultural areas, there is much less of a consensus.

As far as I know, no one has approached this issue systematically. I have noted above Margolis' comment: "Any effort to elucidate this connection [between thought and action] is forced to develop its own way of going about things." I believe that we must begin with a thesis that has been fundamental to the Western tradition of philosophy and theology, namely the identity or mutual coinherence of the true and the good.[88] Ellen Chary has put it this way: "In the thought world of ancient Greece that was inherited by the Church Fathers, truth and goodness coincided. For both Clement of Alexandria and Origen, the good that Christianity brought in its wake testified to its truth. For St. Augustine, to

---

87. See Steven Beller, "Herzl, Wagner, and the Ironies of 'True Emancipation,'" in Nancy A. Harrowitz, ed., *Tainted Greatness,* ch. 7.
88. See Plato, *Phil* 64f; *Rep* 6, 505, et passim; John 1:1-18, 14:6, et passim; Thomas Aquinas, *S. T.,* I, Q.6, 16, a. 4, 5, et passim.

232

increase in the knowledge of God is to increase in goodness and virtue; both of these were embodied in Christian salvation."[89]

Theologically this means that God is the ultimate truth and the ultimate good, in traditional terms the unity of the two transcendentals, truth and goodness. Humanly speaking this means that to know God is the ultimate truth and to love and obey God is the ultimate good.[90] Rockmore touches on this in his discussion of the French debate about Heidegger. He writes:

> According to [the traditional] view, philosophy is the source of reason in the highest sense, productive of truth, intrinsically linked to goodness. Yet Heidegger failed to come to grips with Nazism, the main instance of evil in our time — eminent philosopher though he was. His own thought led him to Nazism. If the true is the good and Nazism is evil, then by implication Nazism is also false, certainly false as a political option. Judged by that standard, Heidegger's thought is neither useful nor true. The result is a paradox, for how can a great philosopher be a proponent of Nazism? Unless we simply overlook Nazism, turn away from one of the central political problems of our epoch, it is impossible to hold that great philosophy preserves the link between truth and goodness and to describe Heidegger as a great philosopher. We cannot ignore the puzzle.[91]

I will return to this puzzle shortly.

Now what are the elements whose relations we are exploring? They are (1) the true, (2) the good, (3) thought, that is, the thinker's conscious philosophy or theology and ethics, (4) functional factors, that is, the thinker's conscious and unconscious convictions, desires, and drives that are the sources of conduct, and (5) conduct, that is, the thinker's statements and moral and political actions.

Now it is clear that a great deal could be and needs to be said about the meaning of the true and the good, terms which have been the main fields of

---

89. Ellen T. Charry, "Is Christianity Good for us?" in *Reclaiming Faith: Essays on Orthodoxy in the Episcopal Church*, ed. Ephraim Radner and George R. Summer (Grand Rapids, MI: William B. Eerdmans, 1993): 227.

90. For ways in which this has been interpreted in contemporary theology see Tillich, *Systematic Theology I:166*, 206f; Robert C. Nevill, *God the Creator: On the Transcendence and Presence of God* (Chicago: University of Chicago Press, 1968): 116-9; Bernard J. F. Lonergan, *Insight: A Study of Human Understanding* (New York: Harper & Row, 1958): 657f.

91. Rockmore and Margolis, *The Heidegger Case*, p. 398.

contention in human thought from the beginning. However, I will postpone that until it becomes critical. But let me expand a bit on the fourth element, namely, what I have called the functional factors. Among ethicists James Gustafson has elaborated on these factors the most fully. He distinguishes those factors for which we are not accountable from those for which we are accountable. Among the former he lists genetic endowment, unconscious motives, and social-cultural conditioning. Among the latter he lists beliefs, perspectives, dispositions, affections or sensitivities, and intentions. All of these factors are related through the imagination. They are the conditions for the possibility of agency that is the capacity to provide self direction in these conditions. But how they produce particular conduct is obscure and beyond our capacity to know.[92]

Now what are the possible relations among these elements? Let us assume that the true and the good are, in Rockmore's phrase, "intrinsically linked," that is, mutually implicative and coinherent. The ideal possibility is that thought is perfectly coherent with the true, that thought is perfectly coherent with functional factors (the unconscious is completely conscious), that thought leads logically to conduct, and that conduct is perfectly coherent with the good. In this ideal situation one could argue from the relation of conduct to the good to the relation of thought to the true.

Now what about the actual situation? It is probably that thought participates in the true fragmentarily and changeably, that thought and functional factors overlap in varying degrees, that thought and conduct are related in quite variable degrees of coherence, and that conduct participates fragmentarily and changeably in the good.

Then what about our fundamental question, namely, the relevance of conduct for the assessment of thought? Can you argue from the relation of conduct to the good to the relation of thought to the true? For example, can you

---

92. James Gustafson, *Can Ethics Be Christian* (Chicago: University of Chicago Press, 1975): 32-47. Max Weber refers to the "infinity" of factors involved in any event. See "Objective Possibility and Adequate Causation in Historical Explanation," *The Methodology of the Social Sciences*, trans. & ed. Edward A. Shils and Henry A. Fink (Glencoe, IL: The Free Press, 1949): 164, 169, 171.

argue that since conduct is remote from the good, that therefore thought must be remote from the true?

Probably not, because of the probable incoherences we have noted between thought and functional factors and therefore between thought and conduct. It might be possible to argue from the relation of conduct to the good to the relation of functional factors (or at least the conscious convictions among them) to the true, but only very indirectly to the relation of thought to the true. So the key relation is that between thought and functional factors, between thought and the sources and determinants of conduct. We know that this relation is extremely complex, variable, and obscure. It may be, as the psychoanalytic tradition and Whitehead, for example, among others, have argued, that the determinants of conduct are largely unconscious and thus only tangentially related to thought. This fits with the deconstructionist attack on the unity of thought, person, and conduct. Thus it is probably our dark awareness of the ideal situation sketched above that leads us to believe that conduct should somehow reflect thought.

Tillich has offered a rather different approach to the relation of the true and the good. He notes that Plato teaches that the doing of the good follows from true knowledge of the good. He interprets this to mean that knowledge involves union with the object of knowledge, openness to receive that with which one unites. "He who knows the essential structure of things in the sense of having received their meaning and power acts according to them; he does the good, even if he has to die for it."[93]

According to Tillich, however, knowledge involves distance or detachment as well as union. Under the conditions of existence the elements of union and detachment are separated and move against each other. The overemphasis on union, on receiving knowledge and ontological reason, leads to dogmatism. The overemphasis on detachment, on controlling knowledge and technical reason, lead to the errors of liberalism. "Out of this conflict the quest arises for a knowledge which unites the certainty of existential union with the

---

93. Tillich, *Systematic Theology*, 1:96.

openness of cognitive detachment. This is the quest for the knowledge of revelation."[94] This quest is fulfilled in the final revelation in Christ. Tillich implies that in so far as one receives, affirms, and participates in the final revelation in Christ, that is, in the truth, one will do the good. This participation and action, however, are understood to be "preliminary, fragmentary, . . . changeable" and "ambiguous."[95] Thus the correlation between knowledge of the truth and doing of the good is partial and variable on Tillich's view.

A rather different approach to these issues is offered by rhetoricians. In a study of the relevance of the tradition of classical rhetoric to Christian theology, David Cunningham stresses the importance of the character of the theologian for the persuasive nature of his/her theology. "The entire life of the theologian can provide a warrant whereby the audience evaluates a theological argument."[96] Cunningham, however, does not offer an argument for the validity such a warrant. Furthermore, Tillich stated in an essay entitled "Heidegger and Jaspers" that "one cannot identify the worth of a philosophy merely with the personal decisions of daily existence, the terms and circumstances of which are constantly changing."[97]

Now let us return to Rockmore's "puzzle:" "How can a great philosopher be a proponent of Nazism?" What are the possible ways out of Rockmore's puzzle? They are as follows: (I) that Heidegger's philosophy is incoherent with his conduct; (II) that Nazism is not evil; (III) that Heidegger's philosophy is not true; and (IV) that the true and the good are not a unity.

Now if we rule out (II) and (IV) and assume that Heidegger's philosophy is on the whole true, then our only option is (I) that Heidegger's philosophy does not lead to his conduct. This would involve a negative assessment of the arguments to the contrary of Habermas, Rockmore, Caputo, and others including Heidegger himself.

---

94. Ibid., p. 97; cf. pp. 94-100.
95. Ibid., pp. 146f.
96. David S. Cunningham, *Faithful Persuasion: In Aid of a Rhetoric of Christian Theology* (Notre Dame: University of Notre Dame Press, 1991): 106.
97. Paul Tillich, Heidegger and Jaspers," in *Heidegger and Jaspers*, ed. Alan M. Olson (Philadelphia: Temple University Press, 1994): 25.

This option should be attractive to Christians if they are Heideggerians, because it is implied by the doctrine of sin, which asserts the potential and actual corruption of thought and life and a variable discontinuity between thought and life, between rational theories and good intentions on the one hand and evil actions on the other. Christians should not be surprised (but should regret) that a person's life is incoherent with that person's thought.

Another option would be a version of (I), namely, that Heidegger's philosophy and ethics are internally incoherent. It has often been suggested that there is an early and a later Heidegger separated by a "turn." The early Heidegger is that of *Being and Time* (1927) and the later that of *Introduction to Metaphysics* (1953), *Holzwege* (1950) and so forth. (The theologians deeply influenced by Heidegger have been mainly dependent on the early Heidegger, with the exception of Macquarie.) We have noted, however, the argument of several commentators that the early as well as the later Heidegger led to Nazism.

A complication of any theory of the kind we are exploring is the case of the thinker about whose life we know nothing or nothing historically sound, such as Dionysius. The options here would seem to be either to reject the thought because of its possible dangers, which is hardly plausible, to assume that thinker is innocent until proven guilty, to assess the thought on (the usual) other grounds, and to accept the possible danger of adopting ideas which may have destructive consequences.

Another necessary element in any theory will be a recognition of the fact that the significance of the moral/political life of the thinker will vary with the field of thought. For example, if Andrew Wiles had led a morally dissolute and reprehensible life, this would presumably not be a relevant consideration in the assessment of his solution of Fermat's Last Theorem. However, if his father, Maurice Wiles, had led such a life in Cambridge and Oxford, this might be a relevant factor in the assessment of this theology, but perhaps less so in regard to his historical work.

I am suggesting that Rorty is wrong in putting Heidegger and Einstein in the same boat, and that there is a spectrum of areas of creative thought. At one end the moral/political life of the thinker might be considered entirely irrelevant to the assessment of the thought, and at the other end the opposite might obtain. In the middle would fall areas of thought in which varying degrees of relevance might be the case.

Emil Brunner formulated this idea in his concept of the "law of the closeness of relation."[98] In discussing the problem of a Christian philosophy he suggests that there is a spectrum of intellectual disciplines in which there is an increasing relevance of faith and sin from mathematics, logic, and linguistics through the natural and human sciences to philosophy and theology. He proposes "a proportional statement: The nearer anything lies to that center of existence where we are concerned with the whole, that is, with man's relation to God and the being of the person, the greater is the disturbance of rational knowledge by sin; the farther away anything lies from this center, the less the disturbance is felt, and the less difference there is between knowing as a believer or as an unbeliever. This disturbance reaches it maximum in theology and its minimum in the exact sciences, and zero in the sphere of the formal."[99]

This last assertion would probably be debated by the followers of Thomas Kuhn and by those who claim that all intellectual disciplines are tradition- and value-laden. In any case if the moral/political life of a thinker is relevant to the assessment of the thought, then this relevance will vary from a minimum to a maximum on such a spectrum. In the cases of Heidegger and Tillich this relevance will be at a maximum.

Where does all this leave us in regard to our question about the relevance of the moral life of the thinker to the assessment of the thought? We have not received much help on this question from the philosophers and theologians we have considered. As we have noted, one philosopher (Sluga) has come to a "skeptical conclusion," namely, that "no theoretical framework would ever

---

98. Emil Brunner, *Revelation and Reason: The Christian Doctrine of Faith and Knowledge* (Philadelphia: Westminster Press, 1946): ch. 25. See also W. T. Jones, *The Romantic Syndrome: Toward a New Method in Cultural Anthropology and History of Ideas* (The Hague: Martinus Nijhoff, 1961): p. 44 and ch. 3; and also David S. Cunningham, *Faithful Persuasion*, p. 102.
99. Brunner, *Revelation and Reason*, p. 383.

account for the tangle of facts that has concerned us" (see note 84.) The only theologian who has dealt with the issue is vague and tentative and implies that the moral life of the thinker may only alert us to problems in the thought.

I will conclude with some brief and tentative theses indicating where I have come out so far on this question.

1. There is an identity of the true and the good in God. To know God is the ultimate truth, and to love and obey God is the ultimate good. (At least for Christians.)

2. Following the good increases one's chances of knowing the truth, and not following the good decreases one's chances of knowing the truth.

3. Because of finitude and sin there is at most only a fragmentary and occasional unity of the true and the good in human life and thought.

4. The unity of thought and life is a proper human goal, but it is never achieved in history except fragmentarily. (Was it achieved in Jesus?)

5. The relevance of the moral life of the thinker to the assessment of the thought will vary with the field of thought, and it will be at a maximum in philosophy and theology.

6. In assessing the moral life of a thinker the moral perspective must be our own, but we must take into account the moral context, namely, the time, culture, and community of the thinker.

7. Therefore, the moral life of the thinker will not be decisive in the assessment of the thought, but it may indicate problems and areas of invalidity.

CUP: This is not exactly a resounding conclusion; it is ending with a whimper rather than a bang; pretty slim pickings from such an extended exploration. We may have to conclude with Sluga that the relation of philosophy and theology to the moral life is "intrinsically historical and understandable only in its narrative uniqueness."[100] Perhaps we theologians need to be more open to minimalist conclusions from our research.

---

100. Hans Sluga, *Heidegger's Crisis*, p. 253.

CHAPTER 11

RELIGIOUS PLURALITY
AND CONTEMPORARY PHILOSOPHY

The fact of religious plurality and how to interpret this fact have in recent decade become central issues in contemporary theology and philosophy of religion. The discussion in recent years has been focused on the debate between the pluralists and the inclusivists, as represented respectively in the volume edited by John Hick and Paul F. Knitter, *The Myth of Christian Uniqueness: Toward a Pluralistic Theology of Religions* and that edited by Gavin D Costa, *Christian Uniqueness Reconsidered: The Myth of a Pluralistic Theology of Religions.*[1]

There is a range of definitions of pluralism and inclusivism, and the relation between the two obviously depends on these definitions. A reading of current literature, and especially the above-mentioned volumes, leads to these definitions: inclusivism is the view that sees truth and salvation in other religious traditions but understands these as manifestations of the truth and salvation that are known normatively in one's own tradition. Pluralism is the point of view that holds all the great religious traditions to be roughly equal in regard to truth and salvation; furthermore, pluralism maintains that no one religion is superior to or normative for the others.

In this chapter I want to explore the question of whether there can be a coherent pluralist theory and, if not, whether all pluralist theories reduce to varieties of inclusivism. I shall suggest that the underlying question that has not been addressed is whether there can be a theory of world views that is not also

---

1. John Hick and Paul F. Knitter, eds., *The Myth of Christian Uniqueness: Toward a Pluralistic Theology of Religions* (Maryknoll, NY: Orbis, 1987); Gavin D'Costa, ed., *Christian Uniqueness Reconsidered: The Myth of a Pluralistic Theology of Religions* (Maryknoll, NY: Orbis, 1990).

one of the world views. I shall further suggest that we may find some help in a hitherto untapped source, namely, contemporary American philosophy.

I am led to this tentative conclusion about the reduction of pluralism to inclusivism by several considerations. I believe that there is something of a consensus in contemporary philosophy of religion and theology that one can interpret the phenomena of religion, and religious plurality in particular, only from some particular religious or philosophical perspective, and, further, that a neutral, objective, unbiased, universal interpretation — a "view from nowhere," or a "God's eye view" — is not possible. As Schubert Ogden has stated recently, "Pluralism in no way offers an alternative to employing some norm of religious truth, and thus to making some one religion or philosophy normative for judging all the rest."[2] Therefore, a pluralist view or theory of religious plurality will be elaborated on the basis of a particular religious and/or philosophical position, which is thus at least implicitly proposed as the most adequate, valid, or true position.

While this pluralist view may sound like inclusivism as defined above, pluralists would probably deny that it does. They claim that they are not making the Christian tradition normative for all other religious traditions as the inclusivists do. Pluralists, however, are presumably making their own perspective normative for all religious traditions. How then do they really differ from inclusivists?

The pluralists argue that their interpretation of religious plurality is both the correct one and also that it does not make the Christian tradition normative for other traditions. Yet all the authors in the volume edited by Hick and Knitter, *The Myth of Christian Uniqueness*, are Christians (with perhaps one exception), and they interpret religious plurality from the point of view of their interpretation of the Christian tradition. Their denial of this common ground derives from the fact that they are all liberal Christians who are critical of the tradition and believe that they have thus transcended or distanced themselves from it. For example,

---

2. Schubert M. Ogden, *Is There Only One True Religion or Are There Many?* (Dallas: Southern Methodist University Press, 1992): 77.

although John Hick interprets religious plurality from a Kantian Christian perspective in this volume, this does not put him outside the Christian tradition.

The pluralists, then, interpret religious plurality from a liberal Christian perspective which they thus make normative for the interpretation of other religious traditions, including the more orthodox version of the Christian tradition. This deludes them into thinking that they are not making any religious tradition normative for the others. Of course, it is possible to make a pluralist interpretation of religious plurality from a philosophical perspective that does not make any religious tradition normative for the others. This has been done many times from Ludwig Feuerbach to the present from the perspective of naturalistic humanism or positivism, which is thus made normative for the religious traditions. The pluralists with whom we are concerned here, however, do not adopt such a perspective.

The pluralists, however, would probably also deny that they make their own perspective normative for all religious traditions. They believe that this is too heavy a term to describe their thought; rather, they would say, they simply propose an interpretation of religious plurality. What I suggest, however, is that their proposal clearly implies that their position is an interpretation of religious plurality that is more adequate, valid, or true than any other. This is what I mean by normative. The pluralists propose that what they believe is the most adequate interpretation; they do not simply describe the situation. My suggestion is that this is exactly what the inclusivists are doing.

I believe that the pluralists make a further point that has to do with attitude. They suggest that the inclusivists are arrogant in claiming that Christianity is normatively true and thus superior to other religions, that inclusivists do not have the proper respect for the dignity and integrity of other religions, and that inclusivists are not open to learning from these other religions. The literature indicates not only that this is an inaccurate picture of inclusivists, but also that pluralists are at least as guilty of such attitudes as inclusivists are. I am not primarily concerned here with attitudes, however, but rather with stated positions on or interpretations of religious plurality.

I should note, moreover, that pluralists arguing against inclusivism tend to define it maximally. John Hick, for example, states that inclusivism

> rests upon the claim to Christianity's unique finality as the locus of the only full divine revelation and the only adequate saving event. Non-Christians can be saved because, unknown to them, Christ is secretly 'in a way united' with them. But the saving truth unknown to them is known to the church which is God's instrument in making redemption known.[3]

This is the official Roman Catholic inclusivist view as stated in the documents of Vatican II and the encyclical *Redemptor Hominis* of John Paul.[4] This maximal form of inclusivism is not the only form, however, nor is it the most representative. The definition that was suggested at the beginning of this chapter describes a more common form of inclusivism, and it is to this form that pluralist theories seem to reduce.

One further clarification is necessary: there seem to be two main interpretations of pluralism, and these are mutually exclusive. One asserts the independent validity and equality of the various religious traditions and denies the possibility of any one of them being universally normative. The other proposes a theory of pluralism that is universally valid. As we have seen, however, the first form of pluralism requires a normative conception of religion — and this requirement implies a theory — but it denies the possibility of such a universal theory. This first form of pluralism, then, seems to be incoherent. The second form proposes a universal theory but implicitly denies that such a theory is based on any of the traditions it is interpreting. This form also seems to be incoherent. Thus it would seem that no coherent pluralistic theory is possible: there cannot be a theory of world views that is not also an interpretation from the perspective of one of the world views.[5]

---

3. Hick and Knitter, *The Myth of Christian Uniqueness*, 22.
4. John Paul II, *Redemptor Hominis* (London: Catholic Truth Society, 1979) § 14. Hick's internal quotation is taken from this document.
5. See Raimundo Panikkar, "The Invisible Harmony: A Universal Theory of Religion or a Cosmic Confidence in Reality?" in Leonard Swidler, ed., *Toward a Universal Theology of Religion* (Maryknoll, NY: Orbis, 1988): 135.

My tentative conclusion from the current literature is that the inclusivists have the better of the debate with the pluralists. The pluralist position seems to be an incoherent one, and the pluralists have turned out, moreover, to be crypto-inclusivists. We may find a source of insight on this issue in contemporary American philosophy.

Certain American philosophers, working on issues closely connected with the question of religious plurality, are concerned in various ways with the relation of objectivity or objectivism and subjectivity or subjectivism. They appreciate the objectivist emphasis, for example, in modern science, but argue against objectivism in its various forms of scientism, metaphysical realism, and what some call the "God's eye view." They perceive the persuasiveness of relativism in its various forms, but they are also clear that relativism is not the solution they are seeking. While arguing for a kind of pluralism, in their final or implied position they seem to support what we have called inclusivism.

In the past decade, Hilary Putnam has been concerned to break the stranglehold of the dichotomy between objective and subjective views of truth and reason. Most philosophers, according to Putnam, hold the copy theory of truth as the correspondence to mind-independent facts, while a minority see systems of thought as subjective and relative.[6]

Putnam presents a conception of truth and rationality that unites objective and subjective components under the title of internal or pragmatic realism. He defines this realism in distinction from external or metaphysical realism; in the latter view, the world consists of a fixed totality of mind-independent objects about which one true and complete description exists. In this "God's eye view," truth is the correspondence between words and things.[7]

For internal realism, truth is not correspondence but rational acceptability, an ideal coherence of beliefs with each other and with our experience. There is no "God's eye view" that we can know or usefully imagine. Objects do not exist

---

6. Hilary Putnam, *Reason, Truth and History* (Cambridge: Cambridge University Press, 1981): ix.

7. Ibid., p. 49.

independently of conceptual schemes; within a conceptual scheme, however, signs can refer to objects, because both are internal to the scheme. It makes no sense to ask whether our concepts refer to or match something uncontaminated by concepts. Experiential inputs are shaped in part by our concepts.[8]

An important consequence of Putnam's internal realism is the possibility of pluralism, the existence of "equally coherent but incompatible conceptual schemes which fit our experiential beliefs equally well." Putnam has stated that "many 'internalist' philosophers, though not all, hold further that there is more than one 'true' theory of the world."[9] Such a pluralism is ruled out by metaphysical realism which affirms the existence of the "one true theory" or "God's eye view."

Putnam explains further that such a theory of truth and rationality is based on one's value system-theory of the good or of human flourishing, as he puts it. This in turn depends on one's assumptions about human nature, society, the universe, including one's metaphysical and theological assumptions.[10]

Finally, Putnam holds that relativism is not the right reaction to the failure of metaphysical realism and the "God's eye view." Relativism is inconsistent, incoherent, and self-refuting; some conceptual schemes are better than others. Furthermore, Putnam presents a complex argument — which he calls "transcendental" — to the effect that rationality is transcultural and that there exists a convergence toward ideal or limit concepts of truth and goodness.[11]

What are the implications of Putnam's views for the question of religious plurality and the relation of inclusivism and pluralism? His most suggestive point mentioned above concerns the possibility of a plurality of "equally coherent but incompatible conceptual schemes which fit our experiential beliefs equally well."

---

8. Ibid., pp. 50, 52, 54.
9. Ibid., pp. 73, 49.
10. Ibid., pp. 201, 215.
11. See the summary of this position in Jeffrey L. Johnson, "Making Noises in Counterpoint or Chorus: Putnam's Rejection of Relativism"; and William Throop and Katheryn Doran, "Putnam's Realism and Relativity: An Uneasy Balance"; *Erkenntnis* 34 (1991): 323-45, 357-69, respectively.

This possibility emerges out of his formulation of internal realism and its implication of conceptual relativism, a point to which we shall return below.

On the face of it, Putnam's theory would seem to be a possible basis for affirming the first form of pluralism discussed above, namely, the rough parity of the great religious traditions with regard to truth. In addition, Putnam's denial of the "God's eye view" or "one true theory" of the world implies that the second form of pluralism — which involves a universal theory — is illegitimate.

One may ask, however, whether a theory of the possibility of pluralism requires a theory of pluralism, that is, a universal theory that explains and interprets the plurality of conceptual schemes or religious world views. As we shall see below, Donald Davidson has argued that the idea of the plurality of conceptual schemes is intelligible only on the basis of the existence of a "common coordinate system on which to plot them."[12] Thus the assertion of the possibility of pluralism may implicitly involve a theory of pluralism that approaches the "God's eye view." Furthermore, Putnam has insisted that some conceptual schemes are better than others, that a transcendental argument can be made for a transcultural rationality, and that there is a convergence toward ideal or limit concepts of truth and goodness. These assertions suggest a move away from a pluralism of the first form toward a pluralism of the second form, which we have found to be the same as a moderate inclusivism.

Nelson Goodman describes his book *Ways of Worldmaking* as belonging to that

> mainstream of modern philosophy that began when Kant exchanged the structure of the world for the structure of the mind, continued when C. I. Lewis exchanged the structure of the mind for the structure of concepts, and that now proceeds to exchange the structure of concepts for the structure of the several symbol systems of the sciences, philosophy, the arts, perception, and everyday discourse. The movement is from unique truth and a

---

12. Donald Davidson, *Inquiries into Truth and Interpretation* (Oxford: Clarendon, 1984): 184.

world fixed and found to a diversity of right and even conflicting versions or worlds in the making.[13]

Goodman's volume is a study of the ways in which visions and versions of the world are created in the sciences, arts, philosophy, and our perceptions. They are not possible alternatives to a single actual world but are multiple actual worlds. We cannot test a version by comparing it with a world undescribed or unperceived. In a famous turn of phrase, Goodman states, "All we learn about the world is contained in right versions of it; and while the underlying world, bereft of these, need not be denied to those who love it, it is perhaps on the whole a world well lost."[14]

Goodman has undertaken a "critique of worldmaking," a comparative study of these world versions and how they are made. He has done so by means of what he calls composition and decomposition, weighting, ordering, deletion, supplementation, and deformation. The truth of a version is not defined by agreement between it and a world apart from it. Rather a version is true "when it offends no unyielding beliefs and none of its own perceptions."[15] Truth, however, is neither a necessary nor a sufficient condition for choosing a version. Goodman subsumes truth under the general notion of "rightness of fit" or, alternatively, "truth of statements and rightness of descriptions, representations, exemplifications, expressions — of design, drawing, diction, rhythm — is primarily a matter of fit."[16]

As in the case of our first impression of Putnam, Goodman's approach seems to be a possible basis for the assertion of the first form of pluralism, a plurality of true or right world versions. Is Goodman's analysis, however, based on a particular way of world making? We must inquire regarding the world version on which Goodman has based all these claims about worlds and their making. He provides us some clues to the answer.

---

13. Nelson Goodman, *Ways of Worldmaking* (Indianapolis: Hackett, 1978): x.
14. Ibid., 4. See Richard Rorty, "The World Well Lost," *Journal of Philosophy* 69 (1972): 649-65.
15. Goodman, *Ways of Worldmaking,* 17.
16. Ibid., 132, 138.

Goodman maintains that the typical adversary of his pluralism is the "monopolist materialist or physicalist who maintains that one system, physics, is preeminent and all-inclusive, such that every other version must eventually be reduced to it or rejected as false and meaningless."[17] He states that the evidence for the reducibility of all versions to one is negligible. Rather, "unity is to be sought not in an ambivalent or neutral *something* beneath these versions but in an overall organization embracing them. . . . My approach is rather through an analytic study of types and functions of symbols and symbol systems."[18] Finally, he refers to his work as "metaphilosophy" and to his "dogged and deflationary nominalism."[19]

It seems to me that here Goodman emerges as the monopolist symbolist who has reduced all world versions to the symbolic order and to a nominalist overall organization embracing them. This means that his pluralism is seen from the point of view of a monism — a theory of versions that is also one of the versions — and thus, in the terms of religious plurality, an inclusivism.[20]

In his book *Beyond Objectivism and Relativism,* Richard Bernstein explores what he perceives as the uneasiness that has spread throughout our intellectual and cultural life. This uneasiness is expressed in the opposition between objectivism and relativism, and while, according to Bernstein, this opposition is a dead end, we can move beyond it.

Bernstein defines objectivism as the conviction that there is some permanent ahistorical framework to which we can appeal in order to determine the nature of rationality, knowledge, truth, reality, and goodness. Relativism is the conviction that all of these latter concepts can be understood only as deriving from and thus relative to some specific conceptual scheme, form of life, or culture. According to relativism, therefore, there is an irreducible plurality of such conceptual schemes, and no overarching framework exists by which we can

---

17. Ibid., p. 4.
18. Ibid., p. 5.
19. Ibid., p. 21.
20. For a similar critique see Harvey Siegel, *Relativism Refuted: A Critique of Contemporary Epistemological Relativism* (Dordrecht: Reidel, 1987): chap. 7, esp. p. 153.

rationally evaluate or choose between these competing claims. Bernstein outlines a solution to this dilemma based on the insights of hermeneutics and the analysis of social practices.[21]

I shall use Bernstein's analysis of objectivism and relativism and their relations to clarify the relation between inclusivism and pluralism. Objectivism and relativism are analogous to inclusivism and pluralism, but the relations are rather complex. On the one hand, pluralism sounds like a relativism of equally valid viewpoints, and inclusivism sounds like an objectivism of one normative viewpoint. This is confirmed by the fact that from the point of view of inclusivism, pluralism is a relativism, and from the point of view of pluralism, inclusivism is an objectivism. On the other hand, however, pluralists consider their position to be the objective one — the way things really are — and they reject the inclusivists' view as hopelessly subjective and relative to their own bias.

Moreover, when we distinguish the two forms of pluralism as we have done above, the situation changes. Whereas the first form of pluralism remains a relativism, the second form, which involves an overarching framework, becomes an objectivism. Likewise, when we distinguish the maximal and moderate forms of inclusivism, we find that a similar modification begins to emerge. The maximal form of inclusivism remains an objectivism, but the moderate form becomes more like a relativism in that it is the proposal of a universal framework but from a particular perspective.

Now what is Bernstein's solution to this puzzle? He claims that he will not take sides in the debate between objectivism and relativism. He says that this debate is misleading and distorting, because it is caused by what he calls Cartesian anxiety about the inability to find a secure foundation for knowledge, truth, and goodness. He claims that we can exorcise this anxiety and move beyond objectivism and relativism.

In fact, Bernstein's solution is to side with relativism and to attempt to show how we can live with it. All his arguments are against objectivism.

---

21. Richard Bernstein, *Beyond Objectivism and Relativism: Science, Hermeneutics, and Praxis* (Philadelphia: University of Pennsylvania Press, 1983).

Although there exist many arguments against relativism, Bernstein employs none of them. His positive proposal is to seek a new and moderate form of practical rationality employing dialogue, undistorted communication, communal judgment, and what he calls "rational wooing." In other words, Bernstein modifies his basic relativism by emphasizing the hermeneutical and practical dimensions in all the natural and social sciences. He asserts that we have never had certainties, but only the capacity to reflect, to discuss, and if possible to come to some viable consensus about the way things are and what we should do. Translated into the situation of interreligious relations, Bernstein's solution offers a perspective in which various inclusivisms can enter into fruitful dialogue.

Although Bernstein mentions moral relativism in passing, this is not the focus of his concern. It is important to note, however, that pluralists, especially those who argue for the first form of pluralism, are very sensitive to the charge of moral relativism and reject it. Half of the authors in *The Myth of Christian Uniqueness* deny the charge of moral relativism and argue against it; there is much discussion about relativizing one's own perspective but not apparently one's moral perspective. Langdon Gilkey argues that we must resist the intolerable. Marjorie Suchocki asserts that justice must be the norm and goal of interreligious relations, and she strives to find a definition of justice that would be acceptable to the various religious traditions.[22] Knitter clearly claims that his commitment to justice takes precedence over his commitment to pluralism: "The absolute, that which all else must serve and clarify . . . is . . . the kingdom and its justice."[23] Likewise, Tom Driver maintains that pluralism is not an ultimate concern but rather an ethically necessary step.[24]

What is the significance of pluralists denying moral relativism and affirming universal moral norms? It seems that this constitutes another example

---

22. Langdon Gilkey, "Plurality and Its Theological Implications"; and Marjorie Hewitt Suchocki, "In Search of Justice"; in Hick and Knitter, *Myth of Christian Uniqueness*, 44, 149-50, respectively.
23. Paul F. Knitter, "Toward a Liberation Theology of Religion," in Hick and idem, *Myth of Christian Uniqueness*, 190.
24. Tom F. Driver, "The Case for Pluralism," in Hick and Knitter, *Myth of Christian Uniqueness*, 207.

of pluralism reducing to inclusivism. Gilkey states it quite clearly: "In order to resist . . . we must ourselves stand somewhere. . . . We must assert some sort of ultimate values. . . . And to assert our ultimate value or values is to assert a 'world,' a view of all reality. . . . And it presupposes an absolute commitment to this understanding of things."[25] Here pluralism is abandoned, although Gilkey also calls for the recognition of the relativity of our standpoint. This is again an example of the moderate form of inclusivism.

In his book *The View from Nowhere* Thomas Nagel addresses what he believes to be the most fundamental issue about morality, knowledge, freedom, self, mind, and world. This is the problem of how to combine the subjective and objective, or internal and external, perspectives and of how to combine the perspective of a particular person with an objective view of the world that includes the person and the person's perspective. He explores this issue in relation to the problems of mind, knowledge, freedom, ethics, and the meaning of life and death, arguing that the two perspectives are irreducible, that neither can be successfully absorbed into the other. Although he looks at possibilities of integration, he concludes that we cannot reconcile the two perspectives and achieve a unified world view.

It seems to me, however, that Nagel tilts finally toward the subjective perspective as the more fundamental. For example, he states that the aim of the pursuit of objective knowledge is unintelligible: "We must get outside ourselves, and view the world from nowhere in it."[26] He explains further that

> however often we may try to step outside ourselves, something
> will have to stay behind the lens. . . . The idea of objectivity seems
> to undermine itself. . . . It seems to follow that the most objective
> view we can achieve will have to rest on an unexamined subjective
> base, and that since we can never abandon our point of view, but

---

25. Gilkey, "Plurality and Its Theological Implications," in Hick and Knitter, *Myth of Christian Uniqueness*, 45.

26. Thomas Nagel, *The View From Nowhere* (New York: Oxford University Press, 1986): 67.

can only alter it, the idea that we are coming closer to the reality outside it with each successive step has no foundation.[27]

Although Nagel goes on to refine his view by taking full account of the objective perspective, this passage seems to represent his final position. The subjective perspective is ultimate and final and includes the objective perspective within it as a mode of the subjective.

What are the implications of Nagel's work for the understanding of religious plurality and the relation of inclusivism and pluralism? In discussing Bernstein, I suggested that inclusivism seemed to be a subjective view, and pluralism in its second form an objective one. If Nagel's argument affirms the subjective view as the more fundamental, then it constitutes another argument that inclusivism is likewise more fundamental. On the one hand, this is confirmed when we realize that every pluralist universal theory or overarching framework is always the elaboration of a particular perspective and thus has the form of an inclusivism.

On the other hand, it should be noted that the objective perspective holds an important place in the Western religious dialectic. In one sense, the objective perspective is the infinite capacity of the subjective perspective to transcend itself, to gain self-awareness and responsibility, a capacity which is often identified with the idea of the image of God in humanity. Putnam and others refer to the ideal goal of the objective perspective, the view from nowhere, as the "God's eye view"; this, however, is the temptation of the serpent, that one can be like God. Finally, the pursuit of objectivity can also be understood as the attempt to see all things sub *specie aeternitatis*. As Nagel states, "The wish to live as far as possible in full recognition that one's position in the universe is not central has an element of the religious impulse about it"; and "the most general effect of the objective stance ought to be a form of humility."[28]

One way in which pluralism can be elaborated is by means of the theory of conceptual relativism, a concept to which most of the philosophers we have considered have referred. This theory holds that assertions are relative to "the

---

27. Ibid., p. 68.
28. Ibid., 210, 222.

intellectual or conceptual background which the individual brings to his problems from the cultural milieu to which he belongs."[29] More specifically, conceptual relativism is the theory that one's view of objects, reality, and truth is relative to one's conceptual scheme, and that there is no scheme that transcends other schemes by which one can choose among schemes. As we have noted, this has led Putnam and Goodman to conclude that there is more than one true theory of the world.

Are pluralists affirming or implying conceptual relativism? The first form of pluralism asserts the parity in regard to truth of the various religious traditions and denies the possibility of any one of them being universally normative; conceptual relativism is one interpretation of such claims. As we have noted, however, some pluralists go on to assert a universal scheme that interprets the various conceptual schemes of the religious traditions. This approach is excluded from the usual interpretation of conceptual relativism, which denies the possibility of a scheme that transcends all other schemes.

What conceptual scheme provides a point of view from which one can assert conceptual relativism? It would seem that the very understanding of conceptual relativism would imply that the various possible schemes are interpreted by some scheme that apparently transcends all other schemes. This would in effect reduce any pluralism allegedly supported by conceptual relativism to a form of inclusivism.

Furthermore, conceptual relativism has not gone unchallenged and is the focus of an intense debate in contemporary philosophy. The usual criticism is that it is self-contradictory and therefore self-refuting. Conceptual relativists presumably hold their theory to be not only relatively true nor merely true for themselves, but rather true universally, which is contradictory to the stance of conceptual relativism.

---

29. Maurice Mandelbaum, "Subjective, Objective, and Conceptual Relativisms," in Jack W. Meiland and Michael Krausz, eds., *Relativism: Cognitive and Moral* (Notre Dame: University of Notre Dame Press, 1982): 36.

In a famous essay, "On the Very Idea of a Conceptual Scheme,"[30] Donald Davidson has argued not only against conceptual relativism but also against the intelligibility of the idea of a conceptual scheme itself. He does so by claiming that there can be no grounds for determining that a conceptual scheme is different from our own.

Davidson identifies conceptual schemes with languages or sets of inter-translatable languages. Different conceptual schemes would then correspond to languages among which translation is not possible. He concludes, however, that it is impossible to make sense of a partial or total failure of translatability and thus of the idea of different conceptual schemes and finally, therefore, of the idea of a conceptual scheme itself. Thus we could never be in the position to judge that others had concepts or beliefs radically different from our own.

The present philosophical consensus, however, seems to be against Davidson on this question, upholding instead the intelligibility of the existence of different conceptual schemes.[31] The existence of different conceptual schemes would seem to be fairly obvious, and many examples have been given. The main difficulty in Davidson's argument is his identification of conceptual schemes with languages and, in particular, his identification of differences between conceptual schemes with the untranslatability of languages. Why must such differences require untranslatability and thus unintelligibility?

Whereas there may be radically different conceptual schemes the existence of which we are unaware,[32] there would also seem to be clear examples of differences between conceptual schemes that are quite intelligible, especially among religions. Most of the theologians and philosophers of religion whom we are considering understand religions to involve different conceptual schemes for organizing and interpreting experience. These schemes, moreover, are understood to be largely translatable into the language and concepts of the interpreter.

---

30. Davidson, *Inquiries*, essay 13.
31. See Jack W. Meiland and Michael Krausz, "Introduction to 'On the Very Idea of a Conceptual Scheme,'" in idem, *Relativism*, 62-5; and Siegel, *Relativism Refilled*, 40-2.
32. For examples, see Meiland and Krausz, "Introduction," 62-5.

Davidson does, however, make some points that are relevant to the question of religious plurality. He writes,

> Different points of view make sense, but only if there is a common coordinate system on which to plot them. . . . Languages we will not think of as separable from souls; speaking a language is not a trait a man can lose while retaining the power of thought. So there is no chance that someone can take up a vantage point for comparing conceptual schemes by temporarily shedding his own.[33]

Presumably, this common coordinate system is part of the conceptual scheme that one cannot shed. Thus Davidson presents an argument not for the first form of pluralism, but for its second form, which we have found to be indistinguishable from the moderate form of inclusivism.

John B. Cobb, Jr., also deals with the question of conceptual relativism. According to Cobb, the aspects of reality that people come to see through various religious traditions differ profoundly, but they are not therefore contradictory and mutually exclusive, but rather may be complementary. This does not lead, however, to a universal scheme of reality, because there is no universal norm for assessing religious claims. "Each tradition is best by its own norms and there is no normative critique of norms," Cobb asserts. "This is the doctrine of conceptual relativism. It seems to do justice to each tradition, but in fact it vitiates the claims of all, since all claim at least some elements of universality."[34] Cobb seems to mean here that conceptual relativism undercuts all universal claims.

Cobb then proposes a way to overcome or go beyond conceptual relativism: "The belief that there is more to truth and wisdom than one's own tradition has thus far attained is the basis for overcoming the alternatives of essentialism and conceptual relativism."[35] The problem with conceptual relativism, according to Cobb, is not that it sees the circularity between beliefs and norms, which is simply the human condition, but that it sees this as a static, self-enclosed situation. In the situation of interreligious dialogue, however, the

---

33. Davidson, *Inquiries*, 184-85.

34. John B. Cobb, Jr., "Beyond Pluralism," in D'Costa, *Christian Uniqueness Reconsidered*, 85.

35. Ibid., p. 86.

situation can be open and dynamic: "Normative thinking within each tradition can be expanded and extended through openness to the normative thinking of others."[36] Therefore, we can see a "relatively objective norm" for the assessment of religious traditions, namely, "their ability, in faithfulness to their heritage, to expand their understanding of reality and its normative implications."[37] This seems to be an appropriate and realistic response to the issue of conceptual relativism in interreligious relations.

Finally, let us consider the work of Nicholas Rescher, who, speaking directly to the issues we are exploring, has drawn together many of the threads of the discussion and treated some of the questions left unanswered by the other authors we have investigated. In his book *The Strife of Systems*, Rescher inquires about the source and significance of philosophical diversity.[38]

Offering a theory of the inevitability of philosophical diversity, Rescher claims that this diversity does not discredit philosophy or undermine its validity or usefulness. He rejects methodological, epistemological, psychological, socio-logical, and eliminative explanations of philosophical disagreement, arguing instead that the cause of such disagreement lies in conflicting cognitive values, such as importance, significance, centrality, weight, priority, and urgency, which set the standards for the assessment of philosophical positions. Our cognitive values emerge from the many causal determinants of nature and nurture, culture and individual experience. They vary because human experience is variable.

Rescher claims that philosophy begins with what he calls an aporetic cluster, a family of contentions for which good reasons exist but which are mutually incompatible and inconsistent. The resolution of an aporetic cluster necessarily involves the abandonment of one of the contentions, but this decision cannot be made by logic or evidential reasoning. It can be achieved only by value considerations. Determining which solution is optimal requires the bringing into operation of a cognitive value orientation.

---

36. Ibid.
37. Ibid., p. 87.
38. Nicholas Rescher, *The Strife of Systems: An Essay on the Grounds and Implications of Philosophical Diversity* (Pittsburgh: University of Pittsburgh Press, 1985).

258

Since a plurality of resolutions of an aporetic cluster is always available, pluralism is a necessary feature of philosophy. This is what Rescher calls "orientational pluralism," defining it as "a position that maintains that philosophical positions hinge on diverse views regarding matters of cognitive value, so that philosophical disagreements become inevitable."[39] Furthermore, there is no neutral "God's eye view" from which all philosophical positions can be assessed.

This pluralism, however, does not mean that one can assert that all philosophical positions are equally valid. The reason for this is that while "the community is inherently pluralistic, . . . the individual is inherently monistic. He has, or can develop only one particular set of weights and priorities."[40] Rescher's point here is that "in *evaluating* positions we have, of course, no alternative to doing so from the perspective of our cognitive values — our own cognitive point of view." The result is that "orientational pluralism does *not* put everyone's position on a par, save from the unachievable olympian point of view of the community at large."[41] Thus, according to Rescher,

> we are enjoined and entitled to see our own theory as correct. All we are called on to do is to acknowledge that *relative to their own orientations* (which we, of course, see as misguided), others are equally entitled to see their versions of the truth as equally warranted. We are certainly not called to see other orientations as equal to our own.[42]

Therefore, "an orientational *monism* is the obverse side of orientational *pluralism.*"[43]

Rescher places his view among four other models of accounting for philosophical differences: the multifaceted reality view, which makes each view a subordinate part of an overarching whole; the no reality view, which asserts that all views are illusory; the unique reality view, which affirms that there is only one

---

39. Ibid., p. 125.
40. Ibid., p. 145.
41. Ibid., pp. 148-9.
42. Ibid., p. 192.
43. Ibid., p. 147.

true position; and the perspectival reality view, which is that of Rescher's orientational pluralism. He emphasizes the difference between the multifaceted and the perspectival views. In the former, the various facets can be combined into one coherent view; in the latter, there is an irreducible plurality of incompatible views.[44]

Finally, Rescher outlines the various approaches to the rival philosophical possibilities. First, one may adopt none of the possibilities, the view of skepticism, agnostic or nihilistic. Second, one may adopt one possibility, a view that Rescher names doctrinalism. It takes two forms: arationalism, which is represented by psychologism, historicism, and historical convergentism; and rationalism, which is represented by absolutism and value-orientational monism. Third, one may adopt all possibilities, the view of syncretism. Among these alternatives, only the rationalist form of doctrinalism, represented by orientational pluralism, is self-applicative. Skepticism and irrationalism are self-contradictory. Syncretism includes itself among the alternatives, but that does not entitle it to a privileged position as. the best way to choose. Orientational pluralism alone has an adequate interpretation of both philosophical plurality and its own superiority on the basis of its own cognitive value orientation. This is the necessary and unavoidable circularity of all philosophical argument.[45]

Rescher concludes by noting that orientational pluralism takes a two-tiered stance as a theory of normative metaphilosophy. At the doctrinal level, it envisages a monism or dogmatic commitment based on one's own cognitive value perspective. At the metadoctrinal level it envisages a pluralism that recognizes that other perspectives exist and are rationally grounded, albeit on other cognitive value perspectives. He explains, "Orientational pluralism at the descriptive level is perfectly consonant with orientational monism at the substantive level; there is no clash or conflict between the two. Philosophical partisanship is not

---

44. Ibid., pp. 173-9.
45. Ibid., pp. 223-39.

incompatible with metaphilosophical tolerance and need not be undermined by it."[46]

What are the implications of Rescher's work for the issues raised by the other philosophers and for the question of religious plurality? Rescher's main contribution to the philosophical discussion is, I believe, a theory of pluralism and relativism, something that none of the others offers. Like Putnam, he notes the plurality of different conceptual schemes and rejects the "God's eye view," relativism, and the conviction that all conceptual schemes are equally good, but he would disagree with Putnam's idea of convergence toward an ideal of truth. Whereas Putnam lacks a theory of pluralism, Rescher supplies one in his concept of cognitive value orientation.

Similarly, Goodman affirms pluralism but offers no theory. Rescher interprets Goodman's pluralism to be the multifaceted view.[47] I believe, however, that he is mistaken in view of the fact that Goodman denies the intelligibility or at least the usefulness of the world underlying the versions of it, the "world well lost." In any case, Rescher would disagree with Goodman's assertion of the validity, truth, and rightness of many world versions. Again Rescher offers a theory of pluralism, whereas Goodman does not.

Bernstein describes the conflict between objectivism and relativism but offers no theory of it. Rescher offers such a theory, namely, that relativism applies at the metaphilosophical level and objectivism at the substantive philosophical level. Bernstein would probably reject this theory, but it is implied by his practical solution to the conflict, namely, rational conversation between opposing viewpoints. The same applies to Nagel. Rescher offers a theory of the relation of the objective and subjective perspectives that explains Nagel's claim that these are irreducible. "Objectivity is a matter of degree rather than an absolute," Rescher states, noting Nagel's work; "viewed in this light philosophical

---

46. Ibid., p. 267.
47. Ibid., pp. 174-5.

reasonings are not strictly subjective but hold objectively for all who share a certain cognitive-value orientation."[48]

Finally, Rescher's position in the debate about conceptual relativism is to affirm it epistemologically and deny it metaphysically. Orientational pluralism involves conceptual relativism at the metaphilosophical level but not at the substantive philosophical level. "The crucial fact is that orientational pluralism, while indeed seeing itself as one position among others, is not committed to regarding them all as having equal merit. It does not see its rivals. . . as *correct*, but merely as *tenable* — that is, arguable from some 'available' orientation."[49] He explains further, "Relativism is only viable when it takes an epistemological form; *ontological* relativism is ultimately incoherent."[50]

In regard to the question of religious plurality, it is clear that Rescher offers a theory that supports our tentative conclusion that pluralist theories are incoherent and reduce to inclusivist theories, and that therefore inclusivism is the proper solution to the problem of religious plurality. Rescher sees the validity of pluralism at the epistemological or metaphilosophical level but denies it at the ontological or philosophical level proper.

As to our final conclusion, however, Rescher's view is too static and does not allow for any progress beyond the situation of a variety of value-orientational viewpoints. Here his view needs to be modified by the point made by Cobb. Cobb's criticism of conceptual relativism can be applied to Rescher, and with this we can conclude.

> The problem with conceptual relativism is not that it sees a circularity between beliefs and the norms by which they are judged. This is the human condition. The weakness is that it pictures this as a static, self-enclosed system, whereas the great religious traditions can be open and dynamic. This does not justify someone claiming to stand outside all the relative positions and to be able to establish a neutral, objective norm over all. But it does mean that normative thinking within each tradition can be

---

48. Ibid., 193.
49. Ibid., p. 184.
50. Ibid., p. 192.

expanded and extended through openness to the normative thinking of others.[51]

---

51. Cobb, "Beyond Pluralism," p. 86.

CHAPTER 12

CHRISTIANITY AND THE PERENNIAL PHILOSOPHY

I used to think that the main option in the West to the biblical religions, Judaism and Christianity, was naturalistic humanism. This is the worldview which affirms the uniquely human values of freedom, community, justice, equality, and so forth, in the context of a naturalistic philosophy, a metaphysic in which nature is the highest or broadest category. Now, I believe that this is no longer the case, and probably never was (except in the academy, and perhaps not even there). I am persuaded that the main option to the biblical religions today is what Aldous Huxley and many others call the perennial philosophy.

Huxley defines the perennial philosophy as "the metaphysic that recognizes a divine reality substantial to the world" and "the psychology that finds in the soul something similar to, or even identical with, divine Reality."[1] It has been exemplified in the West in Neoplatonism, the mysticism of the Pseudo-Dionysius, modern idealism, and such religious movements as Gnosticism, Rosicrucianism, Swedenborgianism, Theosophy, Spiritualism, and Christian Science, as well as imports from the East.[2] It has also become an important school of thought led by such authors as Titus Burckhardt, Réne Guénon, S. H. Nasr, Jacob Needleman, Frithjof Schuon, and Huston Smith.

There is something of a consensus among interpreters that the world religions fall into two main types, what Max Weber called the emissary and the exemplary types, and what Peter Berger has called the confrontation and

---

1. *The Perennial Philosophy* (New York: Harper and Row, 1944): vii.
2. See the study of thirty-six contemporary groups of this type by Robert S. Ellwood in his book *Religious and Spiritual Groups in Modern America* (Englewood Cliffs, NJ: Prentice-Hall, 1973).

interiority types. The first or emissary type is exemplified in the Jewish prophet, the Christian apostle, and the Muslim prophet; the second or exemplary, in the Hindu holy man, the Buddhist monk, and the Taoist sage. And the question is often raised and discussed about the relation between these two types of religion and whether or not a synthesis is possible.

It is usually assumed that Christianity generally falls within the emissary type and the perennial philosophy in the exemplary type. It would seem on the face of it that they represent quite distinct types of religious experience and religious tradition. But I want to suggest that Christianity has always in fact been a synthesis or amalgam, sometimes stable, sometimes unstable, of what I will call biblical religion and the perennial philosophy.

I first became aware of this issue in the forties through the neo-orthodox polemic against liberal theology and, in particular, against the elements in it of mysticism and idealism. In my graduate study, I did a good deal of work on the English Hegelians and especially on the debates between the absolute idealists and the personal idealists in which these issues figured. Then I began to notice that people from all walks of life were fascinated both intellectually and existentially by the perennial philosophy. I recall Reinhold Niebuhr once remarking that if a Christian theologian were invited to lecture at Columbia University, the philosophy department would be outraged, but if a Buddhist monk or a Hindu swami were invited, they would all purr like kittens.

Then, several years ago, I participated in a group of theologians and psychiatrists in Boston assembled by Erich Lindemann. I discovered to my astonishment that the majority of the psychiatrists were rather disdainful of biblical religion but were quite fascinated with the perennial philosophy. In the 1960's, I noticed that much of the counter-culture movement was deeply informed by the perennial philosophy. Finally, I have often been surprised to discover that the operative faith of theological students and other Christians turns out to be some form of the perennial philosophy, that Christian people often assume that Christian faith and the perennial philosophy are the same thing. So, in a word, I have been continually impressed by the power and the pervasiveness of the perennial philosophy, and I continue to be curious about its relation to Christianity.

I want to approach this question by looking at the perennial philosophy and biblical religion as two ideal types, two heuristic constructs which may serve to organize certain historical data. By this, I mean that I will try to indicate the fundamental elements of each, not all of which, however, may be present in any particular example of them. In speaking of biblical religion, I am not referring to Judaism or Christianity in any of their specific forms, but rather to an ideal construct which may underlie any particular form of either of them. The same applies to my description of the perennial philosophy.

The perennial philosophy is a religious worldview which, like all worldviews, involves a particular understanding of reality, including the divine, and the place of humanity in reality. It affirms that ultimate reality, the divine, is the nameless, ineffable One about which nothing else can be said except perhaps by negations. For example, it is not a person or personal. Then, there is the world, but its origin is obscure or problematic. In the Gnostic version of the perennial philosophy, the origin of the world is the result of a mythic accident or misunderstanding. In the Neoplatonic version, the world is the result of the emanation or overflowing of the divine substance, the reason for which is obscure. It is sometimes described as involuntary and sometimes as a reckless falling away from the One.

This means that the world is essentially divine, or, as Huxley puts it, the divine reality is substantial to the world. It also means that reality is ordered in a great hierarchy of levels of being stretching from the divine down through the spiritual, the psychic, and the organic, to the inorganic. This is a hierarchy of reality, power, and value. The higher or closer a level of being is to the divine, the greater its reality, power, value; the lower or farther from the divine, the lesser its reality, power, and value.

Humanity includes all the levels of being and, thus, is called a microcosm, the whole of reality in miniature. Humanity includes the inorganic, the organic, the psychic, the spiritual, and the divine. This means that the highest and essential level of human being is identical with the divine. The problematic character of the human situation is that the human spirit which is essentially divine is involved in the lower levels of being and as a result is confused, led astray, and forgets about its essential divine nature.

The way of salvation is for the human spirit to discover its true nature, to turn away from the lower levels of being and to rise up until it is perfectly united with the divine in mystical union. This way of salvation is pursued in many different ways in the different versions of the perennial philosophy, but they usually involve some kind of asceticism or suppression of the bodily and the psychic through disciplines of meditation.

I pause to note that this is what many people believe Christianity is, especially people raised in the traditions of liberal Protestantism, Roman Catholicism, or Eastern Orthodoxy. The reason for this is that these traditions (and all other Christian traditions in varying degrees) are in fact syntheses or amalgams of biblical religion with various forms of the perennial philosophy.

From these fundamental elements of the perennial philosophy certain results tend to emerge. First, because of the monistic and hierarchical character of reality, individuality in general and human individuality or personhood in particular tends to become at least ambiguous in character, if not actually unreal or evil. The reason for this is that the more individuality or distinctness something has, the further it is from the divine, and thus the less reality, power, and value it will have. This is also indicated by the fact that the fulfillment of the individual is to become perfectly united with the divine in an identity in which there is no distinct individuality at all. Huston Smith puts it this way: "Only persons who sense *themselves* to be not finally real — *anatta*, no-self — will sense the same of the God of theism. And for them it does not matter that in the last analysis God is not the kind of God who loves them, for at this level there is no 'them' to be loved."[3]

A second tendency is that bodily life is viewed with suspicion. The reason is the same. Physical bodies are even further removed from the divine than the

---

3. *Forgotten Truth: The Primordial Tradition* (New York: Harper and Row, 1976): 52.

human psyche and they are, moreover, the source of human confusion and ignorance about its true nature, and thus are the source of evil. (Thus monism always tends to produce a dualism in regard to the body and the physical world.) Since human individuality and embodiment are the basis of human personal relations, human association and community become ambiguous, of little value, and subject to suspicion. Finally, since human history is the story of human communities and their relations, the significance of history becomes questionable. The significant movement of human life is not forward into the future in personal, communal, and historical development, but rather upwards out of bodily, communal, historical life in the direction of the divine.

The ideal type or construct of "biblical religion" has one point of agreement with the perennial philosophy, namely, the ultimate reality of the divine One. But even here there is a fundamental difference. In biblical religion, the divine is ineluctably personal and thus a differentiated or organic unity on the analogy of integrated human personhood, whereas in the perennial philosophy the divine One is absolutely simple and undifferentiated. Moreover, the divine in biblical religion is not nameless or ineffable, but has many names and must be spoken about.

Furthermore, the origin of the world is not obscure, but is understood to be the result of the divine will and action, namely, creation. This means that the world is not essentially divine, but rather creaturely, a kind of reality which is neither divine nor illusory, but contingent and real. There is a sense in which the created world is ordered in a hierarchy of levels of being, but this is not a hierarchy of degrees of reality, but rather one of mutual service and honor.

As in the perennial philosophy, humanity includes all the levels of reality, but with one exception: humanity has no divine element, but is entirely creature. Furthermore, the problematic character of human life is not the involvement of humanity in bodily life, but is rather a matter of the perversity of the human will, of turning away from the divine will. The seat of the problem is in the human spirit, not in the human body. So, the way of salvation is the transformation of the will through the divine presence. The merciful and forgiving divine love draws the human will out of bondage into freedom.

From the fundamental affirmations of biblical religion, certain tendencies emerge which are the opposite of those of the perennial philosophy. In biblical religion, individuality in general and human individuality in particular are not ambiguous, but are affirmed as very good. The goal of individual fulfillment is not to be absorbed into the divine undifferentiated unity, but to live in personal communion with the divine and with one's fellow creatures. Accordingly, human bodily life is not to be turned away from, but is to be affirmed and will be transfigured in the fulfillment. (Thus a duality between creator and creature always tends to produce a monism or holism in regard to the body and the physical world.) Similarly, human personal relations and community are not seen as ambiguous, but rather as of the highest importance and value. Finally, therefore, history as the story of human communities and their relations is taken very seriously as the arena of human responsibility and divine activity aiming at the fulfillment of all the creation.

These are the ideal types or constructs of the perennial philosophy and biblical religion. They have never existed in their pure forms as described. In any particular historical form of either one, the fundamental themes will be described in different ways and the tendencies mentioned will be modified accordingly. As I have suggested, Christianity has never existed as simply biblical religion, but has always been from the very beginning a mixture, amalgam, or synthesis of biblical religion with some form of the perennial philosophy. (Occasionally, the mixture has occurred with other types of philosophy, such as Stoicism. But most often it has been with some form of the perennial philosophy, which has been the dominant form of Western philosophy from Plato to Hegel.)

This amalgamating began in the Bible, and first in the Wisdom literature, and especially in the Wisdom of Solomon which was influenced by Middle Platonism, and also in the Gospel of John (although this is debated). It continued in Philo and the early Christian theologians, such as Clement of Alexandria, in whose writings the perennial philosophy was dominant. A real synthesis was achieved by such thinkers as Augustine, Bonaventure, and Aquinas. Pseudo-Dionysius represents the perennial philosophy in almost pure form. Very few theologians exemplify biblical religion in pure form, but Irenaeus, Luther, and, on the Jewish side, Martin Buber, come close.

A historical sidelight is that by the time of the Renaissance most people identified Christianity with the individual and world-denying aspects of the perennial philosophy, which we have noted above. So the Renaissance can be interpreted as the cultural manifestation of some of the individual and world-affirming themes of biblical religion, as seen, for example, in Renaissance humanism, Renaissance naturalism in art, the beginnings of modern science, and the emergence of a progressive view of history. These were seen, therefore, as anti-Christian in character. Finally, since the Renaissance can in many ways be seen as the birth of the modern world, we have the strange reversal in which the modern world sees itself as an anti-Christian rebirth of classical culture, whereas it is in fact more the result of the cultural working out of the fundamental themes of biblical religion. All of this can be seen as the result of the fact that Christianity was widely understood to be a form of perennial philosophy.

A continuing manifestation of the perennial philosophy since the medieval period can be seen in Romanticism. Denis de Rougemont has argued that Catharism, a religious movement based on the perennial philosophy with a Christian veneer, was the source of the tradition of courtly love which exalted the passion of Romantic love and looked down on marriage.[4] According to de Rougemont, this tradition of Romanticism influenced many areas of Western culture, flowered in the Romantic movement of the last century, and emerged philosophically in German idealism, the main modern Western version of the perennial philosophy.

---

4. *Love in the Western World* (New York: Harper and Row, 1956).

Today, we are experiencing a new Romantic movement which is also pervasively informed by the perennial philosophy.[5] Beginning with the youth culture movement of the 1960's and continuing down to the present in many religious and cultural manifestations, this new Romantic movement has influenced all of us and produced a new popularity for the many religious and philosophical groups which embody the perennial philosophy today.[6] As a result, many are drawn today to the perennial philosophy in these groups and also to the forms of Christianity in which the perennial philosophy is dominant, in particular the mystical traditions. Much of the interest in spirituality in the churches today grows out of the current Romantic movement and its grounding in the perennial philosophy. Also, many have argued that the new physics and the hallucinogenic drug experience both support the validity of the perennial philosophy, especially in the form of Eastern mysticism. But this is hotly debated.[7]

So, as I suggested at the beginning, the perennial philosophy seems to be the main option to Christianity today. This demonstrates the universal appeal and power of this tradition. The fundamental question emerges whether the authentic Christian tradition lies in biblical religion, in the perennial philosophy, or in a synthesis of the two. This raises the further question whether a true and stable synthesis of these two traditions is possible. Many students of religion have struggled with this question, but no consensus has emerged.[8]

Few theologians see this as a critical issue in theology. In the last century, Karl Barth did see the issue and came down on the side of biblical religion. This is also generally true of the theologians in the tradition of political and liberation theology. Huston Smith sees the authentic Christian tradition to be squarely in the

---

5. See the works of Theodore Roszak, *The Making of a Counter Culture* (Garden City: Doubleday and Co., 1969) and *Where the Wasteland Ends* (Garden City: Doubleday and Co., 1972).

6. See the Ellwood study mentioned above and also his more recent work *Alternative Altars* (Chicago: University of Chicago Press, 1979); see also chapter 5.

7. For a critique of the former, see Ken Wilber, "Physics, Mysticism, and the New Holographic Paradigm," *The Holographic Paradigm*, ed. Wilber (Boulder, CO: Shambala, 1982). For a critique of the latter see R. C. Zaehner, *Mysticism Sacred and Profane* (London: Oxford University Press, 1957).

8. See *The Other Side of God: A Polarity in World Religions*, ed. Peter Berger (Garden City: Anchor Press, 1981).

perennial philosophy. Some theologians engaged in the inter-religious dialogue have begun to explore the possibility of a synthesis of Christianity with Buddhism, which stands generally in the perennial philosophy tradition.[9]

Other interpretations of the relation of these two traditions from the point of view of one of them tend to explain away the other tradition or treat it as a lower level of understanding. (Radhakrishnan and Buber are examples of this approach.) But religious traditions of such widespread power and appeal can hardly be distinguished in terms of truth and error. They must both have a firm hold on some aspects of ultimate reality. Complementarity and synthesis seem to be the more appropriate way of understanding their relation. Needless to say, any synthesis would have to be carried out from the point of view of one of the traditions.

Paul Tillich is the main theologian in this century who has argued forcefully that the authentic Christian tradition lies in a stable synthesis of the two traditions. He has carried this out in his *Systematic Theology,* and I will conclude by indicating briefly how he does this.[10] Tillich's synthesis appears clearly at three main points in the system: God as being itself and personal, creation and fall as the transition from essence to existence, and the fulfillment as essentialization or the transition from existence back to essence. I will speak only of the first.

As I suggested above, the One of perennial philosophy is the ineffable, nameless, undifferentiated ultimate reality which is substantial to the world. The divine reality in biblical religion is the transcendent and immanent personal God who creates the world. Tillich synthesized these views by means of his ontology. In his three sets of polar ontological elements which characterize all of finite being, the key one in this connection is the polarity of individualization and participation. All of finite reality from the sub-atomic particle to the human being

---

9. See John B. Cobb, Jr., *Beyond Dialogue: Toward a Mutual Transformation of Christianity and Buddhism* (Philadelphia: Fortress Press, 1982).

10. See *Systematic Theology*, 3 vols. (Chicago: University of Chicago Press, 1951-63): 1, 174-8, 243-5. Others who have attempted such a synthesis are John A. T. Robinson in *Truth is Two-Eyed* (Philadelphia: Westminster Press, 1979), and George Rupp in *Beyond Zen and Existentialism* (New York: Oxford University Press, 1979).

is informed by this polarity. On the human level, it takes the form of person and community. Since God is the ground of finite being, aspects of finite being can and must be used to speak symbolically of God. When the polarity of individualization and participation is applied to God symbolically, God is seen not as a person but as the ground of everything personal, not as the substance of all things but as the ground of all things. God is, thus, both the absolute individual and the absolute participant.

The human experience of the divine is informed by and varies according to this polarity of individualization and participation. Sometimes, as in biblical religion, it is nearer the individualization end of the polarity and is understood as a relation to the personal God. Other times, as in the perennial philosophy tradition, it is nearer the participation pole and is understood as a participation in or union with God. But Tillich's point is that, according to his ontology, individualization and participation can be actualized only in relation to each other. There can be no pure individualization which does not involve participation, and vice versa. Therefore, the religious experiences of these two traditions are not entirely alien, but rather constitute complementary views of the divine reality.

This, at least, is the implication of Tillich's synthesis. It is carried out primarily from the point of view of the biblical religion tradition. Other syntheses have been attempted on the basis of the perennial philosophy tradition. What I am suggesting is that Christianity, in line with its earliest formulations, should proceed to clarify its self-understanding as a synthesis of the biblical tradition and perennial philosophy traditions, and thus broaden its appeal to those whose experience stands more in the latter tradition.[11]

---

11. For a further elaboration of Tillich's view, see chapter 13.

CHAPTER 13

TILLICH AND THE PERENNIAL PHILOSOPHY

In chapter 12 I proposed the paradoxical theses that the main religio-philosophical alternative in the West to Judaism and Christianity has always been the perennial philosophy in its various forms, and that Christianity (and less so Judaism) has always been an amalgam or synthesis of the ideal types, biblical religion and the perennial philosophy. An example of the former is the concept delineated by the biblical theology movement of the 1940s and 1950s.[1] By the latter I mean the religio-philosophical world view exemplified by Neoplatonism and Vedanta, and by the philosophical foundation of Gnosticism, Rosicrucianism, and Theosophy, and propounded by such authors as Réne Guénon, Frithjof Schuon, S. H. Nasr, and Huston Smith.

The distinction between these ideal types is closely related to that which interpreters of religion often make between what Weber called the emissary and exemplary types,[2] or Berger the confrontation and interiority types.[3] These interpreters have noted that each religious tradition has elements of both of these types, but each also emphasizes one type or the other. The issue of the relationship between these types has become of fundamental importance today as many religious traditions have become aware of, and involved with, other

---

1.   James Barr and Brevard Childs have criticized the work of this movement. See James Barr, "Biblical Theology," *IDBSup* 104-11; and Brevard Childs, *Biblical Theology in Crisis* (Philadelphia: Westminster, 1970). Werner E. Lemke ("Theology [OT]," *ABD* 6 [1992]: 453-4, 468-9) has defended the movement against this criticism.
2.   Max Weber, *The Sociology of Religion*, trans. E. Fischoff (Boston: Beacon, 1963) 46-50.
3.   Peter Berger, ed., *The Other Side of God: A Polarity in World Religions* (Garden City, NY: Anchor, 1981): vii-viii, 3-6.

religions, and as it has become clear that religious differences often underlie social and political conflict and war.

I shall address the issue of the relationship between the ideal types of biblical religion and the perennial philosophy in Paul Tillich's interpretation of Christianity. Christian history can be seen as a continuing debate as to whether Christianity is essentially the perennial philosophy (Clement of Alexandria, Dionysius, Eckhart, Huston Smith), essentially biblical religion (Irenaeus, Calvin, Barth), or essentially a synthesis of the two (Augustine, Aquinas, Tillich). As I proposed at the end of chapter 12, Tillich is the main theologian in this century who has argued that the authentic Christian tradition is a stable synthesis of the two types, although he writes from the point of view of the biblical religion type.

Tillich's commitment to the biblical religion type derives from his Lutheranism and his affinity with neoorthodox theology. It is perhaps clearest in his stress on the Protestant principle and on the personalism and historical character of biblical religion in his book *Biblical Religion and the Search for Ultimate Reality.*[4] Tillich's commitment to the perennial philosophy type derives from the strong influence on him of Platonism, Neoplatonism, the mystical tradition of Cusanus, Eckhart, and Böhme, and the idealism of Schelling. It is manifest in his assertions that God is not a person, but rather being-itself, and that the mystical is a necessary element in understanding the divine and the human relationship to the divine. In his *Systematic Theology*, Tillich carries out his synthesis of these two types at three main points: God as being-itself and personal, creation and fall as the transition from essence to existence, and the fulfillment as essentialization or the transition from existence back to essence.[5]

The first point deals with the nature of the divine and the human relationship to it. In the perennial philosophy type, the divine or ultimate reality is the ineffable, undifferentiated One which is substantial to the world and about which nothing can be said except by negations. For example, the divine is not a

---

4. Paul Tillich, *Biblical Religion and the Search for Ultimate Reality* (Chicago: University of Chicago Press, 1955).

5. Paul Tillich, *Systematic Theology*, 3 vols. (Chicago: University of Chicago Press, 1951-63): 1.174-8, 243-5; 2.29-44; 3.406-22.

person or personal. The human relationship to the divine is based on the identity of the human soul or spirit with the divine. In the biblical religion type, however, ultimate reality is the transcendent and immanent personal creator God whose relation to humanity is analogous to human personal relationships. Tillich attempts to synthesize these views by means of his ontology.

According to Tillich, there are four levels of ontological concepts, including that of the basic ontological structure of self and world and that of the elements of the structure of being. There are three sets of polar ontological elements which apply to all levels or dimensions of being: individualization and participation, dynamics and form, and freedom and destiny. Because God is the ground of being, the ontological elements can be appropriate symbols of the divine. The subjective side of the polarities can symbolize the existential relation between God and humanity; thus humans can see God as personal, dynamic, and free. Tillich states, "The symbol 'personal God' is absolutely fundamental because an existential relation is a person-to-person relation. Man cannot be ultimately concerned about anything that is less than personal."[6] Tillich, however, goes on to state, "'Personal God' does not mean that God is a person. It means that God is the ground of everything personal. . . . He is not a person, but he is not less than personal."[7]

The other side of the polarities is, moreover, present in the side used as symbolic material. We can, therefore, call God the "absolute individual" only if we also call God the "absolute participant": "This can only mean that both individualization and participation are rooted in the ground of the divine life and God is equally 'near' to each of them while transcending them both."[8]

The human experience of the divine is informed by and varies according to this polarity. Tillich describes it as follows:

> Since the relation of man to the ground of his being must be expressed in symbols taken from the structure of his being, the polarity of participation and individualization determines the

---

6. Ibid., 1.244.
7. Ibid., 1.245.
8. Ibid., 1.244-5.

special character of this relation. . . . If participation is dominant, the relation to being-itself has a mystical character, if individualization prevails the relation to being-itself has a personal character. . . . In mysticism the individual strives for a participation in the ground of being which approaches identification. . . . The pole of individualization expresses itself in the religious experience as a personal encounter with God. . . . Although the two types are in contrast they do not exclude each other. For they are united by the polar interdependence of individualization and participation.[9]

Tillich's point is that every experience of the divine involves both individualization and participation. Thus, the religious experience of the biblical religion and perennial philosophy types are complementary experiences and interpretations of the divine.

Since Tillich approaches this issue primarily from the point of view of biblical religion, he believes that the union of personal encounter and mystical union can be called "faith." He states, "If both poles [individualization and participation] are accepted and transcended, the relation to being-itself has the character of faith."[10] Biblical religionists have criticized Tillich for dissolving faith into a mystical ontology alien to the Bible, while perennialists fault him for not perceiving that the divine transcends being-itself and for elevating faith as personal encounter to the level of mystical union. His approach, however, seems to me to be a valid and creative synthesis of the two types.[11]

The second point at which Tillich attempts a synthesis of the biblical religion and perennial philosophy types is in his interpretation of creation and fall. In the perennial philosophy type, the world originates from an emanation or overflowing of the divine substance analogous to light from the sun or water from a fountain. This origin does not depend on the will or purpose of the divine. This means that the world is essentially divine, or that the divine reality is "substantial

---

9. Paul Tillich, *The Courage To Be* (New Haven: Yale University Press, 1952): 156-7, 160.

10. Ibid., 156-7.

11. While on this point Tillich interprets the relationship between the biblical religion and perennial philosophy types as a polarity, perennialists interpret this relation as a hierarchy. They see the interpretation of the divine in biblical religion as an incomplete understanding which is valid on a lower level, but which is transcended in the perennial philosophy. See, for example, Huston Smith, *Forgotten Truth: The Primordial Tradition* (New York: Harper & Row, 1976): 48-53.

to the world," as Huxley has put it.[12] The world is ordered in a hierarchy, a great chain of being, stretching from the divine down through the spiritual, the psychic, and the organic to the inorganic. This is a hierarchy in which the closer a level of being is to the divine, the greater its reality, power, and value; the farther from the divine, the lesser its reality, power, and value.

In this hierarchy of being, humanity is a microcosm containing within itself all the levels of being from the divine down to the inorganic. The highest level of a human being is identical with the divine. So the problematic character of the human situation ("the fall") is due to the involvement of the human spirit, which is essentially divine, in the lower levels of being and its resulting confusion and ignorance of its essential divine nature.[13]

In the biblical religion type, on the other hand, the world originates from the divine purpose and will of love in creation out of nothing. The created world is thus essentially good in all its aspects. The world is not essentially divine but rather creaturely, a reality that is neither divine nor illusory, but rather contingent yet real. There is a sense in which the world is ordered in a hierarchy of levels of being, but it is not a hierarchy of degrees of reality, but rather one of degrees of complexity and spiritual possibility.

In the biblical religion type, as in the perennial philosophy type, humanity includes all levels of being with one exception: humanity has no divine element but is entirely creaturely. The problematic situation of humanity is, moreover, due not to involvement in the lower levels of being, but to the will's perverse turning away from the divine love. The problem lies not in the body but in the human spirit. There are also some suggestions in the biblical religion type of the fall of the natural world, seen mythologically in the divine cursing of the earth in punishment for Adam's disobedience or in the fall of angels, which also results from the perversity of the will or spirit. The fulfillment will include the

---

12. Aldous Huxley, *The Perennial Philosophy* (New York: Harper & Row, 1944): vii.
13. See Paul Ricoeur, "The Myth of the Exiled Soul and Salvation Through Knowledge," in *The Symbolism of Evil* (reprint, 1967; Boston: Beacon, 1969): 279-305.

transformation of the creation, which may imply either that it is fallen or that the fulfillment will transcend the original creation.

These two types regard creation and fall very differently. Tillich attempts to synthesize their views by describing creation and fall as the transition from essence to existence. He states that God is essentially creative and describes this in terms of freedom and destiny, which is the third set of polar ontological elements constituting the structure of being. This polarity is grounded in God as being-itself and can therefore be applied symbolically to God. Tillich states that creation is a matter of neither necessity nor contingency but rather of God's freedom and destiny. He emphasizes the divine freedom by describing the Word as the medium of creation: "Creation through the Word, in contrast to a process of emanation as elaborated in Neoplatonism, points symbolically both to the freedom of creation and to the freedom of the created. The manifestation of the ground of being is spiritual, not mechanical."[14]

Tillich affirms, moreover, the doctrine of creation not out of God nor out of matter but out of nothing which he describes as protecting Christianity against any type of ultimate dualism such as he finds in Platonism. "The *me-ontic* matter of Platonism represents the dualistic element which underlies all paganism and which is the ultimate ground of the tragic sense of life."[15]

Thus far Tillich's interpretation stands clearly on the side of the biblical religion type. When he proceeds to interpret creation and fall as the transition from essence to existence, however, the emphasis changes. Tillich interprets essence to mean the true nature of things, "the original goodness of everything created."[16] Essence, however, is only potential, not actual. Tillich interprets existence, on the other hand, to mean actuality, especially its distorted character. He emphasizes the centrality of his doctrine of essence and existence: "A complete discussion of the relation of essence and existence is identical with the entire theological system. The distinction between essence and existence, which

---

14. Tillich, *Systematic Theology*, 1.158.
15. Ibid., 1.188.
16. Ibid., 1.202.

religiously speaking is the distinction between the created and the actual world, is the backbone of the whole body of theological thought."[17]

The transition from essence to existence means that "man and the rest of reality are not only 'inside' the process of the divine life but also 'outside' it."[18] Tillich states,

> This is the point at which the doctrine of creation and the doctrine of the fall join. It is the most difficult and the most dialectical point in the doctrine of creation. . . . It is the most mysterious point in human existence. Fully developed creatureliness is fallen creatureliness. . . . To be outside the divine life means to stand in actualized freedom, in an existence which is no longer united with essence.[19]

This is the end of creation and the beginning of the fall. It is also a universal situation true for all of creation. It is a matter of neither individual contingency nor structural necessity, but of freedom and destiny. Tillich's interpretation of this transition is thus close to that of the perennial philosophy type.

Thus far I have summarized the discussion of this issue in the first volume of the *Systematic Theology*. Tillich treats it in more detail in the second volume, where he takes up the question of how the transition from essence to existence is possible. The answer is clear but surprising: "One can say that nature is finite necessity, God is infinite freedom, man is finite freedom. It is finite freedom which makes possible the transition from essence to existence."[20] Tillich repeats this statement and begins to explain: "Man is responsible for the transition from essence to existence because he has finite freedom and because all dimensions of reality are united in him."[21] Is Tillich suggesting that humanity rather than God is responsible for the creation and fall of the universe? He seems to assert here that humanity is a kind of Platonic universal and/or microcosm acting for all of finite

---

17. Ibid., 1.204.
18. Ibid., 1.255.
19. Ibid.
20. Ibid., 2.31. This passage is absent in the German translation; see Paul Tillich, *Systematische Theologie*, 3 vols. (Stuttgart: Evangelische Verlag, 1956-66): 2.38. Since this translation was largely approved by Tillich, it constitutes a revised edition.
21. Tillich, *Systematic Theology*, 2.40; this passage is also absent from Tillich, *Systematische Theologie*, 2.47.

reality and thus enacting the universal transition from essence to existence which is creation and fall.

How can Tillich make this claim given the late appearance of humanity in cosmic history and the microscopic character of humanity in the cosmos? Tillich's answer to this question is three-fold. Human freedom is possible only in the context of a universal destiny, the universal transition from essence to existence; humanity and nature participate in each other; and there are analogies in nature to human good and evil actions. The capacity of finite freedom to contradict itself in existence is "possible only within the context of the universal transition from essence to existence. There is no individual fall. . . . The transition from essence to existence is possible because finite freedom works within the frame of a universal destiny."[22] Furthermore,

> The universe participates in every act of human freedom. It represents the side of destiny in the act of freedom. . . . Man reaches into nature, as nature reaches into man. They participate in each other and cannot be separated from each other. This makes it possible and necessary to use the term 'fallen world' and to apply the concept of existence (in contrast to essence) to the universe as well as to man.[23]

Tillich goes beyond this concept of mutual participation to assert that there are also analogies to human good and evil in all parts of the universe. He refers to various biblical passages to argue that nature is not innocent. He concludes, "Just as, within man, nature participates in the good and evil he does, so nature, outside man, shows analogies to man's good and evil doing."[24] Tillich gives no example here of the fallenness of nature, but in a sermon he refers to the Romantic interpretation of suffering, death, and decay in nature.[25]

Thus Tillich suggests that creation and fall take place because of finite human freedom, either because of the universal polarity of freedom and destiny,

---

22. Tillich, *Systematic Theology*, 2.32. The last sentence is absent from Tillich, *Systematische Theologie*, 2.39.

23. Tillich, *Systematic Theology*, 2.43

24. Ibid.

25. See Paul Tillich, "Nature, also, Mourns for a Lost Good," in *The Shaking of the Foundations* (New York: Harper & Row, 1948): 81-2.

or the mutual participation of humanity and nature, or the analogies to human good and evil action in nature. These are distinct explanations for the universal transition. Only the first seems to explain the universality satisfactorily given the late appearance and minuteness of humanity in the cosmos. Why then the emphasis on human responsibility for the universal transition? There seem to be serious problems in Tillich's argument here, perhaps indicated by the extensive rewriting carried out in the German translation.

In another section Tillich states that the unity of ethical freedom and tragic destiny is "the great problem of the doctrine of man."[26] The Christian tradition has struggled to keep the balance between these two emphases but "must simultaneously acknowledge the tragic universality of estrangement and man's personal responsibility for it."[27] "It" clearly refers here to human estrangement. Does it also refer to universal estrangement? If so, the problem remains.

Some interpreters have attempted to resolve or at least ease this problem by noting that Tillich seems to claim that creation and fall are not identical but simply coincide at one point.[28] Thus, when describing the reality of standing outside the divine life in actualized freedom, Tillich says: "Seen from one side, this is the end of creation. Seen from the other side, it is the beginning of the fall."[29] He later asserts, however: "Creaturely freedom is the point at which creation and the fall coincide."[30]

Tillich, moreover, does not understand creation and fall mythologically as distinct processes such that the end of one coincides with the beginning of the other. Both creation and fall consist in the transition from potential essentiality inside the divine life to existential actuality outside the divine life. In the second volume of *Systematic Theology*, Tillich continues to speak of a point of coincidence between creation and fall, but he drops any reference to the end of creation and the beginning of the fall. He states simply, "Creation and the Fall

---

26. Tillich, *Systematic Theology*, 2.38.
27. Ibid., 2.39.
28. See, for example, John E. Smith, "Comments," in Jacquelyn Ann K. Kegley, ed., *Paul Tillich on Creativity* (Lanham, MD: University Press of America, 1989): 25-7.
29. Tillich, *Systematic Theology*, 1.255.
30. Ibid., 2.256.

coincide in so far as there is no point in time and space in which created goodness was actualized and had existence. . . . Actualized creation and estranged existence are identical."[31]

Tillich's picture of creation and fall as the transition (in which God is apparently not active) from essential potentiality within the divine life to existential actuality outside the divine life is coherent with the perennial philosophy type. On the other hand, the emphasis on God's freedom expressed in creation out of nothing and on human responsibility for the fall are coherent with biblical religion. Tillich does not seem, however, to have achieved a synthesis or unified interpretation of the two types on this second point.

The third point at which Tillich attempts a synthesis lies in his interpretation of the fulfillment as essentialization or the transition from existence to essence. In the perennial philosophy type the way of fulfillment is through knowledge (*gnosis*). The human spirit comes to know its divine nature, turns away from its involvement in the lower levels of being, and by means of ascetical disciplines rises up to such a perfect mystical union that its individuality is entirely transcended in the undifferentiated unity of the divine, as a drop of water returns to the ocean. In the biblical religion type, fulfillment comes (fragmentarily in history, fully at the end of history) to the perverse human will and spirit through transformation by the divine presence in forgiveness and reconciliation, leading to perfect communion with God and the whole creation in the reign of God. The difference between the views of the fulfillment in these two types is seen in the contrast between the natural symbol of the drop of water returning to the ocean and the socio-political symbol of the reign of God.

Although Tillich notes the contrast between the biblical religion and perennial philosophy types throughout his *Systematic Theology* and other works,[32] it is in this area that he perceives the greatest contrast between them. In his

---

31. Ibid., 2.44.
32. See, for example, Paul Tillich, *A History of Christian Thought* (ed. Carl E. Braaten; New York: Harper & Row, 1968): 6, 13, 50-5, 109. Tillich's theological dissertation also treats the same issue: *Mysticism and Guilt Consciousness in Schelling's Philosophical Development* (Lewisburg, PA: Bucknell University Press, 1974).

interpretation of time and eternity, history and the kingdom of God, Tillich notes that there has been what he calls "a basic split in the valuation of history and life itself" between

> the two contrasting types of interpreting history— the nonhistorical and the historical. The nonhistorical . . . presupposes that the 'running ahead' of historical time has no aim either within or above history. . . . One can distinguish three forms of such nonhistorical interpretations of history: the tragic, the mystical, and the mechanistic.[33]

The mystical is the perennial philosophy type:

> Although it appears in Western culture (as, for example, in Neoplatonism and Spinozism) it is most fully and effectively developed in the East, as in Vedanta Hinduism, in Taoism, and in Buddhism. Historical existence has no meaning in itself. One must live in it and act reasonably, but history itself can neither create the new nor be truly real. This attitude, which demands elevation above history while living in it, is the most widespread of all within historical mankind. . . . The emphasis is on the individual and particularly on the comparatively few illuminated individuals who are aware of the human predicament.[34]

There are also three inadequate historical interpretations of history: the progressivist, utopian, and transcendental. For his own interpretation of history and the fulfillment, Tillich takes the symbol of the kingdom of God which stands in stark contrast with the nonhistorical interpretations, especially the mystical. Tillich concludes, "The consequences of this difference for religion and culture in East and West are world-historical, and it would seem that there is no other symbol in Christianity which points to the ultimate source of the differences as clearly as the symbol 'Kingdom of God,' especially when it is contrasted with the symbol 'Nirvana.'"[35]

Tillich attempts to synthesize the views of fulfillment in the biblical religion and perennial philosophy types by means of his concepts of eternity and essentialization. First, he describes the fulfillment as the constant transition from

---

33. Tillich, *Systematic Theology*, 3.350.
34. Ibid., 3.351.
35. Ibid., 3.357.

the temporal to the eternal. He approaches the perennial philosophy type by interpreting the end or goal of history "as ever present, and as the permanent elevation of history into eternity, the permanent transition of the temporal to the eternal."[36] "The eternal is not a future state of things. It is always present."[37] Tillich, however, also points to the contribution of the temporal to the eternal in accordance with the biblical religion type. "The ever present end of history elevates the positive content of history into eternity."[38] "Life in the whole of creation and in a special way in human history contributes in every moment of time to the Kingdom of God and its eternal life."[39]

Then Tillich introduces the concept of essentialization and comments on its relation to the perennial philosophy type. He asks how the positive in history is related to essential being.

> A first and somewhat Platonizing answer is that being, elevated into eternity, involves a return to what a thing essentially is; this is what Schelling called 'essentialization.' This formulation can mean return to the state of mere essentiality or potentiality, including the removal of everything that is real under the conditions of existence. Such an understanding of essentialization would make it into a concept which is more adequate to the India-born religions than to any of the Israel-born ones. The whole world process would not produce anything new. It would have the character of falling away from and returning to essential being. But the term 'essentialization' can also mean that the new which has been actualized in time and space adds something to essential being, uniting it with the positive which is created within existence.'[40]

In this passage the first meaning of essentialization is that of the perennial philosophy type pervasive in the "India-born" religions. The second meaning is closer to the biblical religion type, fundamental in the "Israel-born" religions, although the question about the finitude of time is not addressed. I will return to this later.

---

36. Ibid., 3.398-9.
37. Ibid., 3.400.
38. Ibid., 3.397.
39. Ibid., 3.398.
40. Ibid., 3.400.

One of the main issues between the two types is the ultimate status of individuality, which the perennial philosophy type transcends and the biblical religion type affirms. Here Tillich sides with the latter and affirms that "the centered, self-conscious self cannot be excluded from eternal life," but not as "the endless continuation of a particular stream of consciousness in memory and anticipation."[41] "Christian theology could not go this way [of Plotinus' mystical union of the one with the One] because of its emphasis on the individual person and his eternal destiny."[42]

The final point in Tillich's attempt to synthesize the two types on the fulfillment is in his symbolism of time. He notes the Pythagorean-Platonic image of time as a circle and the Augustinian image of time as a straight line and proposes a compromise, the image of a curve:

> I would suggest a curve which comes from above, moves down as well as ahead, reaches the deepest point which is the *nunc existentiale*, the 'existential now,' and returns in an analogous way to that from which it came, going ahead as well as up. This can be drawn in every moment of experienced time, and it can also be seen as the diagram for temporality as a whole. It implies the creation of the temporal, the beginning of time, and the return of the temporal to the eternal, the end of time.[43]

Tillich is careful, however, to state that the beginning and end of time are not definite moments of time in past or future. "Beginning from and ending in the eternal are not matters of a determinable moment in physical time but rather a process going on in every moment. . . . There is always creation and consummation, beginning and end."[44]

Tillich seems ambivalent on this point. On the one hand, he affirms the theme of the biblical religion type that time moves from beginning to end, from creation to fulfillment, and that time contributes to the eternal. He states that the curve can be seen as "the diagram for temporality as a whole." This implies that time has a beginning in the past and an end in the future. On the other hand, he

---

41. Ibid., 3.414.
42. Ibid., 3.411.
43. Ibid., 3.420.
44. Ibid.

also wants to deny a literal beginning and end of time and to focus on the continuous character of creation and consummation in the present, as affirmed in at least some versions of the perennial philosophy type.

It is clear that on this third point Tillich has achieved a partial synthesis of the two types. He accomplishes this by accepting the thesis of the perennial philosophy type that the fulfillment is the transition from existence to essence, and then adding the affirmation of the biblical religion type that historical existence contributes to essence or the eternal. He avoids, however, the question of the finitude of temporality.

In conclusion, one can say that Tillich's synthesis of the biblical religion and perennial philosophy types, from the point of view of the former, is partially successful. It is satisfactory on the first point (God as being-itself and personal), somewhat less satisfactory on the third point (the fulfillment as the transition from existence to essence), and even less satisfactory on the second point (creation and fall as the transition from essence to existence).

What then can one conclude from this investigation about the possibility of a synthesis of the two types? There seem to be three possible answers to this question: first, a synthesis is impossible because of fundamental contradictions between the two types. This is the view of many neoorthodox or evangelical Protestants. Second, a complete synthesis is possible, because the two types are fully complementary in their main affirmations. This is the view of many Roman Catholic, Orthodox, and liberal Protestant thinkers, whose traditions have always been amalgams of the two types. And third, a partial synthesis is possible, because the two traditions are complementary on some issues and contradictory on others. This seems to be the implication of Tillich's answer to the question.

Because of the richness of the various religious traditions and of the dangers of separation, misunderstanding, and hostility among them, it is to be hoped that further reflection on this issue will lead to progress on the question of whether a synthesis is possible between these two great religio-philosophical types.

Appendix: Paul Ricoeur

In his well-known book *The Symbolism of Evil*,[45] Paul Ricoeur presents the same theses that I proposed in chapter 12, but in the mode of the phenomenological analysis of the myths of evil. He suggests a typology of the four myths of the origin and end of evil that have informed Western sensibility and reflection: the drama of creation out of chaos, the tragic vision of the evil god, the Adamic myth of the fall, and the myth of the exiled soul. The latter two correspond exactly to my biblical religion and perennial philosophy types. Although Ricoeur describes them as "profoundly heterogeneous,"[46] he indicates ways in which they have been synthesized.

Ricoeur states that the myth of the exiled soul "presided, if not over the birth, at least over the growth of Greek philosophy."[47] It "differs from all the others in that it divides man into *soul* and *body* and concentrates on the destiny of the soul, which it depicts as coming from elsewhere and straying here below."[48] The myth "tells how the 'soul,' divine in its origin, became human — how the 'body,' a stranger to the soul and bad in many ways, falls to the lot of the soul. . . . Divine as to his soul, earthly as to his body, man is the forgetting of the difference; and the [Orphic myth of Dionysos] tells how that happened."[49] In this myth the way of salvation and fulfillment is knowledge: "The myth of the exiled soul is *par excellence* the principle and promise of 'knowledge,' of 'gnosis.' . . . In this awareness, in this awakening to itself of the exiled soul, all 'philosophy' of the Platonic and Neo-Platonic type is contained."[50]

Then Ricoeur describes "the struggle between the Adamic myth and the myth of exile"[51] and their confusion in Christian history: "Whatever may be the later confusions of Christianity and Neoplatonism, which in a certain fashion retains the essential traits of the Orphic myth, the dualistic myth [of the exiled

45. Paul Ricoeur, *The Symbolism of Evil* (New York: Harper & Row, 1967).
46. Ricoeur, *The Symbolism of Evil*, 174.
47. Ibid.
48. Ibid.
49. Ibid., 280.
50. Ibid., 300.
51. Ibid., 330.

288

soul] and the [Adamic] myth of the fall are radically heterogeneous."[52] He later continues:

> The history of the use in Christianity of a Neo-Platonic mode of expression offers . . . many examples of contamination of the myth of the fall by the myth of the exiled soul. . . . It is only by discovering in each of these myths an affinity for the other that we shall be able to account for their confusion.[53]

The affinity of the Adamic myth for the myth of exile can be seen in the givenness and externality of evil symbolized by Eve and the serpent; the themes of banishment from the garden, captivity in Egypt, and exile in Babylon; the image of the body as the symbol of externality in the prophetic image of the heart of stone and as the seat of seduction and defilement; and the twice-born religious experiences of Paul, Augustine, and Luther which lead to quasi-dualistic symbolic language about the body.

The later development of the myth of the exiled soul shows affinities with the Adamic myth. Ricoeur gives as an example the shift in Plato "from the evil body to the unjust soul," which appears in the Phaedo, the Phaedrus, and the Republic.[54]

Ricoeur concludes,

> In its ascetic form as well as in its mystical form, Platonizing Christianity adopts the opposition between contemplation and concupiscence, which, in its turn, introduces the opposition between the spiritual soul and the mortal and raving body; the old fear of defilement and the old fear of the body and sexuality are taken over by the new wisdom. . . . Thus there will be assembled, within the Christian experience, the conditions for a fusion with Neo-Platonic spirituality, the remote heir of the myth of exiled soul and the body-prison.[55]

---

52. Ibid., 281.
53. Ibid., 330.
54. Ibid., 336-45.
55. Ibid., 335.

CHAPTER 14

BEATRICE OR ISEULT?
THE DEBATE ABOUT ROMANTIC LOVE

Several years ago my wife and I were on leave in Rome doing some writing and teaching. Through a friend we joined a group of four Roman Catholic priests who met weekly to study various historical texts. The first one was the *Vita Nuova* of Dante, a text which I had never read before. Its subject matter was entirely new to me, namely, the experience of romantic love as an experience of God. My neo-orthodox theological education in the late forties had not left me open to this possibility. The study of Denis de Rougemont's *Love in the Western World* had confirmed my uneasiness about such an idea. But since the meetings in Rome, I have often wondered about it. More recently some research on romanticism has led me to the writings of Charles Williams on the theology of romantic love which focuses on Dante's *Vita Nuova* as well as the *Commedia*. The contrast between Williams and de Rougemont intrigued me — thus this chapter.

In the 1930s and 1940s there arose a largely silent debate about the meaning and significance for human life of romantic love. On the one hand, Charles Williams (1886-1945), the English poet, novelist, literary critic, and theologian, proposed an orthodox Christian theology of romantic love. Following Dante he saw it as an experience of grace and salvation.[1] On the other hand,

---

1. The works in which Williams elaborates his theology of romantic love are as follows, with dates of writing: "Outlines of Romantic Theology" (1925), in *Outlines of Romantic Theology*, ed. Alice Mary Hadfield (Grand Rapids: William B. Eerdmans, 1990); "The Theology of Romantic Love" (1938) in *He Came Down from Heaven* (Grand Rapids: William B. Eerdmans, 1984), reprinted in *Charles Williams: Essential Writings in Spirituality and Theology*, ed. Charles C. Hefting, Jr. (Cambridge, MA: Crowley Publications, 1993); "Religion and Love in Dante: The

Denis de Rougemont (1906-1985), the Swiss historian, literary critic, and theologian, proposed an interpretation of what he called the myth of romantic love which had its origin in heretical Catharist sources. This myth interpreted the experience of the passion of romantic love as one which promised the exaltation and destruction of the lovers.[2] As far as I know, neither Williams nor de Rougemont knew of the work of the other, with a single exception to which I will refer later.

The theses of Williams and de Rougemont on romantic love appear to be quite contradictory. They refer to much of the same historical and literary material and come to what seem to be exactly opposite conclusions. Let us consider their theses.

According to de Rougemont, in the twelfth century a Christian heresy known as Catharism arose in southern France which involved a dualism of body and soul. The divine soul has been tempted by the Woman and is imprisoned in the body. It longs to be delivered from the body so that it can be reunited with the divine. This longing is directed at an ideal woman named Maria, the mother of a docetic Jesus who teaches an ascetic way of deliverance from the body. This deliverance occurs finally in death. So the passionate longing of the soul for deliverance is essentially a longing for death. Thus, Catharism transformed natural sexual desire into passion, limitless aspiration and longing.

Catharism was persecuted by the Inquisition, went underground, and appeared again in the guise of courtly love. This was expounded in the poems and songs of the troubadours who were its evangelists. The fundamental myth of courtly love is the story of Tristan and Iseult. This is the legend of the passionate adulterous love of these two which was inflamed by numerous obstacles, the main

---

Theology of Romantic Love" (1941) in *Outlines*, ed. Hadfield; *The Figure of Beatrice: A Study in Dante* (1943) (New York: Octagon Books, 1983).

2. De Rougemont's main work on the myth of romantic love was published as *L'Amour et L'Occident* in Paris in 1938. An English translation entitled *Passion and Society* was published in England in 1940. A revised edition entitled *Love in the Western World* was published in New York by Harper & Row in 1956. De Rougemont published an extended recasting of the argument in the introductory chapter of *Love Declared*, trans. Richard Howard (New York: Pantheon Books, 1963). An augmented edition of *Love in the Western World* was published by Princeton University Press in 1983 with a 53-page postscript. The pagination of this and the 1956 edition is the same.

one being that Iseult was married to King Mark. The message of the myth is that passionate romantic love is the true human fulfillment which exalts and transforms the lovers through death. De Rougemont interprets this myth to be in direct contradiction to the Christian understanding of love as Agape.

According to Williams the modern view of romantic love had its source in Dante's experience of falling in love with Beatrice and his interpretation of this as an experience of grace and salvation. "He is the spring of all modern love literature."[3] Williams claims that the common experience of falling in love can be an experience of the unfallen state of original perfection, of the kingdom of God, and especially an experience of the love and grace of God incarnate in Christ, an experience of salvation. It depends upon what is done with the experience. If it is not seen as an end in itself but rather a beginning, it can be a following of the Christian way, especially in marriage.

Williams gives the larger context for his theology of romantic love. "It has been part of the work of Christianity in the world to make men aware of the spiritual significance of certain natural experiences. . . . [But this] has been attempted very little with romantic love. Yet an human energy which can be so described is capable of being assumed into sacramental and transcendental heights — such is the teaching of the Incarnation."[4] The lack of such an attempt in regard to romantic love in the past has been due to apocalypticism, the concentration upon another world, suspicion of any sacrament involving human delight, the haunting of Manicheanism, the asceticism necessary for the mystical life, and clerical celibacy.[5]

The beginning of romantic love was Beatrice's appearance to Dante and his response. "A flame of *caritas* possessed me, which made me pardon anyone who had offended me."[6] Williams comments, "The experience . . . arouses a sense of intense significance, a sense that an explanation of the whole universe is

---

3. *Outlines*, p. 55.
4. Ibid., p. 9.
5. Ibid., pp. 9-10.
6. Charles Williams, p. 79, quoting *Vita Nuova*, 11:1.

being offered."[7] This requires a response of intellect, will, and emotions. "Is it serious? Is it capable of intellectual treatment? Is it capable of belief, labor, fruition? Is it (in some sense or other) *true*? . . . . Can this state of things be treated as the first matter of a great experiment? . . . . The end of course is known by definition of the kingdom: it is the establishment of a state of *caritas*, of pure love, the mode of expression of one moment into eternity."[8] This is the Way of Romantic Love.

(In connection with de Rougemont's thesis about Catharism as the source of the myth of romantic love, it is intriguing to note that about 1917 Williams was initiated into an occult group, the hermetic Order of the Golden Dawn, which had been founded in 1887 by three English Rosicrucians, a tradition which has similarities to Catharism.)

Now what are we to make of this fundamental disagreement? Is it simply a matter of differing interpretations of some medieval literature? It certainly is that. But does it also involve deeper disagreements? I shall look first at the differences in historical interpretation, especially in regard to Dante and the Arthurian romances, and then move on to other questions.

I have noted that for Williams, Dante is the main source of his theology of romantic love, and Williams interprets him to be an orthodox catholic Christian. De Rougemont, however, sees Dante quite differently, namely, as continuing the heretical tradition of the myth of romantic love.

De Rougemont's main point is that for Dante, Beatrice is "entirely symbolical."[9] He states, "In Dante the images are the more passionate and 'realistic' in proportion to Beatrice's progressive rise in the hierarchy of mystical abstraction, where she becomes first Philosophy, then Wisdom, and finally Divine Knowledge."[10] De Rougemont suggests that in *Vita Nuova* 19 where Dante describes Beatrice as heaven's only lack and one whom the saints entreat, he is not referring to Beatrice as "a real woman" but rather as "the Holy Ghost in the

---

7. Ibid., p. 75.
8. Ibid., pp. 72-3.
9. *Love in the Western World*, p. 178.
10. Ibid., p. 98.

act of upholding His Church with the charity of Christ."[11] He grants that Beatrice existed and that Dante loved her, but he states that this is a case of sublimation. "Love is [essentially] mystic passion" and "it is perilous to stop short at the terrestrial forms [of love] which are *merely its image*."[12] Thus de Rougemont interprets Dante as standing in the tradition of the heretical myth of romantic love.

It is important to note that Williams explicitly denies such an interpretation of Dante. He criticizes the allegorists who "deny altogether the mortal identity of Beatrice and turn her wholly into Theology or Divine Grace or what not," and also the spiritualizers for whom Beatrice "becomes so dim that she is, in fact, nothing but a kind of vapor of the soul, a mist that goes up out of the ground of the heart. . . . To spiritualize Beatrice away from the earth into a pseudo-Romanticism is, in criticism, very like mortal sin."[13]

Williams's quite different interpretation of Dante emphasizes the very earthy and concrete reality of Beatrice and involves a very different understanding of symbols and images. According to Williams, Dante always affirms and never loses sight of the fact that Beatrice is a real flesh-and-blood woman from birth to death. But for Dante she is also an image of the kingdom of God. Here Williams's doctrine of images comes into play. An image, unlike an allegory, is not constructed but discovered. An image exists independently of its imaging function and thus has its own uniqueness and integrity. Finally, an image is both identical with and not identical with its basis or referent.[14]

According to Williams, therefore, for Dante Beatrice has a specific identity which is unique and integrated, and her whole being is a revelation of God. As Williams puts it, "She has a double nature."[15] "Beatrice was, in her degree, an image of nobility, of virtue, of the Redeemed Life, and in some sense

---

11. Ibid., p. 179.
12. Ibid.; emphasis added.
13. *Figure of Beatrice*, p. 101.
14. For a summary of William's doctrine of images, see Mary McDermott Shideler: *The Theology of Romantic Love: A Study in the Writings of Charles Williams* (New York: Harper & Row, 1962): ch. 1.
15. *Charles Williams*, pp. 85-6.

of Almighty God Himself. But she also remained Beatrice right to the end."[16] "This is the law of symbolism — that the symbol must be utterly itself before it can properly be a symbol."[17] It is clear that Williams's view of imagery is quite different from that of de Rougemont, and that for Williams Beatrice can hardly be described as "entirely symbolical" or "merely an image."

(It should be noted that C. S. Lewis, in his book on courtly love entitled *The Allegory of Love* (1938), which Williams quotes at length in "The Theology of Romantic Love," agrees with de Rougemont that Dante stands in the tradition of courtly love but at one extreme. In Dante, according to Lewis, courtly love "find[s] a *modus vivendi* with Christianity and produce[s] a noble fusion of sexual and religious experience."[18])

De Rougemont's main thesis is that the myth which dominates the imagination of modern western people is a secularized version of the myth of the adulterous love of Tristan and Iseult. Since the Tristan romance is one of the Arthurian romances, they are at the center of de Rougemont's argument. He considers them to be largely a translation of courtly love from southern to northern France and England with new features added from the Celtic background but manifesting the same heretical dualistic idea of love.

According to de Rougemont, the main new theme which is found in the Arthurian romances is the occurrence of a sin against courtly love, namely, the adultery of Tristan with Iseult and of Lancelot with Guinevere. In the thirteenth century the Tristan myth was revived by Gottfried of Strasbourg who was Wagner's source for his opera *Tristan and Isolde,* which is the classic modern form of the myth of romantic love.

Again Williams's interpretation of the Arthurian romances is quite different from that of de Rougemont. Williams sees them, and in particular Malory's *Morte D'Arthur,* as one of the main documents after Dante supporting

---

16. *Figure of Beatrice,* pp. 7-8.
17. Charles Williams, *Reason and Beauty in the Poetic Mind* (London: Oxford University Press, 1933), quoted in Shideler, *Theology of Romantic Love,* p. 40.
18. C. S. Lewis, *The Allegory of Love: A Study in Medieval Tradition* (New York: Oxford University Press, 1958): 21.

and exemplifying his theology of romantic love, and as "the supreme invention in Christendom of a story concerned with the adventure and ineffable destiny of romantic love."[19] In addition, Williams published two volumes of poetry on the Arthurian romances in which he expounds and interprets his theology of romantic love.

Both de Rougemont and Williams claim that their interpretations of romantic love have implications for all of human life and culture. De Rougemont argues that in the course of the last eight centuries, the myth of romantic love has been secularized and that the heretical dualistic religious context has been lost. The result has been not only the pervasive influence of the myth in novels, plays, and films, but also the spread of passion into every sphere of life. This has led not only to the breakdown of middle-class marriage but also to the emergence of passion in politics, nationalism, and war.

De Rougemont focuses especially on marriage. The Catharists had condemned procreation and therefore marriage, claiming that it was not a sacrament but rather a collaboration with the evil power which had created the world. They honored the passionate mystical love which led the soul out of the world to the divine. In the guise of courtly love, it took the form of passionate love of the Lady. It was gradually secularized and transformed into the myth of romantic love which honored the passionate love which was inflamed by obstacles. This led to the despising of marriage and the glorification of adulterous passion as the true human fulfillment. According to de Rougemont, however, Agape or Christian love can "rescue" Eros or passionate love, and "contain" it in marriage.[20]

Williams also sees his theology of romantic love as applying to all of life. Although its main focus is sexual love in marriage, "its principles are true in relation to other romantic occupations of men."[21] He refers to what he calls virginal love, friendship, and also "any relation of man into which the element of

---

19. *Outlines*, p. 60.
20. *Love in the Western World*, pp. 312, 315.
21. *Outlines*, p. 67.

sincere and single attraction enters."[22] He mentions learning, art, nature, politics, sport, and even stamp collecting. "Any occupation exercising itself with passion, with self-oblivion, with devotion, towards an end other than itself, is a gateway to divine things."[23] In particular, the image of the city and its relation to the state is a central concern of Williams. "The principles of [Dante's writings on the city of man] . . . are a necessary part of the Beatrician way. Politics are, or should be, a part of *caritas*; they are the matter to which the form of *caritas* must be applied."[24]

Williams's central concern, however, is also marriage. He is clear that it is an error to hold that romantic love should be the only basis for marriage or that it should necessarily lead to marriage. However, "the clearest possibility of this Way [of romantic love] and perhaps the most difficult, may be in marriage."[25] Williams's theology of marriage views it as a microcosm of the church as well as of the state.

Williams also treats what is often assumed to be the problem which romantic love causes in marriage, namely, one partner falling in love with another person. Here there is a sharp contrast with de Rougemont who argues that the myth of romantic love exalts adulterous passion and derogates marriage. According to Williams, if a married person falls in love with another person (as happened to Williams), this person must not discard the first image of love in the spouse. Yet neither may this person deny the new love. The way of romantic love requires that one use the energy found in the second image of love for the heightening of the first. "One continues to love the second image, which is as much a revelation as the first, but restricts the expression of that love and its position in the total structure of one's life."[26]

And what should be the response of the spouse to this second image of love? Here Williams is a rigorist. Jealousy and the condoning of infidelity are

---

22. Ibid., p. 70
23. Ibid.
24. Ibid., p. 97.
25. *Figure of Beatrice*, p. 15.
26. Shideler, *Theology of Romantic Love*, p. 208.

both wrong. The spouse is called "to rejoice in every revelation the other receives, whatever it be, because 'he who hates the manifestation of the kingdom hates the kingdom; he is an apostate to the kingdom.'"[27] Williams points to the ideal of the way of romantic love: "The aim of the Romantic Way is the two great ends of liberty and power. . . . If it were possible to create in marriage a mutual adoration towards the second image, whenever and however it came, and also a mutual limitation of the method of it, I do not know what new liberties and powers might not be achieved."[28]

Both Williams and de Rougemont make gestures toward the other's position. Williams states that one reaction to falling in love is to "lose ourselves in it,"[29] which means to treat it as an end in itself which excuses any response to it, rather than treating it as the beginning of a new way of life. He also states that among the attacks which Hell has made on the Way of Romantic Love is the assumption that the state of love is a personal possession of the lover, and that it is sufficient to have known the state of love and to consider oneself as one of the elect.[30]

On his side de Rougemont states that Agape, Christian love, can rescue Eros, passionate love, from the myth of romantic love. Agape makes the bondage of Eros evident and thus delivers from this bondage. He states, "All pagan religions deify Desire. All seek to be upheld and saved by Desire, which is thus instantly transformed into the greatest enemy of Life, the seduction of Nothingness. . . . *In ceasing to be a god, [Eros] ceases to be a demon.* And he finds his proper place in the provisional economy of Creation and of what is human."[31] De Rougemont does not elucidate what he means by this "proper place" of Eros, except to add that "fidelity secures itself against unfaithfulness by

---

27. Ibid., pp. 208-9; quoting *Figure of Beatrice*, p. 50.
28. *Figure of Beatrice*, pp. 49-50.
29. Ibid., p. 100.
30. *Charles Williams*, pp. 86-9.
31. *Love in the Western World*, p. 312.

298

becoming accustomed not to separate desire from love," and to define marriage as *"the institution in which passion is 'contained,' not by morals, but by love."*[32]

De Rougemont goes on to state that in Christian marriage "fidelity is a refusal *on oath* 'to cultivate' the illusions of passion, to render them a secret worship or to expect from them any mysterious intensification of life."[33] Furthermore, "when a man is faithful to one woman, he looks on other women in quite another way, a way unknown to the world of Eros: other women turn into other persons instead of being reflections or means. This 'spiritual exercise' develops new powers of judgement, self-possession, and respect. . . . The sway of the myth [of romantic love] is by so much weakened, and although this sway is unlikely ever to be entirely abolished without leaving traces in hearts drugged by images, hearts such as men harbour today, at least it loses its efficacy."[34]

De Rougemont seems to be quite negative about passion. He views it as the ultimate enemy of humanity and Christianity and also as an unavoidable element in human life which needs to be "contained." Williams, on the other hand, sees passion as "a gateway to divine things."

The exception mentioned above to the silence of the debate between Williams and de Rougemont is a brief review by Williams of the first English edition of de Rougemont's main work. In this review he dismisses much of de Rougemont's historical interpretation and argues for his own quite different view that the experience of falling in love can be one of grace and thus should not be identified with de Rougemont's passion myth. "The great tradition of romantic love — renewed like the phoenix in each generation — is quite other than the desire of death. The passion myth is a heresy of it: at moments a temptation; in moments of agony a very great temptation. . . . By virtue of the Incarnation Eros and Agape are no longer divided, though they may be again at the next moment."[35]

32. Ibid., pp. 313, 315.
33. Ibid., p. 312.
34. Ibid., p. 313.
35. "One Way of Love," in Charles Williams, *The Image of the City and Other Essays*, ed. Anne Ridler (London: Oxford University Press, 1958): 161.

In an earlier work Williams stated, "Eros need not forever be on his knees to Agape; he has a right to his delights; they are part of the Way. The division is not between the Eros of the flesh and the Agape of the soul; it is between the moment of love which sinks into hell and the moment of love which rises to the in-Godding."[36]

Now in conclusion what is the relation between these two interpretations of romantic love? Are they contradictory or complementary? Williams states that de Rougemont's myth of romantic love is a heresy of and also a permanent temptation of the tradition of romantic love which he is expounding. De Rougemont also asserts that it is a heresy. Although he sees romantic love in the modern world as dominated by the myth, de Rougemont allows that Agape can "rescue" and "contain" Eros and thus allow it to find its "proper place" in human life. Although he does not explain what a rescued Eros would look like or what its proper place would be, it is clear that he views passion with suspicion and could not with Williams understand it as an important way of the Christian life. He would probably want to see Eros always "on his knees" to Agape, whereas Williams apparently wants to see them as equals. Like their differing views of images, their contrasting views of passion and romantic love surely derive, at least in part, from Williams's participation in the catholic Anglican tradition and de Rougemont's participation in the Reformed tradition.

Thus de Rougemont and Williams seem to represent, respectively, the protestant emphasis on the distinction between Agape and Eros, and the catholic emphasis on the synthesis of Agape and Eros in *caritas*. If a synthesis is possible between these two traditions and if the above-mentioned gestures which Williams and de Rougemont have made toward the other's position are kept in mind, then their views of romantic love can be considered to be complementary.

Finally, it should be noted that this half-century-old debate about romantic love seems quite sexist and elitist in the contemporary context. Williams and de Rougemont focus on male experience, men looking at and falling in love with women, although both are clear that their theories apply to women as well.

---

36. *Outlines*, p. 111.

Neither refers to homosexual love, gays and lesbians falling in love, although there is no reason why their theories could not apply to any falling in love.

CHAPTER 15

MODERN SCIENCE AND CHRISTIAN FAITH

Times have changed. Early in the year 1600 Giordano Bruno, one of the most distinguished philosophers and scientists of his age, was condemned by the Church in the city of Rome primarily for his belief and teaching that the earth goes around the sun. And on February 17, 1600, he was publicly burned at the stake in the Campo dei Fiori. But, some three and a half centuries later the Christian Church through one of its schools is dedicating a building to be devoted to the use of scientists and the teaching of science.

Times have changed. I must say that dedicating science buildings is nowhere near as exciting as burning scientists. I'm afraid I can't compete with anything like that.

Times have changed. The battles of science and Christianity are over. These battles can be compared to the battles fought between two countries in a dispute over the border between them. There have been forays by both sides into the territory of the other. But finally a truce is established and a frontier defined which is now guarded carefully by both sides and the forays of the past are understood as bad mistakes based on misunderstanding about where the boundary really lay.

So it is between science and Christianity. The Church was in error when it believed that the Bible and the Christian faith gave any information about astronomy, geology, or biology. And later, science was in error when it claimed to be a savior and to answer questions about the ultimate meaning of human life. (I'm afraid that I still hear some scientists or scientific popularizers talking that way, but they, should know better by now.)

Times have changed. But how has this tremendous change come about in the Church's attitude toward science?

One view is that the rise of modern science has forced the Church to retreat step by step until science has won a complete victory, which is symbolized by what we are doing here this morning, a complete victory symbolized by the Church's dedicating science buildings instead of burning scientists.

We must confess that there is a great deal of truth in this picture. Most of you are aware of what the Church did to Galileo and what it tried to do to Darwin and his colleagues, but these examples are just peanuts when you begin to look at the whole dreary record in detail. It took Andrew White two fat volumes of his *A History of the Warfare of Science and Theology* just to survey this sad story. There is no doubt that the Christian Church fought desperately and fanatically against the rise of modern science in all of its forms.

Confession is good for the soul. And we Christians have not confessed fully enough and often enough this black record of the Church's attitude toward science. So let us take this occasion to confess it again. We have been miserable offenders here.

But let's not overdo it. The Church's attitude toward Galileo, for example, was simply the majority view of the scientists of his day whom in fact the Church had consulted. But we might hope that the Church would be more forward looking than it was, and at least realize that the revelation of God testified in the Bible gives us no information about astronomy.

But there is another side of the story of how we got from burning scientists to dedicating science buildings. And it is about this that I want to speak to you for a few minutes this morning.

One of the most fascinating points here is that the Christian Church is beginning to realize that it has a greater responsibility for science than it ever dreamed of before. An increasing number of the historians of modern science are coming to the surprising conclusion that modern science is in fact the offspring of Christian faith, that it was primarily the impact of Christian faith on the mind of Western people which led to the rise of science as we know it today. Everyone knows that it was the Greeks who invented the idea of science, but the historians are beginning to realize that modern science cannot be understood simply as the rediscovery of Greek science at the time of the Renaissance, but that modern science is derived from the transformation of Greek science through the impact of Christian faith. This is an astounding discovery and would have certainly been quite a shock to the medieval churchmen who were so busy persecuting the scientists.

Now how can it be that modern science is largely the child of Christianity? First we must recall that modern science is a combination of mathematics and experiments. The Greeks developed the mathematical side of science a good deal but they did very little with the experimental side. And this is the main difference between Greek and modern science, the appearance of the experimental method as one of its foundations. Now it is exactly the appearance of this experimental side of modern science which the historians attribute to the influence of Christian faith. I know this probably sounds far-fetched, but let me try to explain how it happened.

Greek science was based squarely on the pagan religion of the Greeks. In their religion God or ultimate reality was understood to have produced the world, as animals produce their offspring or as light radiates from the sun, that is, by generation or emanation. The world was sometimes seen as the spilling over of the divine substance. So all the things in the world were considered to be materializations of God's essence. The result was that the simplest way to understand the things in the world (science) was to contemplate God or ultimate reality. Then the properties and the behavior of the things in the world could be derived from the nature of God by deduction, by the mathematical method. It was not really necessary to examine the things themselves. They could be considered as illustrations but the investigation of them was not considered really necessary to the work of science.

But then Christianity came along and destroyed the pagan religion of the Greeks. And now the world was seen no longer as the spilling over of the divine substance but as something very different, as the creation of God. The world is not the offspring or emanation of God but his creature, the result of the free act of the will of God the creator. And now there is no way of telling what the structure of the world is going to be like. As St. Paul put it, God's acts and judgments are unsearchable and his ways inscrutable. The Lord might well have been addressing a Greek scientist when he begins his four-chapter tongue-lashing of Job with the words, "Where were you when I laid the foundation of the earth?" What he means is that Job wasn't around then, so he doesn't really understand the mystery of the structure of the world.

Modern science has a deep faith that the structure of the world can be expressed in mathematical equations, but it also knows that there is no way of telling what the equations are beforehand, without actually examining nature itself. John Kepler believed that the planets must move around the sun in some geometrical figure and he worked out several possibilities. But he had no way of knowing which one was the true one without turning to his telescope. Now here is the difference: the Greeks would have known beforehand which figure it was. They would have thought like this. God is perfect. And the planets are the offspring of God or inhabited by gods. Therefore they must move in a perfect figure. Now the only perfect figure is a circle. So they must move in a circle. So it wasn't necessary to look and see how they actually moved. But of course when Kepler did look, he discovered they didn't move in circles but in ellipses. Kepler was a devout Christian, and he knew that the planets weren't divine in any sense but simply God's creatures. And he also realized that he had no way of knowing how God had created them to move. So he had to look at them. And thus modern science arose with its tremendously powerful method of empirical or experimental investigation.

But there was another aspect of Greek culture which prevented the development of the experimental side of science. As we have seen, nature was considered to be essentially divine or "full of gods" as Plato put it. So the Greeks approached nature with a religious caution which made experimenting and monkeying around with nature highly inappropriate if not downright dangerous. The later Greek world became demon-ridden, full of evil spirits who had to be handled very carefully with the correct religious practices or else they would cause misfortune and illness. And this made the pulling apart of natural objects even less appropriate.

But then along came Christianity and did away with the divinity of nature. The Christian God is the creator of the universe. He alone is divine and holy and worthy of worship. So the natural world is in no sense divine but creature. Thus Christianity secularized the natural world. Christians need no longer stand in religious awe of nature as a divine thing. It is just our fellow creature with whom we are to rejoice before the Lord. Moreover, God has given to us responsibility for our fellow creature to care for it and mold it for our benefit and the glory of God. And so began the whole new way of looking at the world, the secular way, which is manifest in modern science and which has appeared nowhere else in the history of the world.

To the pagan the world was like a religious powerhouse. You had to watch your step. You couldn't just go monkeying around with it, touching this and pulling that apart. You might get a shock or even get electrocuted. But then Christianity came along and turned off the main switch and made the religious powerhouse safe and secular, so that Christians could touch it and examine it to our heart's content.

But besides secularizing the world God in Christ also conquered the demons and freed us from slavish fear and bondage to them. As St. Paul put it in his letter to the Christians in Colossae: "[God] disarmed the principalities and powers and made a public example of them triumphing over them in [Christ] . . . With Christ you died to the elemental spirits of the universe" (2:15, 20).

Let me read to you a couple of sentences written by the distinguished Russian philosopher Nicholas Berdyaev.

> However paradoxical it may seem, (he writes) I am convinced that Christianity alone made possible both positive science and [technology] . . . It is impossible to build railways, invent the telegraph or telephone, while living in fear of the demons. Thus, for man to be able to treat nature like a mechanism, it is necessary for the demonic inspiration of nature and man's communion with it to have died out in the human consciousness. The mechanical

conception of the world was to lead to a revolt against Christianity, but it was itself the spiritual result of the Christian act of liberating man from elemental nature and its demons."[1]

This spiritual result of Christianity, as Berdyaev calls it, was illustrated perfectly a year ago last winter at the time of the alignment of the planets and the eclipse of the sun. The striking thing was the contrast between the reaction in Asia, and the reaction in the West. And the Asians reacted the way the Greeks would have reacted. Let me quote from the front page of the *Boston Globe* of February 5, 1962.

> For the Asians the eclipse presented a period of great danger, coming as part of an alignment in the Zodiac sign of Capricorn of five other planets as well — Mercury, Venus, Mars. Jupiter, and Saturn. Hindu, Moslem, and Buddhist communities throughout the Far East held non-stop prayer sessions and sacrifices as the eight heavenly bodies began moving into line yesterday. Miners refused to enter the shafts at Dhanbad in northeast India. An Indian Airlines plane traveled empty to Bombay when passengers failed to show up at New Delhi. Market places closed down and merchants gave free food to beggars to placate the planets. But the eclipse was a welcome event for Americans and other western scientists who gathered at Lae in Australian New Guinea to watch the moon blot out the sun. They were able to carry out planned experiments as the moon moved into position between the earth and the sun at 8:51 a.m. local time (5:51 p.m. EST yesterday).

For the Asians (as it would have been for the Greeks) the eclipse and the alignment of the planets was a time of great danger. But for the Western scientists it was a welcome event because they were able to perform experiments. And this is the spiritual result of Christianity which conquered the demons, secularized the world, and made the world safe for modern science.

There is another interesting sidelight here, as to why the Greeks never developed the experimental or empirical side of science. They had a very low view of manual labor. The Greek free man should not do any kind of work with his hands, because that would have a bad effect on his soul. Manual labor was for slaves, not for the Greek free man.

---

1. *The Meaning of History* (Meridian Books, 1962): 106.

But along came Christianity and upset this attitude. The God of the Bible was a worker, beginning with his work of creation. In the second chapter of Genesis God is depicted as a manual laborer. "The Lord formed man of the dust of the ground." God works and so man who is created in the image of God must work too: His first work is to take care of the Garden of Eden. And so the whole Greek attitude toward work is undercut. This was not worked out fully until Luther announced that all kinds of work were equal before God. This made the lowliest manual labor as fully a part of the divine service as the work of the scholar or the prayers of the monk. So now it was no longer considered bad taste for the scientist to get his hands dirty in the laboratory.

In the light of all this, it is not surprising that Christian faith can illuminate and make more sense of the great phenomenon of modern science than any other perspective. For example, the faith of modern science is that the universe embodies a rational order or an intelligible structure which our minds can grasp and understand and express mathematically. That is to say, it would never occur to a scientist when he discovered a datum which did not fit into any previously held theory, to say, "Oh well, this is probably an irrational aspect of reality which we will never be able to understand," and then turn to other problems. Now this is an amazing thing. And the fact that the world process produces minds which can understand the whole universe probably tells us more about the nature of the whole universe than anything else. So Christian faith understands this when it affirms that God is the creator of nature and of humanity, and that God gives both to nature and to the human mind the same kind of structure so that we can grasp and understand the structure of nature. Furthermore, it is our God-given destiny to do exactly this, to grasp the structure of the world, to know it, and in knowing it to know also the "eternal power and deity" of God, as St. Paul puts it. (Rom. 1:20). And it is also our destiny under God to exercise care for the creation, and to use it according to God's purpose and for our benefit. The Psalmist exclaims over the wonder of humanity: "Thou makest him to have dominion of the works of thy hands; and thou has put all things in subjection under his feet" (8:6). You would never catch a Greek talking like that.

So scientists can understand their work as a divine calling and service. Then loyalty to truth, honesty, humility before the facts, openness to new truth, tolerance of the views of others, loyalty to the scientific tradition and community can be seen as faithful obedience to God. As Emil Brunner has written:

> All science could be and ought to be a divine service, a reverent following the traces — *lineamenta*, as Calvin says — of God's creation. Behind the postulate of scientific objectivity we find nothing less than awe in the face of God's order. What the scientist discovers are materialisations of God's thought and will. Man is not mistaken but supremely right if he feels science to be a high, divine, vocation closely linked up with his human dignity, a sacred cause which requires surrender, loyalty and obedience, a duty which is laid upon him and which he cannot forsake arbitrarily."[2]

One author has gone so far as to suggest that not only can science be seen from the point of view of Christian faith as a divine calling but that science is in fact the typical Christian calling. John Macmurray describes modern science and the technology based upon it not only as "the product of Christianity" but also as "its most adequate expression so far" and as "the full achievement of the Christian intention." He continues, "Its capacity for cooperative progress, which knows no frontiers of race or nationality or sex, its ability to predict, and its liability to control, are the fullest manifestation of Christianity that Europe has yet seen."[3] What he means is that science and technology are the fulfillment of God's calling of humanity to exercise care for the creation, that they are the expression of a life in the world devoted to the knowledge, care, and transformation of the world for our benefit and for the glory of God.

In the sixteenth century the question was whether the infant modern science could maintain itself in the face of the persecution of the Christian Church. But in the light of what we have considered this morning we must raise quite the opposite question of whether or not mature modern science can maintain itself if its Christian basis should disappear, if Western culture should slip back

---

2. *Christianity and Civilization* (Nisbet, 1949): II, p. 21.
3. *The Clue to History* (SCM, 1938): pp. 86, 192.

again into the pagan darkness of deifying the world, the race, the state, or the party.

One interpreter is quite clear on this:

> The virtues necessary to [the] advancement of [modern science] (writes John Baillie) are . . . the Christian virtues of humility, self-effacement, tolerance, impartiality, and a community of thought that transcends all distinctions of class or race or nation; and when those lose their ancient status as absolute standards, the effect on scientific progress may well be disastrous . . . I am convinced that if Christian faith should languish, the scientific impulse would in the end languish no less.[4]

Perhaps our responsibility as Christians for the maintenance and advance of modern science is greater than we have ever dreamed. So I congratulate St. George's School and its benefactors. And this, I submit, is why we do well this morning when in the name of God we dedicate a building for the study of science.

---

4. *Natural Science and the Spiritual Life* (Scribners, 1952): 36f, 34.

BIBLIOGRAPHY

Abbot, Walter M., ed. *The Documents of Vatican II.* New York: American Press, 1966.

Alston, W. P. "God's Action in the World," in *Evolution and Creation,* edited by E. McMullin. Notre Dame: University of Notre Dame Press, 1985.

Armstrong, A. H., ed. *The Cambridge History of Later Greek and Early Medieval Philosophy.* Cambridge: Cambridge University, 1967.

Attwater, Donald, trans. *Lay People in the Church: A Study for a Theology of the Laity.* Westminster, MD: Newman, 1955.

Augustine. *In evangelium Joannis* 65.2.

----------. *On the Predestination of the Saints [De Prædestinatione Sanctorum],* in *Nicene and Post-Nicene Fathers of the Christian Church. Volume 4: Saint Augustine: Anti Pelagian Writings,* edited by P. Schaff. New York: Charles Scribner's Sons, 1902.

Baillie, D. M. *God Was in Christ.* New York: Charles Scribner's Sons, 1978.

Barth, Karl. *Church Dogmatics,* vol. 2: *The Doctrine of God,* ed. G. W. Bromiley and T. F. Torrance. Edinburgh: Clark, 1957.

Barth, Markus. *Ephesians,* vol. 34 of *The Anchor Bible.* Garden City, NY: Doubleday, 1974.

Bayne, Stephen F., ed. *Theological Freedom and Social Responsibility.* New York: Seabury, 1987.

Beller, Steven. "Herzl, Wagner, and the Ironies of 'True Emancipation,'" in Nancy A. Harrowitz, ed., *Tainted Greatness: Antisemitism and Cultural Heroes.* Philadelphia: Temple University Press, 1994.

Berger, Peter. *The Heretical Imperative: Contemporary Possibilities of Religious Affirmation.* Garden City, NY: Anchor, 1979.

----------., ed. *The Other Side of God: A Polarity in World Religions.* Garden City, NY: Anchor, 1981.

Bernasconi, Robert. *Heidegger in Question: The Art of Existing.* Atlantic Highlands, NJ: Humanities Press, 1993.

Bernstein, Richard. *Beyond Objectivism and Relativism: Science, Hermeneutics, and Praxis.* Philadelphia: University of Pennsylvania Press, 1983.

----------. *Philosophical Profiles: Essays in a Pragmatic Mode.* Cambridge: Polity Press, 1986.

Biersdorf, John E. *Hunger for Experience: Vital Communities in America.* New York: Seabury, 1975.

Blackstone, William T. *The Problem of Religious Knowledge: The Impact of Philosophical Analysis on the Question of Religious Knowledge.* Englewood Cliffs, NJ: Prentice-Hall, 1963.

Bonhoeffer, Dietrich. *Ethics,* ed. Eberhard Bethge. New York: Macmillan, 1955.

----------. *Letters and Papers from Prison: The Enlarged Edition,* ed. Eberhard Bethge. New York: Macmillan, 1971.

Bonting, Sjoerd L. *Chaos Theology: A Revised Creation.* Ottawa: Novalis, 2002.

Bouveresse, Jacques. *Le mythe de l'intériorité: Expérience, signification et langage privé chez Wittgenstein.* Paris: Les Éditions de Minuit, 1976.

Brinton, Crane. "Romanticism," *The Encyclopedia of Philosophy* 8 vols. New York: Macmillan, 1967.

Brown, Delwyn; Ralph E. James, Jr., and Gene Reeves, eds. *Process Philosophy and Christian Thought.* Indianapolis: Bobbs-Merrill, 1974.

Browning, Don, ed. *Practical Theology.* San Francisco: Harper & Row, 1983.

Brunner, Emil. *Revelation and Reason: The Christian Doctrine of Faith and Knowledge.* Philadelphia: Westminster Press, 1946.

----------. *The Christian Doctrine of God.* Philadelphia: Westminster, 1950.

Burrell, David. *Analogy and Philosophical Language.* New Haven: Yale University Press, 1973.

Burton-Christie, Douglas. "The Wild and the Sacred," *Anglican Theological Review* 85:3 (2003).

Campbell, Colin. *The Romantic Ethic and the Spirit of Modern Consumerism.* Oxford: Basil Blackwell, 1987.

Caputo, John D. *Demythologizing Heidegger.* Bloomington, IN: Indiana University Press, 1993.

Carey, John J. "Life on the Boundary: The Paradoxical Models of Tillich and Pike," *Duke Divinity School Review* 42:3 (Fall, 1977).

----------. "Response to Alexander C. Irwin's *Eros Toward the World, Papers from the Annual Meeting of the North American Paul Tillich Society,* San Francisco, CA, November, 1992. Charlottesville: Department of Religious Studies, University of Virginia, 1993.

Carrette, Jeremy and Richard King. *Selling Spirituality: The Silent Takeover of Religion.* London: Routledge, 2005.

Cavell, Stanley. *The Claim of Reason: Wittgenstein, Skepticism, Morality, and Tragedy.* New York: Oxford University Press, 1979.

Chandler, Stuart. "When the World Falls Apart: Methodology for Employing Chaos and Emptiness as Theological Constructs," *Harvard Theological Review* 85:4 (1992).

Charry, Ellen T. "Is Christianity Good for us?" in *Reclaiming Faith: Essays on Orthodoxy in the Episcopal Church,* ed. Ephraim Radner and George R. Summer. Grand Rapids, MI: William B. Eerdmans, 1993.

Childs, Brevard. *Biblical Theology in Crisis.* Philadelphia: Westminster, 1970.

Clayton, John Powell. *The Concept of Correlation.* Berlin: De Gruyter, 1980.

Cobb, Jr., John B. *A Christian Natural Theology Based on the Thought of Alfred North Whitehead.* Philadelphia: Westminster, 1965.

----------. *Beyond Dialogue: Toward a Mutual Transformation of Christianity and Buddhism.* Philadelphia: Fortress Press, 1982.

----------. "Beyond Pluralism," in D'Costa, *Christian Uniqueness Reconsidered: The Myth of a Pluralistic Theology of Religions.* Maryknoll, NY: Orbis, 1990.

Cobb Jr., John B. and Franklin L. Gamwell, eds. *Existence and Actuality: Conversations with Charles Hartshorne.* Chicago: University of Chicago Press, 1984.

Cohen, Debra Nussbaum. "A Surge in Popularity in Jewish Mysticism," *The New York Times,* December 13, 2003.

Congar, Yves M. J. *Tradition and Traditions: A Historical and Theological Essay.* London: Burns and Oates, 1966.

Cooper, Michael. "Ignatian Spirituality: Unitative Action with Christ on Mission," *Presence: An International Journal of Spiritual Direction* 2, no. 3. September 1996.

Cousins, Ewert, ed. *World Spirituality: An Encyclopedic History of the Religious Quest,* 25 vols. New York: Crossroad, 1985-.

----------. "A Spirituality for the New Axial Period," *Christian Spirituality Bulletin* 2, no. 2, Fall 1994.

Crossman, Richard, ed. *The God That Failed.* New York: Bantam, 1950.

Cunningham, David S. *Faithful Persuasion: In Aid of a Rhetoric of Christian Theology.* Notre Dame: University of Notre Dame Press, 1991.

D'Costa, Gavin, ed. *Christian Uniqueness Reconsidered: The Myth of a Pluralistic Theology of Religions.* Maryknoll, NY: Orbis, 1990.

Davidson, Arnold I. "Archeology, Genealogy, Ethics," in *Foucault: A Critical Reader,* ed. David Couzens Hoy. Oxford: Basil Blackwell, 1986.

Davidson, Donald. *Inquiries into Truth and Interpretation.* Oxford: Clarendon, 1984.

de Rougemont, Denis. *Love in the Western World.* New York: Harper and Row, 1956.

Deming, W. Edwards. "Sample Surveys" in *The International Encyclopedia of the Social Sciences,* ed. David L. Sills; 17 vols. New York: Macmillan/Free Press, 1968.

Dentan, R. C. "Heart," in *Interpreter's Dictionary of the Bible,* ed. George Arthur Buttrick et al., 4 vols. New York: Abingdon, 1967.

Dewart, Leslie. *The Future of Belief. Theism in a World Come of Age.* New York: Herder, 1966.

----------. *The Foundations of Belief.* New York: Herder, 1969.

Dilley, F. "Does the 'God Who Acts' Really Act?" in *God's Activity in the World,* edited by O. C. Thomas. Chico: Scholar's Press, 1983.

Downey, Michael. *Understanding Christian Spirituality.* New York: Paulist Press, 1992.

Dreyfus, Herbert L. and Paul Rabinow. *Michel Foucault: Beyond Structuralism and Hermeneutics* 2nd ed. Chicago: Univ. of Chicago Press, 1983.

Driver, Tom F. "The Case for Pluralism," in Hick and Knitter, *The Myth of Christian Uniqueness: Toward a Pluralistic Theology of Religions.* Maryknoll, NY: Orbis, 1987.

----------. Review of *Naming the Whirlwind. USQR* 25 (1970).

Drury, Shadia. *The Political Ideas of Leo Strauss.* London: Macmillan, 1988.

----------. *Alexandre Kojève: The Roots of Postmodern Politics.* New York: St. Martin's Press, 1994

----------. *Leo Strauss and the American Right.* New York: St. Martin's Press, 1997.

DuBois, Page. "Subjected Bodies, Science, and The State: Francis Bacon, Torturer," in *Body Politics: Disease, Desire, and the Family,* ed. Michael Ryan and Avery Gordon. Boulder, CO: Westview Press, 1994.

Dulles, A. *Models of Revelation.* Garden City: Doubleday and Company, 1983.

----------. "Faith, Church and God: Insights from Michael Polanyi," *Modern Theological Studies* 45, no. 3, September, 1984.

Duméry, Henry. *The Problem of God in the Philosophy of Religion: A Critical Examination of the Category of the Absolute and the Scheme of Transcendence,* tr. Charles Courtney. Evanston, IL: Northwestern University, 1964.

Durrant, Michael. *Theology and Intelligibility.* London: Routledge and Kegan Paul, 1973.

Ebeling, Gerhard. "Die Klage über das Erfahrungsdefizit in der Theologie als Frage nach ihrer Sache," *Wort und Glaube* 3. Tübingen: Mohr-Siebeck, 1975.

Ellwood, Robert S. *Religious and Spiritual Groups in Modern America.* Englewood Cliffs, NJ: Prentice-Hall, 1973.

----------. *Alternative Altars.* Chicago: University of Chicago Press, 1979.

Emmet, Dorothy. *The Nature of Metaphysical Thinking.* London: Macmillan & Co., 1953.

----------. "The Ground of Being," *JTS* n.s.15 (1964).

316

Erickson, Robert P. *Theologians Under Hitler: Gerhard Kittel, Paul Althaus, and Emmanuel Hirsch.* New Haven: Yale University Press, 1985.

Farley, Edward. *Ecclesial Reflection: An Anatomy of Theological Method.* Philadelphia: Fortress, 1982.

----------. *Theologia.* Philadelphia: Fortress, 1983.

Farrer, Austin. *Finite and Infinite: A Philosophical Essay.* Westminster: Dacre Press, 1943.

Felski, Rita. *Beyond Feminist Aesthetics: Feminist Literature and Social Change.* Cambridge: Harvard University Press, 1989.

Ferré, Frederick. *Language, Logic and God.* New York: Harper and Brothers, 1961.

----------. "Analogy in Theology," *Encyclopedia of Philosophy*, 8 vols., ed. Paul Edwards. New York: Macmillan Co., 1967.

----------. "Metaphors, Models, and Religion," *Soundings* 51 (1968).

----------. "A Renewal of God-Language?" *JR* 52 (1972).

Finch, Henry Le Roy. *Wittgenstein — the Later Philosophy: An Exposition of the "Philosophical Investigations."* Atlantic Highlands, NJ: Humanities Press, 1977.

Fiorenza, Francis Schüssler. *Foundational Theology: Jesus and the Church.* New York: Crossroad, 1984.

Fitzmyer, Joseph A. *The Gospel According to Luke, X-XXIV*, vol. 28 of *The Anchor Bible.* Garden City, NY: Doubleday, 1985.

Fleischner, Eva, ed. *Auschwitz: Beginning of A New Era? Reflections on the Holocaust.* New York: KTAV Publishing House, 1977.

Ford, L. *The Lure of God.* Philadelphia: Fortress Press, 1978.

Forstman, Jack. *A Romantic Triangle: Schleiermacher and Early German Romanticism.* Missoula, MT: Scholars Press, 1970.

----------. *Christian Faith in Dark Times: Theological Conflicts in the Shadow of Hitler.* Louisville, KY: Westminster/John Knox, 1992.

Foucault, Michel. *The Archaeology of Knowledge.* New York: Pantheon, 1972.

Fox, Richard Wightman. *Reinhold Niebuhr: A Biography.* New York: Pantheon Books, 1985.

Fromm, Erich. "Problems of Surplus," in *The Essential Fromm,* ed. Rainer Funk. New York: Continuum, 1995.

Fuller, Robert C. *Spiritual But Not Religious: Understanding Unattached America.* Oxford: Oxford University Press, 2001.

Furnish, Victor Paul. *II Corinthians,* vol. 32A of *The Anchor Bible.* Garden City, NY: Doubleday, 1984.

Gadamer, Hans-Georg. *Truth and Method.* Trans. and ed. Garrett Barden and John Cumming. New York: Seabury, 1975.

Gerson, Lloyd P., ed. *The Cambridge Companion to Plotinus.* Cambridge: Cambridge University Press, 1996.

Gilkey, Langdon. *Naming the Whirlwind: The Renewal of God-Language.* Indianapolis: Bobbs-Merrill, 1969.

----------. *Reaping the Whirlwind: A Christian Interpretation of History.* New York: Seabury, 1976.

----------. "Plurality and Its Theological Implications," in Hick and Knitter, *The Myth of Christian Uniqueness: Toward a Pluralistic Theology of Religions.* Maryknoll, NY: Orbis, 1987.

Gilson, Étienne. *The Unity of Philosophical Experience.* London: Sheed and Ward, 1938.

----------. *The Spirit of Mediaeval Philosophy.,* trans. A. H. C. Downes. New York: Scribner's, 1940.

----------. *God and Philosophy.* New Haven: Yale University, 1941.

----------. *Being and Some Philosophers,* 2nd rev. ed. Toronto: Pontifical Institute of Mediaeval Studies, 1952.

----------. *The Christian Philosophy of St. Thomas Aquinas,* trans. L. K. Shook. New York: Random House, 1956.

----------. *Elements of Christian Philosophy.* Garden City, NY: Doubleday, 1960.

----------. *The Spirit of Thomism.* New York: Harper & Row, 1964.

Goethe, J. W. von. *The Autobiography of Johann Wolfgang von Goethe*, trans. John. V. Oxenburg. New York: Horizon Press, 1969.

Goodman, Nelson. *Ways of Worldmaking*. Indianapolis: Hackett, 1978.

Greeley, Andrew M. *Unsecular Man: The Persistence of Religion*. New York: Schocken, 1972.

Green, Arthur, ed. "Introduction," in *Jewish Spirituality*, vol. 1, *From the Bible through the Middle Ages, World Spirituality*, vol. 13. New York: Crossroad, 1986.

Griffin, David Ray. *A Process Christology*. Philadelphia: Westminster, 1973.

----------. "Creation out of Chaos and the Problem of Evil," in Stephen T. Davis, ed. *Encountering Evil: Live Options in Theology*. Atlanta: John Knox Press, 1981.

----------. "Relativism, Divine Causation, and Biblical Theology," in *God's Activity in the World: The Contemporary Problem*, edited by O. C. Thomas. Chico: Scholars Press, 1983.

----------. *God and Religion in the Postmodern World: Essays in Postmodern Theology*. Albany: SUNY Press, 1989.

Gustafson, James. *Can Ethics Be Christian*. Chicago: University of Chicago Press, 1975.

Gutierez, Gustavo. *A Theology of Liberation: History, Politics and Salvation*, ed. and trans. Sister Caridad Inda and John Eagleson. Maryknoll, NY: Orbis, 1973.

Habermas, Jürgen. "The Public Sphere: An Encyclopedia Article (1964)," *New German Critique* 1 (1974).

----------. "Work and Weltanschauung: The Heidegger Controversy from a German Perspective," *Critical Inquiry* (Winter, 1989).

----------. *The Structural Transformation of the Public Sphere: An Inquiry into a Category of Bourgeois Society* (trans. Thomas Burger and Frederick Lawrence. Cambridge: MIT Press, 1989.

Haddock, Vicki. "Lessons in Human Buy-ology," *San Francisco Chronicle*, 12/19/04.

Hartshorne, Charles. *Man's Vision of God and the Logic of Theism*. Chicago: Willett, Clark & Co., 1941.

----------. *The Divine Relativity: A Social Conception of God*. New Haven: Yale University Press, 1948.

----------. "Tillich and the Other Great Tradition," *ATR* 43 (1961).

----------. *The Logic of Perfection and Other Essays in Neoclassical Metaphysics*. LaSalle, IL: Open Court Publishing Co., 1962.

----------. "Introduction: The Development of Process Philosophy," in *Philosophers of Process*, Douglas Browning, ed. New York: Random House, 1965.

Hebblethwaite, B. L. "The Appeal to Experience in Christology," in S. W. Sykes and J. P. Clayton, eds., *Christ, Faith and History: Cambridge Studies in Christology*. Cambridge: Cambridge University Press, 1972.

Hebblethwaite, B. L. and E. H. Henderson, eds. *Divine Action*. Edinburgh: T and T Clark, 1990.

Hefner, Philip. "God and Chaos: The Demiurge Versus the *Ungrund*," *Zygon* 19:4 (1984).

Heidegger, Martin. *Introduction to Metaphysics*. Garden City, NY: Doubleday, 1961.

Heim, Karl. *Christian Faith and Natural Science*. New York: Harper & Brothers, 1953.

Hick, John and Paul F. Knitter, eds. *The Myth of Christian Uniqueness: Toward a Pluralistic Theology of Religions*. Maryknoll, NY: Orbis, 1987.

Holmes, Urban T. "Theology and Religious Renewal," *The Anglican Theological Review* 62:1 (1980).

Huchingson, James E. *Pandemonium Tremendum: Chaos and Mystery in the Life of God*. Cleveland: Pilgrim Press, 2001.

Huxley, Aldous. *The Perennial Philosophy*. New York: Harper & Row, 1944.

Irenaeus. *Against Heresies* 1.21.4-5; Alexander Roberts and James Donaldson, eds., *Ante-Nicene Fathers*. Buffalo, NY: Christian Literature Publishing, 1885.

Irwin, Alexander. *Eros Toward the World: Paul Tillich and the Theology of the Erotic*. Minneapolis: Fortress Press, 1991.

Jantzen, G. *God's World, God's Body*. Philadelphia: Westminster Press, 1984.

Jaspers, Karl. *The Origin and Goal of History*. New Haven, CT: Yale University Press, 1953.

Jeffner, Anders. *Kriterien christlicher Glaubenslehre: Eine prinzipielle Untersuchung heutiger protestantischer Dogmatik im deutschen Sprachbereich*. Acta Universitatis Upsaliensis, Studia Doctrinae Christiane Upsaliensia 13. Stockholm: Almqvist & Wiksell, 1977.

John Paul II. *Redemptor Hominis*. London: Catholic Truth Society, 1979.

Johnson, Jeffrey L. "Making Noises in Counterpoint or Chorus: Putnam's Rejection of Relativism," *Erkenntnis* 34 (1991).

Jonas, Hans. "Heidegger and Theology," in *The Phenomenon of Life: Toward a Philosophical Biology*. New York: Harper & Row, 1966.

Jones, W. T. *The Romantic Syndrome: Toward a New Method in Cultural Anthropology and History of Ideas*. The Hague: Martinus Nijhoff, 1961.

Kahn, Robert L. and Charles F. Cannell. "Interviewing: Social Research" in *The International Encyclopedia of the Social Sciences* (ed. David L. Sills; 17 vols. New York: Macmillan/Free Press, 1968.

Kakutani, Michiko. "Biography Becomes a Blood Sport," *New York Times*, Friday, May 20, 1994.

Kaufman, Gordon. "Reading Wittgenstein: Notes for Constructive Theologians," *Journal of Religion* 79, no. 3 (July 1999).

Keane, John. *Public Life and Late Capitalism: Toward a Socialist Theory of Democracy*. Cambridge: Cambridge University Press, 1984.

Kegley, W. and Robert W. Bretall, eds. *The Theology of Paul Tillich*. New York: Macmillan, 1952.

Keller, Catherine. *Face of the Deep: A Theology of Becoming*. London & New York, 2003.

Kerr, Fergus. *Theology after Wittgenstein*. Oxford: Blackwell, 1986.

Knitter, Paul F. "Toward a Liberation Theology of Religion," in Hick, John and Paul F. Knitter, eds. *The Myth of Christian Uniqueness: Toward a Pluralistic Theology of Religions.* Maryknoll, NY: Orbis, 1987.

Knox, John. *Romans*, vol. 9 of *Interpreter's Bible*, ed. George Arthur Buttrick et al. New York: Abingdon, 1954.

Lane, Dermot A. *The Experience of God: An Invitation to Do Theology.* New York: Paulist, 1981.

Lash, Nicholas. *Change in Focus.* London: Sheed & Ward, 1973.

----------. *Newman on Development.* London: Sheed & Ward, 1975.

Lawrence Jr., Raymond J. *The Poisoning of Eros: Sexual Values in Conflict.* New York: Augustine Moore Press, 1989.

Lemke, Werner E. "Theology [OT]," *Anchor Bible Dictionary* 6 (1992).

Lewis, C. S. *The Allegory of Love: A Study in Medieval Tradition.* New York: Oxford University Press, 1958.

Lindbeck, George A. *The Nature of Doctrine: Religion and Theology in a Postliberal Age.* Philadelphia: Westminster, 1984.

Lonergan, Bernard J. F. *Insight: A Study of Human Understanding.* New York: Philosophical Library, 1956.

Loomer, Bernard E., ed. *The Future of Empirical Theology.* Chicago: University of Chicago Press, 1969.

Lossky, Vladimir. *The Mystical Theology of the Eastern Church.* London: Clarke, 1957.

Lovejoy, Arthur O. "On the Discrimination of Romanticisms," in *Essays in the History of Ideas.* Baltimore: Johns Hopkins Press, 1948.

MacIntyre, Alasdair. "Being," *The Encyclopedia of Philosophy*, ed. Paul Edwards (8 vols.). New York: Macmillan/Free Press, 1967.

----------. *After Virtue: A Study in Moral Theory.* Notre Dame, IN: University of Notre Dame Press, 1984.

MacKinnon, Donald. *Explorations in Theology*, 5. London: SCM Press, 1979.

Macquarrie, John. *Studies in Christian Existentialism*. Philadelphia: Westminster, 1965.

----------. *Principles of Christian Theology*. New York: Scribner's, 1966.

Maimonides. Quoted in *Tainted Greatness: Antisemitism and Cultural Heroes*, ed. Nancy A. Harrowitz. Philadelphia: Temple University Press, 1994.

Mandelbaum, Maurice. "Subjective, Objective, and Conceptual Relativisms," in Jack W. Meiland and Michael Krausz, eds., *Relativism: Cognitive and Moral*. Notre Dame: University of Notre Dame Press, 1982.

Marcus Aurelius. *Meditations*.

Martin, Bernice. *A Sociology of Contemporary Cultural Change*. New York: St. Martin's Press, 1981.

May, Rollo. *Paulus: Reminiscences of a Friendship*. New York: Harper & Row, 1973.

McCall, Bruce. "Not Scared of Harry Potter," *The New Yorker* (12/10/01).

McCord, James I. "Editorial: The Blurred Vision," *Theology Today* 28:3 (1971).

McDonnell, Colleen. *Material Christianity: Religion and Popular Culture in America*. New Haven, CT: Yale University Press, 1995.

McGuire, Meredith B. "Mapping Contemporary American Spirituality: A Sociological Perspective," *Christian Spirituality Bulletin* 5:1 (1997).

McLain, F. Michael. "On Theological Models," *Harvard Theological Review* 62 (1969).

McShane, Philip, ed. *Language, Truth and Meaning: Papers from the International Lonergan Conference 1970*. Dublin: Gill and Macmillan..

Michalson, Carl. *Worldly Theology: The Hermeneutical Focus of an Historical Faith*. New York: Scribner's, 1976.

Miles, Margaret R. *Fullness of Life: Historical Foundations for a New Asceticism*. Philadelphia: Westminster, 1981.

----------. *Carnal Knowing: Female Nakedness and Religious Meaning in the Christian West*. Boston: Beacon, 1989.

----------. *Desire and Delight: A New Reading of Augustine's Confessions.* New York: Crossroad, 1992.

----------. *Plotinus on Body and Beauty.* London: Blackwell, 1999.

Moltmann, Jürgen. *The Trinity and the Kingdom.* San Francisco: Harper & Row, 1981.

Monk, Ray. *Ludwig Wittgenstein: The Duty of Genius.* New York: Free Press, 1990.

Musgrove, Frank. *Ecstasy and Holiness: Counter Culture and the Open Society.* Bloomington, IN: Indiana University Press, 1974.

Nagel, Thomas. *The View From Nowhere.* New York: Oxford University Press, 1986.

Negt, Oskar and Alexander Kluge. *Öffentlichkeit and Erfahrung.* Frankfurt: Suhrkamp, 1972.

Neske, Carol. Review of a biography of Laura Riding, *New York Times Book Review*, November 28, 1993.

Neville, Robert C. *God the Creator.* Chicago: University of Chicago, 1968.

----------. *Reconstruction of Thinking.* Albany: SUNY Press, 1981.

----------. *The Tao and the Daimon: Segments of a Religious Inquiry.* Albany: SUNY Press, 1982.

----------. *Behind the Masks of God: An Essay Toward Comparative Theology.* Albany: SUNY Press, 1991.

Ó Murchú, Diarmuid. *Religion in Exile: A Spiritual Vision for the Homeward Bound.* Dublin: Gateway, 2000.

O'Regan, Cyril. *Gnostic Return in Modernity.* Albany: State University of New York Press, 2001.

Ogden, Schubert M. *Christ Without Myth: A Study Based on the Theology of Rudolf Bultmann.* New York: Harper & Row, 1961.

----------. *The Reality of God and Other Essays.* New York: Harper & Row, 1963.

----------. "The Authority of Scripture for Theology," *Int* 30 (1976).

----------. *The Point of Christology.* San Francisco: Harper & Row, 1982.

----------. *Is There Only One True Religion or Are There Many?* Dallas: Southern Methodist University Press, 1992.

Ortner, Sherry B. "Theory in Anthropology since the Sixties," *Comparative Studies in Society and History* 26:1 (January 1984).

Otis, Brooks. "Nicene Orthodoxy and Fourth Century Mysticism," *Actes du XIIe Congrès International des Études Byzantines.* Geograd: 1964.

Ott, Heinrich. *Denken and Sein: Der Weg Martin Heideggers and der Weg der Theologie.* Zollikon: Evangelischer Verlag, 1959.

Owens, Joseph. *The Doctrine of Being in the Aristotelian 'Metaphysics.'* Toronto: Pontifical Institute of Mediaeval Studies, 1951.

Palmer, Humphrey. *Analogy: A Study of Qualification and Argument in Theology.* London: Macmillan, 1973.

Panikkar, Raimundo. "The Invisible Harmony: A Universal Theory of Religion or a Cosmic Confidence in Reality?" in Leonard Swidler, ed., *Toward a Universal Theology of Religion.* Maryknoll, NY: Orbis, 1988.

Pannenberg, Wolfhart. *Basic Questions in Theology.* Collected Essays, tr. George H. Kehm. Philadelphia: Fortress, 1971.

Pateman, Carol. "Feminist Critiques of the Public/Private Dichotomy," in S. I. Bern and G. F. Gaus, eds., *Public and Private in Social Life.* London: Croom Helm, 1983.

Pauck, Wilhelm and Marion. *Paul Tillich: His Life and Thought, Volume 1: Life.* New York: Harper & Row, 1976.

Plato. *Phil* 64f; *Rep* 6.

Pluskow, Judith. *Sex, Sin and Grace: Women's Experience and the Theologies of Reinhold Niebuhr and Paul Tillich.* Washington: University Press of America, 1980.

Polak, Joseph. "Tainted Artists/Tainted Texts: Reflections from the Rabbinic Sources," in *Tainted Greatness*, ed. Nancy A. Harrowitz. Philadelphia: Temple University Press, 1994.

Polanyi, M. *Knowing and Being: Essays by Michael Polanyi*, edited by Marjorie Grene. Chicago: University of Chicago Press, 1969.

Putnam, Hilary. *Reason, Truth and History.* Cambridge: Cambridge University Press, 1981.

Rahner, Karl. *Theological Investigations.* Baltimore: Helicon, 1961.

----------. *Hominisation: The Evolutionary Origin of Man as a Theological Problem.* New York: Herder and Herder, 1965.

----------. "Christology Within an Evolutionary View of the World," in *Theological Investigations*, vol. 4. Baltimore: Helicon Press, 1966.

----------. *Theological Investigations*, vol. 5. Baltimore: Helicon Press, 1966.

----------. *Spirit in the World*, trans. William Dych. New York: Herder, 1968.

----------. *Hearers of the Word*, trans. Michael Richards. New York: Herder, 1969.

----------. *Foundations of Christian Faith: An Introduction to the Idea of Christianity.* New York: Seabury Press, 1978.

----------. "The Concept of Mystery in Catholic Theology," *Investigations*, 4.36.

Ramsey, Ian T. *Religious Language: An Empirical Placing of Theological Phrases.* New York: Macmillan Co., 1957.

Ratzinger, Joseph. *Commentary on the Documents of Vatican II.* New York: Herder and Herder, 1969.

Reformation principle, *Praedicatio verbi Dei est verbum Dei.* Second Helvetic Confession, 1566.

Rescher, Nicholas. *The Strife of Systems: An Essay on the Grounds and Implications of Philosophical Diversity.* Pittsburgh: University of Pittsburgh Press, 1985.

Richardson, William J. "Being for Lonergan," in McShane, *Language, Truth and Meaning: Papers from the International Lonergan Conference 1970.* Dublin: Gill and Macmillan.

Ricoeur, Paul. *The Symbolism of Evil.* New York: Harper & Row, 1967.

Rieff, Philip. *The Triumph of the Therapeutic: The Uses of Faith. After Freud.* New York: Harper & Row, 1966.

Riemann, G. F. B. *Über die Hypothesen, welche de Geometrie zu Grunde liegen.* Berlin: Springer, 1923.

Robinson, John A. T. *Truth is Two-Eyed.* Philadelphia: Westminster Press, 1979.

Rockmore, Tom. *On Heidegger's Philosophy and Nazism.* Berkeley: University of California Press, 1992.

Rockmore, Tom and Joseph Margolis, eds. *The Heidegger Case: On Philosophy and Politics.* Philadelphia: Temple University Press, 1992.

Roof, Wade Clark. *A Generation of Seekers: The Spiritual Journey of the Baby Boom Generation.* San Francisco: Harper, 1993.

----------. *The Spiritual Marketplace: Baby Boomers and the Remaking of American Religion.* Princeton: Princeton University Press, 1999.

Rorty, Richard. "The World Well Lost," *Journal of Philosophy* 69 (1972).

----------. *Philosophy and the Mirror of Nature.* Princeton: Princeton University Press, 1979.

----------. "Taking Philosophy Seriously," *The New Republic* 198:15 (April 11, 1988).

Ross, Alex. "The Ring and the Rings," *The New Yorker* (12/22 & 29/ 03).

Ross, James F. "Analogy as a Rule of Meaning for Religious Language," *International Philosophical Quarterly* I (1961).

----------. *Introduction to the Philosophy of Religion.* London: Macmillan Co., 1969.

----------. "A New Theory of Analogy," in *Logical Analysis and Contemporary Theism,* ed. John Donnelly. New York: Fordham University Press, 1972.

----------. *God, Power and Evil: A Process Theodicy.* Philadelphia: Westminster, 1976.

Roszak, Theodore. *The Making of a Counterculture: Reflections on the Technocratic Society and Its Youthful Opposition.* Garden City, NY: Doubleday, 1969.

----------. *Where the Wasteland Ends: Politics and Transcendence in Postindustrial Society.* Garden City: Doubleday and Co., 1972.

Rupp, George. *Beyond Zen and Existentialism.* New York: Oxford University Press, 1979.

Safranski, Rüdiger. *Schopenhauer and the Wild Years of Philosophy.* Cambridge: Harvard University Press, 1990.

----------. *Martin Heidegger: Between Good and Evil.* Cambridge, MA: Harvard University Press, 1998.

Schillebeeckx, Edward. *Christ: The Experience of Jesus as Lord.* New York: Seabury, 1980.

Schor, Juliet. *Do Americans Shop Too Much?* Boston: Beacon Press, 2000.

----------. *Born to Buy: The Commercialized Child and the New Consumer Culture.* New York: Scribner, 2004.

Schor, Juliet B. and Douglas B. Holt. *The Consumer Society Reader.* New York: The New Press, 2000.

Scott, A. O. "A Hunger for Fantasy, an Empire to Feed It," *The New York Times,* (6/16/02).

Shannon, William A. *Silent Lamp: The Thomas Merton Story.* New York: Crossroad, 1992.

Sheehan, Thomas. "Heidegger and the Nazis," *New York Review of Books* 35:10 (June 16, 1988).

----------. "A Normal Nazi," *New York Review of Books* 40:1&2 (January 14, 1993).

Shideler, Mary McDermott. *The Theology of Romantic Love: A Study in the Writings of Charles Williams.* New York: Harper & Row, 1962.

Sidney Hook. *The Quest for Being and other Studies in Naturalism and Humanism.* New York: Dell, 1934.

Siegel, Harvey. *Relativism Refuted: A Critique of Contemporary Epistemological Relativism.* Dordrecht: Reidel, 1987.

Sluga, Hans. *The Break: Habermas, Heidegger, and the Nazis.* San Anselmo, CA: Center for Hermeneutical Studies, 1992.

----------. *Heidegger's Crisis: Philosophy and Politics in Nazi Germany.* Cambridge: Harvard University Press, 1993.

Smith, Huston. *Forgotten Truth: The Primordial Tradition.* New York: Harper & Row, 1976.

Smith, John E. "Comments," in Jacquelyn Ann K. Kegley, ed., *Paul Tillich on Creativity.* Lanham, MD: University Press of America, 1989.

Smart, Ninian. *The Religious Experience of Mankind.* New York: Scribner, 1969.

Smith, Ronald Gregor. *The Doctrine of God,* ed. K. Gregor Smith and A. D. Galloway. Philadelphia: Westminster, 1970.

Sobrino, Jon. *Spirituality of Liberation: Toward Political Holiness.* Maryknoll, NY: Orbis, 1988.

Strawson, P. F. *Individuals: An Essay in Descriptive Metaphysics.* London: Methuen, 1959.

Suchocki, Marjorie Hewitt. "In Search of Justice," in Hick and Knitter, *The Myth of Christian Uniqueness: Toward a Pluralistic Theology of Religions.* Maryknoll, NY: Orbis, 1987.

Sykes, Stephen. *The Identity of Christianity: Theologians and the Essence of Christianity from Schleiermacher to Barth.* Philadelphia: Fortress, 1984.

Tanner, Kathryn. *The Politics of God: Christian Theologies and Social Justice.* Minneapolis: Fortress Press, 1992.

Taylor, Charles. *Sources of the Self: The Making of the Modern Identity.* Cambridge, MA: Harvard University Press, 1989.

Temple, William. *Nature, Man and God.* London: Macmillan, 1934.

Thiemann, Ronald F. *Revelation and Theology: The Gospel as Narrated Promise.* Notre Dame: University of Notre Dame Press, 1985.

----------. *Constructing a Public Theology: The Church in a Pluralistic Society.* Louisville, KY: Westminster/John Knox, 1991.

Thomas, Owen C. "Barth on Non-Christian Knowledge of God," *ATR* 46 (1964).

----------. "Some Problems in Theological Education," *Theological Education* 5 (1969).

----------. "Where Are We in Theology?" in Martin E. Marty and Dean G. Peerman, eds., *New Theology* No. 9. New York: Macmillan, 1972.

----------. *God's Activity in the World: The Contemporary Problem*. Chico: Scholars Press, 1983.

----------. *Introduction to Theology*, rev. ed. Wilton: Morehouse-Barlow Co., 1983.

----------. *Theological Questions: Analysis and Argument*. Wilton, CT: Morehouse-Barlow, 1983.

----------. "Christianity and the Perennial Philosophy," *Theology Today* 43:2 (1986).

----------. "On Stepping Twice into the Same Church: Essence, Development, and Pluralism," *Anglican Theological Review* 70, no. 4 (October 1988).

----------. "Recent Thought on Divine Agency." Edinburgh, Scotland T & T Clark Limited, 1990.

----------. "Tillich and the Perennial Philosophy," *Harvard Theological Review* 89:1 (1996).

----------. "Interiority and Christian Spirituality," *The Journal of Religion* 80:1 (2000).

----------. "Political Spirituality: Oxymoron or Redundancy?" *Journal of Religion and Society* 3 (2001) (an electronic journal).

Throop, William and Katheryn Doran. "Putnam's Realism and Relativity: An Uneasy Balance," *Erkenntnis* 34 (1991).

Tillich, Hannah. *From Time to Time*. New York: Stein and Day, 1973.

Tillich, Paul. "Nature, also, Mourns for a Lost Good," in *The Shaking of the Foundations*. New York: Harper & Row, 1948.

----------. *The Protestant Era*, trans. James Luther Adams. Chicago: University of Chicago, 1948.

----------. *Systematic Theology* 3 vols. Chicago: University of Chicago Press, 1951-63.

----------. *The Courage To Be*. New Haven: Yale University Press, 1952.

----------. *Love, Power and Justice: Ontological Analysis and Ethical Applications*. New York: Oxford University Press, 1954.

----------. *Biblical Religion and the Search for Ultimate Reality.* Chicago: University of Chicago Press, 1955.

----------. *Systematische Theologie* 3 vols. Stuttgart: Evangelische Verlag, 1956-66.

----------. *Theology of Culture*, ed. Robert C. Kimball. New York: Oxford University, 1959.

----------. *A History of Christian Thought*, ed. Carl E. Braaten. New York: Harper & Row, 1968.

----------. *Mysticism and Guilt Consciousness in Schelling's Philosophical Development.* Lewisburg, PA: Bucknell University Press, 1974.

----------. "Heidegger and Jaspers," in *Heidegger and Jaspers*, ed. Alan M. Olson. Philadelphia: Temple University Press, 1994.

Torrell, Jean-Pierre. "New Trends in Fundamental Theology in the Postconcilear Period," in René Latourelle and Gerald O'Collins, eds., *Problems and Perspectives of Fundamental Theology* (trans. Matthew J. O'Connell). New York: Paulist, 1982.

Tracy, David. "Theology as Public Discourse," *The Christian Century* 92 (1975).

----------. *Blessed Rage for Order: The New Pluralism in Theology.* New York: Seabury, 1975.

----------. *The Analogical Imagination: Christian Theology and the Culture of Pluralism.* New York: Crossroad, 1981.

----------. "Defending the Public Character of Theology," in James M. Wall, ed., *Theologians in Transition.* New York: Crossroad, 1981.

----------. *Plurality and Ambiguity: Hermeneutics, Religion, Hope.* San Francisco: Harper & Row, 1987.

----------. "Afterword: Theology, Public Discourse, and the American Tradition," in Michael J. Lacey, ed., *Religion and Twentieth-Century American Intellectual Life.* Cambridge: Cambridge University Press, 1989.

----------. "Theology, Critical Social Theory and the Public Realm," in Don S. Browning and Francis Schüssler Fiorenza, eds., *Habermas, Modernity, and Public Theology.* New York: Crossroad/Continuum, 1992.

Tracy, Thomas F. *God, Action and Embodiment*. Grand Rapids: William B. Eerdmans Publishing Company, 1984.

Troeltsch, Ernst. "What does 'Essence of Christianity' Mean?" in *Ernst Troeltsch: Writings in Theology and Religion*, ed. Robert Morgan and Michael Pye. London: Duckworth, 1977.

Turner, Denys. *The Darkness of God: Negativity in Christian Mysticism*. Cambridge: Cambridge University Press, 1995.

Ulanov, Ann Belford. "Between Anxiety and Faith: The Role of the Feminine in Tillich's Theological Thought," in *Paul Tillich on Creativity*, ed. Jacquelyn Ann K. Kegley. Lanham, MD: University Press of America, 1989.

Wakefield, Gorden S. "Spirituality," in *The Westminster Dictionary of Christian Spirituality*, ed. Gordon S. Wakefield. Philadelphia: Westminster, 1983.

Weber, Max. "Objective Possibility and Adequate Causation in Historical Explanation," *The Methodology of the Social Sciences*, trans. & ed. Edward A. Shils and Henry A. Fink. Glencoe, IL: The Free Press, 1949.

----------. *The Sociology of Religion*, trans. E. Fischoff. Boston: Beacon, 1963.

White, V. *The Fall of a Sparrow: A Concept of Special Divine Action*. Exeter: Paternoster Press, 1985.

Wilber, Ken. "Physics, Mysticism, and the New Holographic Paradigm," *The Holographic Paradigm*, ed. Wilber. Boulder, CO: Shambala, 1982.

Wiles, Maurice. *God's Action in the World: The Brampton Lectures for 1986*. London: SCM Press, 1986.

----------. *The Remaking of Christian Doctrine*. London: SCM, 1974.

Williams, Charles. *Reason and Beauty in the Poetic Mind*. London: Oxford University Press, 1933.

----------. "One Way of Love," in Charles Williams, *The Image of the City and Other Essays*, ed. Anne Ridler. London: Oxford University Press, 1958.

----------. *The Figure of Beatrice: A Study in Dante* (1943). New York: Octagon Books, 1983.

----------. "The Theology of Romantic Love" (1938) in *He Came Down from Heaven*. Grand Rapids: William B. Eerdmans, 1984.

332

----------. "Outlines of Romantic Theology" (1925), in *Outlines of Romantic Theology*, ed. Alice Mary Hadfield. Grand Rapids: William B. Eerdmans, 1990.

----------. *Charles Williams: Essential Writings in Spirituality and Theology*, ed. Charles C. Hefting, Jr. Cambridge, MA: Crowley Publications, 1993.

Williams, Rowan. "The Suspicion of Suspicion: Wittgenstein and Bonhoeffer," in *The Grammar of the Heart: New Essays in Moral Philosophy and Theology*, ed. Richard H. Bell. San Francisco: Harper & Row, 1988.

----------. "Interiority and Epiphany: A Reading in New Testament Ethics," *Modern Theology* 13, no. 1 (January 1997).

Wittgenstein, Ludwig. *Philosophical Investigations*, trans. G. E. M. Anscombe, 3rd ed. New York: Macmillan, 1958.

----------. *Zettel*, ed. G. E. M. Anscombe and G. H. von Wright, trans. G. E. M. Anscombe. Oxford: Blackwell, 1967.

----------. *On Certainty*, ed. G. E. M. Anscombe and G. H. von Wright, trans. Denis Paul and G. E. M. Anscombe. Oxford: Blackwell, 1969.

----------. *Philosophical Grammar*, ed. Rush Rhees, trans. A. J. P. Kenny. Oxford: Blackwell, 1974.

----------. *Wittgenstein's Lectures: Cambridge, 1930-1932*, ed. Desmond Lee. Oxford: Blackwell, 1980.

Wolters, Clifton, ed. and trans. *The Cloud of Unknowing*. New York: Penguin, 1961.

Yollin, Patricia. "New interest in Jewish Mysticism," *San Francisco Chronicle*, (12/26/03).

Young, Iris Marion. "Impartiality and the Civic Public," in Seyla Benhabib and Drucilia Cornell, eds., *Feminism as Critique: On the Politics of Gender*. Minneapolis: University of Minnesota Press, 1987.

Zaehner, R. C. *Mysticism Sacred and Profane*. London: Oxford University Press, 1957.

NAME INDEX

336

INDEX